THE ARCHAEOLOGY
OF KNOWLEDGE

Also by Michel Foucault

MADNESS AND CIVILIZATION:
A HISTORY OF INSANITY IN THE AGE OF REASON

THE ORDER OF THINGS:
AN ARCHAEOLOGY OF THE HUMAN SCIENCES

THE BIRTH OF THE CLINIC:
AN ARCHAEOLOGY OF MEDICAL PERCEPTION

I, PIERRE RIVIERE, HAVING SLAUGHTERED MY MOTHER,
MY SISTER, AND MY BROTHER...A CASE OF PARRICIDE IN
THE NINETEENTH CENTURY

DISCIPLINE AND PUNISH:
THE BIRTH OF THE PRISON

THE HISTORY OF SEXUALITY, VOL. I

HERCULINE BARBIN, BEING THE RECENTLY DISCOVERED
MEMOIRS OF A NINETEENTH-CENTURY FRENCH
HERMAPHRODITE

POWER/KNOWLEDGE:
SELECTED INTERVIEWS AND OTHER WRITINGS 1972–1977

MICHEL FOUCAULT

THE ARCHAEOLOGY
OF KNOWLEDGE

AND

THE DISCOURSE ON LANGUAGE

Translated from the French
by A. M. Sheridan Smith

PANTHEON BOOKS, NEW YORK

Copyright © 1972 by Tavistock Publications Limited

All rights reserved under International and Pan-American Copyright Conventions. Published in the United States by Pantheon Books, a division of Random House, Inc., New York. Originally published in Great Britain by Tavistock Publications, Ltd. Originally published in France under the title *L'Archéologie du Savoir* by Éditions Gallimard. © Éditions Gallimard 1969

The Discourse on Language (Appendix) was originally published in French under the title *L'ordre du discours* by Éditions Gallimard. © Éditions Gallimard 1971. English translation by Rupert Swyer. Copyright © 1971 by *Social Science Information.*

Library of Congress Cataloging in Publication Data
Foucault, Michel.   The archaeology of knowledge.
(World of man)
Translation of L'archéologie du savoir.
Includes the author's The Discourse on Language, translation of L'ordre du discours
1. Learning and scholarship.   I. Foucault, Michel.
L'ordre du discours.   English.   1972.   II. Title.
AZ101.F6813   1972   001.2   72-1135   ISBN 0-394-47118-0 (h.c.)
ISBN 0-394-71106-8 (pbk.)

Manufactured in the United States of America

M 9 8 7 6 5 4 3

Contents

PART I   INTRODUCTION

Introduction   3

PART II   THE DISCURSIVE REGULARITIES

1 The unities of discourse   21
2 Discursive formations   31
3 The formation of objects   40
4 The formation of enunciative modalities   50
5 The formation of concepts   56
6 The formation of strategies   64
7 Remarks and consequences   71

PART III   THE STATEMENT AND THE
ARCHIVE

1 Defining the statement   79
2 The enunciative function   88
3 The description of statements   106
4 Rarity, exteriority, accumulation   118
5 The historical *a priori* and the archive   126

PART IV   ARCHAEOLOGICAL DESCRIPTION

1 Archaeology and the history of ideas   135
2 The original and the regular   141
3 Contradictions   149
4 The comparative facts   157
5 Change and transformations   166
6 Science and knowledge   178

PART V   CONCLUSION

Conclusion   199

Appendix: The Discourse on Language   215

Index   239

PART I

Introduction

Introduction

For many years now historians have preferred to turn their attention to long periods, as if, beneath the shifts and changes of political events, they were trying to reveal the stable, almost indestructible system of checks and balances, the irreversible processes, the constant readjustments, the underlying tendencies that gather force, and are then suddenly reversed after centuries of continuity, the movements of accumulation and slow saturation, the great silent, motionless bases that traditional history has covered with a thick layer of events. The tools that enable historians to carry out this work of analysis are partly inherited and partly of their own making: models of economic growth, quantitative analysis of market movements, accounts of demographic expansion and contraction, the study of climate and its long-term changes, the fixing of sociological constants, the description of technological adjustments and of their spread and continuity. These tools have enabled workers in the historical field to distinguish various sedimentary strata; linear successions, which for so long had been the object of research, have given way to discoveries in depth. From the political mobility at the surface down to the slow movements of 'material civilization', ever more levels of analysis have been established: each has its own peculiar discontinuities and patterns; and as one descends to the deepest levels, the rhythms become broader. Beneath the rapidly changing history of governments, wars, and famines, there emerge other, apparently unmoving histories: the history of sea routes, the history of corn or of gold-mining, the history of drought and of irrigation, the history of crop rotation, the history of the balance achieved by the human species between hunger and abundance. The old questions of the traditional analysis (What link should be made between disparate events? How can a causal succession be established between them? What continuity or overall significance do they possess? Is it possible to define a totality, or must one

3

be content with reconstituting connexions?) are now being replaced by questions of another type: which strata should be isolated from others? What types of series should be established? What criteria of periodization should be adopted for each of them? What system of relations (hierarchy, dominance, stratification, univocal determination, circular causality) may be established between them? What series of series may be established? And in what large-scale chronological table may distinct series of events be determined?

At about the same time, in the disciplines that we call the history of ideas, the history of science, the history of philosophy, the history of thought, and the history of literature (we can ignore their specificity for the moment), in those disciplines which, despite their names, evade very largely the work and methods of the historian, attention has been turned, on the contrary, away from vast unities like 'periods' or 'centuries' to the phenomena of rupture, of discontinuity. Beneath the great continuities of thought, beneath the solid, homogeneous manifestations of a single mind or of a collective mentality, beneath the stubborn development of a science striving to exist and to reach completion at the very outset, beneath the persistence of a particular genre, form, discipline, or theoretical activity, one is now trying to detect the incidence of interruptions. Interruptions whose status and nature vary considerably. There are the *epistemological acts and thresholds* described by Bachelard: they suspend the continuous accumulation of knowledge, interrupt its slow development, and force it to enter a new time, cut it off from its empirical origin and its original motivations, cleanse it of its imaginary complicities; they direct historical analysis away from the search for silent beginnings, and the never-ending tracing-back to the original precursors, towards the search for a new type of rationality and its various effects. There are the *displacements* and *transformations* of concepts: the analyses of G. Canguilhem may serve as models; they show that the history of a concept is not wholly and entirely that of its progressive refinement, its continuously increasing rationality, its abstraction gradient, but that of its various fields of constitution and validity, that of its successive rules of use, that of the many theoretical contexts in which it developed and matured. There is the distinction, which we also owe to Canguilhem, between the *microscopic* and *macroscopic scales* of the history of the sciences, in which events and their consequences are not arranged in the same way: thus a discovery, the development of a method, the achievements, and the failures, of a particular scientist, do not have the same incidence, and cannot be described in the same way at both levels; on each of the two levels, a different history is being written. *Recurrent redistributions* reveal several pasts, several forms of connexion, several hierarchies of importance, several networks of determination, several teleologies, for one and the same science, as its present undergoes change: thus historical descriptions are necessarily ordered by the present state of knowledge, they increase with every transformation and never cease, in turn, to break with themselves (in the field of mathematics, M. Serres has provided the theory of this phenomenon). There are the *architectonic unities* of systems of the kind analysed by M. Guéroult, which are concerned not with the description of cultural influences, traditions, and continuities, but with internal coherences, axioms, deductive connexions, compatibilities. Lastly, the most radical discontinuities are the breaks effected by a work of theoretical transformation 'which establishes a science by detaching it from the ideology of its past and by revealing this past as ideological'.[1] To this should be added, of course, literary analysis, which now takes as its unity, not the spirit or sensibility of a period, nor 'groups', 'schools', 'generations', or 'movements', nor even the personality of the author, in the interplay of his life and his 'creation', but the particular structure of a given *œuvre*, book, or text.

And the great problem presented by such historical analyses is not how continuities are established, how a single pattern is formed and preserved, how for so many different, successive minds there is a single horizon, what mode of action and what substructure is implied by the interplay of transmissions, resumptions, disappearances, and repetitions, how the origin may extend its sway well beyond itself to that conclusion that is never given – the problem is no longer one of tradition, of tracing a line, but one of division, of limits; it is no longer one of lasting foundations, but one of transformations that serve as new foundations, the rebuilding of foundations. What one is seeing, then, is the emergence of a whole field of questions, some of which are already familiar, by which this new form of history is trying to develop its own theory: how is one to specify the different concepts that enable us to conceive of discontinuity (threshold, rupture, break, mutation, transformation)? By what criteria is one to isolate the unities with which one is dealing; what is *a* science? What is an *œuvre*? What is *a* theory? What is *a* concept? What is *a* text? How is one to diversify the levels at which one may place oneself, each of which possesses its own divisions and form of analysis? What is the legitimate

[1] L. Althusser, *For Marx*, London, Allen Lane; New York, Pantheon, 1969, p. 168.

5

level of formalization? What is that of interpretation? Of structural analysis? Of attributions of causality?

In short, the history of thought, of knowledge, of philosophy, of literature seems to be seeking, and discovering, more and more discontinuities, whereas history itself appears to be abandoning the irruption of events in favour of stable structures.

But we must not be taken in by this apparent interchange. Despite appearances, we must not imagine that certain of the historical disciplines have moved from the continuous to the discontinuous, while others have moved from the tangled mass of discontinuities to the great, uninterrupted unities; we must not imagine that in the analysis of politics, institutions, or economics, we have become more and more sensitive to overall determinations, while in the analysis of ideas and of knowledge, we are paying more and more attention to the play of difference; we must not imagine that these two great forms of description have crossed without recognizing one another.

In fact, the same problems are being posed in either case, but they have provoked opposite effects on the surface. These problems may be summed up in a word: the questioning of the *document*. Of course, it is obvious enough that ever since a discipline such as history has existed, documents have been used, questioned, and have given rise to questions; scholars have asked not only what these documents meant, but also whether they were telling the truth, and by what right they could claim to be doing so, whether they were sincere or deliberately misleading, well informed or ignorant, authentic or tampered with. But each of these questions, and all this critical concern, pointed to one and the same end: the reconstitution, on the basis of what the documents say, and sometimes merely hint at, of the past from which they emanate and which has now disappeared far behind them; the document was always treated as the language of a voice since reduced to silence, its fragile, but possibly decipherable trace. Now, through a mutation that is not of very recent origin, but which has still not come to an end, history has altered its position in relation to the document: it has taken as its primary task, not the interpretation of the document, nor the attempt to decide whether it is telling the truth or what is its expressive value, but to work on it from within and to develop it: history now organizes the document, divides it up, distributes it, orders it, arranges it in levels, establishes series, distinguishes between what is relevant and what is not, discovers elements, defines unities, describes

6

relations. The document, then, is no longer for history an inert material through which it tries to reconstitute what men have done or said, the events of which only the trace remains; history is now trying to define within the documentary material itself unities, totalities, series, relations. History must be detached from the image that satisfied it for so long, and through which it found its anthropological justification: that of an age-old collective consciousness that made use of material documents to refresh its memory; history is the work expended on material documentation (books, texts, accounts, registers, acts, buildings, institutions, laws, techniques, objects, customs, etc.) that exists, in every time and place, in every society, either in a spontaneous or in a consciously organized form. The document is not the fortunate tool of a history that is primarily and fundamentally *memory*; history is one way in which a society recognizes and develops a mass of documentation with which it is inextricably linked.

To be brief, then, let us say that history, in its traditional form, undertook to 'memorize' the *monuments* of the past, transform them into *documents*, and lend speech to those traces which, in themselves, are often not verbal, or which say in silence something other than what they actually say; in our time, history is that which transforms *documents* into *monuments*. In that area where, in the past, history deciphered the traces left by men, it now deploys a mass of elements that have to be grouped, made relevant, placed in relation to one another to form totalities. There was a time when archaeology, as a discipline devoted to silent monuments, inert traces, objects without context, and things left by the past, aspired to the condition of history, and attained meaning only through the restitution of a historical discourse; it might be said, to play on words a little, that in our time history aspires to the condition of archaeology, to the intrinsic description of the monument.

This has several consequences. First of all, there is the surface effect already mentioned: the proliferation of discontinuities in the history of ideas, and the emergence of long periods in history proper. In fact, in its traditional form, history proper was concerned to define relations (of simple causality, of circular determination, of antagonism, of expression) between facts or dated events: the series being known, it was simply a question of defining the position of each element in relation to the other elements in the series. The problem now is to constitute series: to define the elements proper to each series, to fix its boundaries, to reveal its own specific type of relations, to formulate its laws, and, beyond this, to

7

describe the relations between different series, thus constituting series of series, or 'tables': hence the ever-increasing number of strata, and the need to distinguish them, the specificity of their time and chronologies; hence the need to distinguish not only important events (with a long chain of consequences) and less important ones, but types of events at quite different levels (some very brief, others of average duration, like the development of a particular technique, or a scarcity of money, and others of a long-term nature, like a demographic equilibrium or the gradual adjustment of an economy to climatic change); hence the possibility of revealing series with widely spaced intervals formed by rare or repetitive events. The appearance of long periods in the history of today is not a return to the philosophers of history, to the great ages of the world, or to the periodization dictated by the rise and fall of civilizations; it is the effect of the methodologically concerted development of series. In the history of ideas, of thought and of the sciences, the same mutation has brought about the opposite effect; it has broken up the long series formed by the progress of consciousness, or the teleology of reason, or the evolution of human thought; it has questioned the themes of convergence and culmination; it has doubted the possibility of creating totalities. It has led to the individualization of different series, which are juxtaposed to one another, follow one another, overlap and intersect, without one being able to reduce them to a linear schema. Thus, in place of the continuous chronology of reason, which was invariably traced back to some inaccessible origin, there have appeared scales that are sometimes very brief, distinct from one another, irreducible to a single law, scales that bear a type of history peculiar to each one, and which cannot be reduced to the general model of a consciousness that acquires, progresses, and remembers.

Second consequence: the notion of discontinuity assumes a major role in the historical disciplines. For history in its classical form, the discontinuous was both the given and the unthinkable: the raw material of history, which presented itself in the form of dispersed events – decisions, accidents, initiatives, discoveries; the material, which, through analysis, had to be rearranged, reduced, effaced in order to reveal the continuity of events. Discontinuity was the stigma of temporal dislocation that it was the historian's task to remove from history. It has now become one of the basic elements of historical analysis. Its role is threefold. First, it constitutes a deliberate operation on the part of the historian (and not a quality of the material with which he has to deal): for he must, at least as a systematic hypothesis, distinguish the possible levels of analysis, the methods proper

8

to each, and the periodization that best suits them. Secondly, it is the result of his description (and not something that must be eliminated by means of his analysis): for he is trying to discover the limits of a process, the point of inflexion of a curve, the inversion of a regulatory movement, the boundaries of an oscillation, the threshold of a function, the instant at which a circular causality breaks down. Thirdly, it is the concept that the historian's work never ceases to specify (instead of neglecting it as a uniform, indifferent blank between two positive figures); it assumes a specific form and function according to the field and the level to which it is assigned: one does not speak of the same discontinuity when describing an epistemological threshold, the point of reflexion in a population curve, or the replacement of one technique by another. The notion of discontinuity is a paradoxical one: because it is both an instrument and an object of research; because it divides up the field of which it is the effect; because it enables the historian to individualize different domains but can be established only by comparing those domains. And because, in the final analysis, perhaps, it is not simply a concept present in the discourse of the historian, but something that the historian secretly supposes to be present: on what basis, in fact, could he speak without this discontinuity that offers him history – and his own history – as an object? One of the most essential features of the new history is probably this displacement of the discontinuous: its transference from the obstacle to the work itself; its integration into the discourse of the historian, where it no longer plays the role of an external condition that must be reduced, but that of a working concept; and therefore the inversion of signs by which it is no longer the negative of the historical reading (its underside, its failure, the limit of its power), but the positive element that determines its object and validates its analysis.

Third consequence: the theme and the possibility of a *total history* begin to disappear, and we see the emergence of something very different that might be called a *general history*. The project of a total history is one that seeks to reconstitute the overall form of a civilization, the principle – material or spiritual – of a society, the significance common to all the phenomena of a period, the law that accounts for their cohesion – what is called metaphorically the 'face' of a period. Such a project is linked to two or three hypotheses; it is supposed that between all the events of a well-defined spatio-temporal area, between all the phenomena of which traces have been found, it must be possible to establish a system of homogeneous relations: a network of causality that makes it possible to derive each of them, relations of analogy that show how they symbolize one another, or how they all express one and the same central core; it is also supposed that one and the same form of historicity operates upon economic structures, social institutions and customs, the inertia of mental attitudes, technological practice, political behaviour, and subjects them all to the same type of transformation; lastly, it is supposed that history itself may be articulated into great units – stages or phases – which contain within themselves their own principle of cohesion. These are the postulates that are challenged by the new history when it speaks of series, divisions, limits, differences of level, shifts, chronological specificities, particular forms of rehandling, possible types of relation. This is not because it is trying to obtain a plurality of histories juxtaposed and independent of one another: that of the economy beside that of institutions, and beside these two those of science, religion, or literature; nor is it because it is merely trying to discover between these different histories coincidences of dates, or analogies of form and meaning. The problem that now presents itself – and which defines the task of a general history – is to determine what form of relation may be legitimately described between these different series; what vertical system they are capable of forming; what interplay of correlation and dominance exists between them; what may be the effect of shifts, different temporalities, and various rehandlings; in what distinct totalities certain elements may figure simultaneously; in short, not only what series, but also what 'series of series' – or, in other words, what 'tables' it is possible to draw up. A total description draws all phenomena around a single centre – a principle, a meaning, a spirit, a world-view, an overall shape; a general history, on the contrary, would deploy the space of a dispersion.

Fourth and last consequence: the new history is confronted by a number of methodological problems, several of which, no doubt, existed long before the emergence of the new history, but which, taken together, characterize it. These include: the building-up of coherent and homogeneous *corpora* of documents (open or closed, exhausted or inexhaustible corpora), the establishment of a principle of choice (according to whether one wishes to treat the documentation exhaustively, or adopt a sampling method as in statistics, or try to determine in advance which are the most representative elements); the definition of the level of analysis and of the relevant elements (in the material studied, one may extract numerical indications; references – explicit or not – to events, institutions, practices; the words used, with their grammatical rules and the semantic fields that they indicate, or again the formal structure of the propositions and the types of connexion that unite them); the specification of a method of analysis (the quantitative treatment of data, the breaking-down of the material according to a number of assignable features whose correlations are then studied, interpretative decipherment, analysis of frequency and distribution); the delimitation of groups and sub-groups that articulate the material (regions, periods, unitary processes); the determination of relations that make it possible to characterize a group (these may be numerical or logical relations; functional, causal, or analogical relations; or it may be the relation of the 'signifier' (*signifiant*) to the 'signified' (*signifié*).

All these problems are now part of the methodological field of history. This field deserves attention, and for two reasons. First, because one can see to what extent it has freed itself from what constituted, not so long ago, the philosophy of history, and from the questions that it posed (on the rationality or teleology of historical development (*devenir*), on the relativity of historical knowledge, and on the possibility of discovering or constituting a meaning in the inertia of the past and in the unfinished totality of the present). Secondly, because it intersects at certain points problems that are met with in other fields – in linguistics, ethnology, economics, literary analysis, and mythology, for example. These problems may, if one so wishes, be labelled structuralism. But only under certain conditions: they do not, of themselves, cover the entire methodological field of history, they occupy only one part of that field – a part that varies in importance with the area and level of analysis; apart from a number of relatively limited cases, they have not been imported from linguistics or ethnology (as is often the case today), but they originated in the field of history itself – more particularly, in that of economic history and as a result of the questions posed by that discipline; lastly, in no way do they authorize us to speak of a structuralism of history, or at least of an attempt to overcome a 'conflict' or 'opposition' between structure and historical development: it is a long time now since historians uncovered, described, and analysed structures, without ever having occasion to wonder whether they were not allowing the living, fragile, pulsating 'history' to slip through their fingers. The structure/development opposition is relevant neither to the definition of the historical field, nor, in all probability, to the definition of a structural method.

This epistemological mutation of history is not yet complete. But it is not of recent origin either, since its first phase can no doubt be traced back to Marx. But it took a long time to have much effect. Even now – and this is especially true in the case of the history of thought – it has been neither registered nor reflected upon, while other, more recent trans-formations – those of linguistics, for example – have been. It is as if it was particularly difficult, in the history in which men retrace their own ideas and their own knowledge, to formulate a general theory of discontinuity, of series, of limits, unities, specific orders, and differentiated autonomies and dependences. As if, in that field where we had become used to seeking origins, to pushing back further and further the line of antecedents, to reconstituting traditions, to following evolutive curves, to projecting teleologies, and to having constant recourse to metaphors of life, we felt a particular repugnance to conceiving of difference, to describing separa-tions and dispersions, to dissociating the reassuring form of the identical. Or, to be more precise, as if we found it difficult to construct a theory, to draw general conclusions, and even to derive all the possible implications of these concepts of thresholds, mutations, independent systems, and limited series – in the way in which they had been used in fact by historians. As if we were afraid to conceive of the *Other* in the time of our own thought.

There is a reason for this. If the history of thought could remain the locus of uninterrupted continuities, if it could endlessly forge connexions that no analysis could undo without abstraction, if it could weave, around everything that men say and do, obscure synthesis that anticipate for him, prepare him, and lead him endlessly towards his future, it would provide a privileged shelter for the sovereignty of consciousness. Continuous history is the indispensable correlative of the founding function of the subject: the guarantee that everything that has eluded him may be restored to him; the certainty that time will disperse nothing without restoring it in a reconstituted unity; the promise that one day the subject – in the form of historical consciousness – will once again be able to appropriate, to bring back under his sway, all those things that are kept at a distance by difference, and find in them what might be called his abode. Making historical analysis the discourse of the continuous and making human consciousness the original subject of all historical development and all action are the two sides of the same system of thought. In this system, time is conceived in terms of totalization and revolutions are never more than moments of consciousness.

In various forms, this theme has played a constant role since the nine-teenth century: to preserve, against all decentrings, the sovereignty of the subject, and the twin figures of anthropology and humanism. Against the decentring operated by Marx – by the historical analysis of the relations of production, economic determinations, and the class struggle – it gave place, towards the end of the nineteenth century, to the search for a total history, in which all the differences of a society might be reduced to a single form, to the organization of a world-view, to the establishment of a system of values, to a coherent type of civilization. To the decentring operated by the Nietzschean genealogy, it opposed the search for an original foundation that would make rationality the *telos* of mankind, and link the whole history of thought to the preservation of this rationality, to the maintenance of this teleology, and to the ever necessary return to this foundation. Lastly, more recently, when the researches of psycho-analysis, linguistics, and ethnology have decentred the subject in relation to the laws of his desire, the forms of his language, the rules of his action, or the games of his mythical or fabulous discourse, when it became clear that man himself, questioned as to what he was, could not account for his sexuality and his unconscious, the systematic forms of his language, or the regularities of his fictions, the theme of a continuity of history has been reactivated once again; a history that would be not division, but development (*devenir*); not an interplay of relations, but an internal dynamic; not a system, but the hard work of freedom; not form, but the unceasing effort of a consciousness turned upon itself, trying to grasp itself in its deepest conditions: a history that would be both an act of long, uninterrupted patience and the vivacity of a movement, which, in the end, breaks all bounds. If one is to assert this theme, which, to the 'immobility' of structures, to their 'closed' system, to their necessary 'synchrony', opposes the living openness of history, one must obviously deny in the historical analyses themselves the use of discontinuity, the definition of levels and limits, the description of specific series, the uncovering of the whole interplay of differences. One is led therefore to anthropologize Marx, to make of him a historian of totalities, and to rediscover in him the message of humanism; one is led therefore to interpret Nietzsche in the terms of transcendental philosophy, and to reduce his genealogy to the level of a search for origins; lastly, one is led to leave to one side, as if it had never arisen, that whole field of methodological problems that the new history is now presenting. For, if it is asserted that the question of discontinuities, systems and transformations, series and thresholds, arises in all the historical disciplines (and in those concerned with ideas or the sciences no less than those concerned with economics and society), how could one oppose with any semblance of legitimacy 'development' and 'system', movement and circular regulations, or, as it is sometimes put crudely and unthinkingly, 'history' and 'structure'?

The same conservative function is at work in the theme of cultural totalities (for which Marx has been criticized, then travestied), in the theme of a search for origins (which was opposed to Nietzsche, before an attempt was made to transpose him into it), and in the theme of a living, continuous, open history. The cry goes up that one is murdering history whenever, in a historical analysis – and especially if it is concerned with thought, ideas, or knowledge – one is seen to be using in too obvious a way the categories of discontinuity and difference, the notions of threshold, rupture and transformation, the description of series and limits. One will be denounced for attacking the inalienable rights of history and the very foundations of any possible historicity. But one must not be deceived: what is being bewailed with such vehemence is not the disappearance of history, but the eclipse of that form of history that was secretly, but entirely related to the synthetic activity of the subject; what is being bewailed is the 'development' (*devenir*) that was to provide the sovereignty of the consciousness with a safer, less exposed shelter than myths, kinship systems, languages, sexuality, or desire; what is being bewailed is the possibility of reanimating through the project, the work of meaning, or the movement of totalization, the interplay of material determinations, rules of practice, unconscious systems, rigorous but unreflected relations, correlations that elude all lived experience; what is being bewailed, is that ideological use of history by which one tries to restore to man everything that has unceasingly eluded him for over a hundred years. All the treasure of bygone days was crammed into the old citadel of this history; it was thought to be secure; it was sacralized; it was made the last resting-place of anthropological thought; it was even thought that its most inveterate enemies could be captured and turned into vigilant guardians. But the historians had long ago deserted the old fortress and gone to work elsewhere; it was realized that neither Marx nor Nietzsche were carrying out the guard duties that had been entrusted to them. They could not be depended on to preserve privilege; nor to affirm once and for all – and God knows it is needed in the distress of today – that history, at least, is living and continuous, that it is, for the subject in question, a place of rest, certainty, reconciliation, a place of tranquillized sleep.

At this point there emerges an enterprise of which my earlier books *Histoire de la folie* (*Madness and Civilization*), *Naissance de la clinique*, and

Les Mots et les choses (*The Order of Things*)[1] were a very imperfect sketch. An enterprise by which one tries to measure the mutations that operate in general in the field of history; an enterprise in which the methods, limits, and themes proper to the history of ideas are questioned; an enterprise by which one tries to throw off the last anthropological constraints; an enterprise that wishes, in return, to reveal how these constraints could come about. These tasks were outlined in a rather disordered way, and their general articulation was never clearly defined. It was time that they were given greater coherence – or, at least, that an attempt was made to do so. This book is the result.

In order to avoid misunderstanding, I should like to begin with a few observations.

—My aim is not to transfer to the field of history, and more particularly to the history of knowledge (*connaissances*),[2] a structuralist method that has proved valuable in other fields of analysis. My aim is to uncover the principles and consequences of an autochthonous transformation that is taking place in the field of historical knowledge. It may well be that this transformation, the problems that it raises, the tools that it uses, the concepts that emerge from it, and the results that it obtains are not entirely foreign to what is called structural analysis. But this kind of analysis is not specifically used;

—my aim is most decidedly not to use the categories of cultural totalities (whether world-views, ideal types, the particular spirit of an age) in order to impose on history, despite itself, the forms of structural analysis. The series described, the limits fixed, the comparisons and correlations made

---

[1] *Madness and Civilization*, New York, Random House, 1965; London, Tavistock, 1967; *The Order of Things*, London, Tavistock; New York, Pantheon, 1970. A translation of *Naissance de la clinique* is in press.

[2] The English 'knowledge' translates the French '*connaissance*' and '*savoir*'. *Connaissance* refers here to a particular corpus of knowledge, a particular discipline – biology or economics, for example. *Savoir*, which is usually defined as knowledge in general, the totality of *connaissances*, is used by Foucault in an underlying, rather than an overall, way. He has himself offered the following comment on his usage of these terms:

'By *connaissance* I mean the relation of the subject to the object and the formal rules that govern it. *Savoir* refers to the conditions that are necessary in a particular period for this or that type of object to be given to *connaissance* and for this or that enunciation to be formulated.'

Throughout this translation I have used the English word, followed, where the meaning required it, by the appropriate French word in parenthesis (Tr.).

are based not on the old philosophies of history, but are intended to question teleologies and totalizations;

—in so far as my aim is to define a method of historical analysis freed from the anthropological theme, it is clear that the theory that I am about to outline has a dual relation with the previous studies. It is an attempt to formulate, in general terms (and not without a great deal of rectification and elaboration), the tools that these studies have used or forged for themselves in the course of their work. But, on the other hand, it uses the results already obtained to define a method of analysis purged of all anthropologism. The ground on which it rests is the one that it has itself discovered. The studies of madness and the beginnings of psychology, of illness and the beginnings of a clinical medicine, of the sciences of life, language, and economics were attempts that were carried out, to some extent, in the dark: but they gradually became clear, not only because little by little their method became more precise, but also because they discovered – in this debate on humanism and anthropology – the point of its historical possibility.

In short, this book, like those that preceded it, does not belong – at least directly, or in the first instance – to the debate on structure (as opposed to genesis, history, development); it belongs to that field in which the questions of the human being, consciousness, origin, and the subject emerge, intersect, mingle, and separate off. But it would probably not be incorrect to say that the problem of structure arose there too.

This work is not an exact description of what can be read in *Madness and Civilization*, *Naissance de la clinique*, or *The Order of Things*. It is different on a great many points. It also includes a number of corrections and internal criticisms. Generally speaking, *Madness and Civilization* accorded far too great a place, and a very enigmatic one too, to what I called an 'experiment', thus showing to what extent one was still close to admitting an anonymous and general subject of history; in *Naissance de la clinique*, the frequent recourse to structural analysis threatened to bypass the specificity of the problem presented, and the level proper to archaeology; lastly, in *The Order of Things*, the absence of methodological signposting may have given the impression that my analyses were being conducted in terms of cultural totality. It is mortifying that I was unable to avoid these dangers: I console myself with the thought that they were intrinsic to the enterprise itself, since, in order to carry out its task, it had first to free itself from these various methods and forms of history; moreover, without the questions that I was asked,[1] without the difficulties that arose, without the objections that were made, I may never have gained so clear a view of the enterprise to which I am now inextricably linked. Hence the cautious, stumbling manner of this text: at every turn, it stands back, measures up what is before it, gropes towards its limits, stumbles against what it does not mean, and digs pits to mark out its own path. At every turn, it denounces any possible confusion. It rejects its identity, without previously stating: I am neither this nor that. It is not critical, most of the time; it is not a way of saying that everyone else is wrong. It is an attempt to define a particular site by the exteriority of its vicinity; rather than trying to reduce others to silence, by claiming that what they say is worthless, I have tried to define this blank space from which I speak, and which is slowly taking shape in a discourse that I still feel to be so precarious and so unsure.

'Aren't you sure of what you're saying? Are you going to change yet again, shift your position according to the questions that are put to you, and say that the objections are not really directed at the place from which you are speaking? Are you going to declare yet again that you have never been what you have been reproached with being? Are you already preparing the way out that will enable you in your next book to spring up somewhere else and declare as you're now doing: no, no, I'm not where you are lying in wait for me, but over here, laughing at you?'

'What, do you imagine that I would take so much trouble and so much pleasure in writing, do you think that I would keep so persistently to my task, if I were not preparing – with a rather shaky hand – a labyrinth into which I can venture, in which I can move my discourse, opening up underground passages, forcing it to go far from itself, finding overhangs that reduce and deform its itinerary, in which I can lose myself and appear at last to eyes that I will never have to meet again. I am no doubt not the only one who writes in order to have no face. Do not ask who I am and do not ask me to remain the same: leave it to our bureaucrats and our police to see that our papers are in order. At least spare us their morality when we write.'

---

[1] In particular, the first pages of this introduction are based on a reply to questions presented by the *Cercle d'Épistémologie* of the E.N.S. (cf. *Cahiers pour l'analyse*, no. 9). A sketch of certain developments was also given in reply to readers of the review *Esprit* (avril 1968).

PART II

The Discursive Regularities

The Unities of Discourse

The use of concepts of discontinuity, rupture, threshold, limit, series, and transformation present all historical analysis not only with questions of procedure, but with theoretical problems. It is these problems that will be studied here (the questions of procedure will be examined in later empirical studies – if the opportunity, the desire, and the courage to undertake them do not desert me). These theoretical problems too will be examined only in a particular field: in those disciplines – so unsure of their frontiers, and so vague in content – that we call the history of ideas, or of thought, or of science, or of knowledge.

But there is a negative work to be carried out first: we must rid ourselves of a whole mass of notions, each of which, in its own way, diversifies the theme of continuity. They may not have a very rigorous conceptual structure, but they have a very precise function. Take the notion of tradition: it is intended to give a special temporal status to a group of phenomena that are both successive and identical (or at least similar); it makes it possible to rethink the dispersion of history in the form of the same; it allows a reduction of the difference proper to every beginning, in order to pursue without discontinuity the endless search for the origin; tradition enables us to isolate the new against a background of permanence, and to transfer its merit to originality, to genius, to the decisions proper to individuals. Then there is the notion of influence, which provides a support – of too magical a kind to be very amenable to analysis – for the facts of transmission and communication; which refers to an apparently causal process (but with neither rigorous delimitation nor theoretical definition) the phenomena of resemblance or repetition; which links, at a distance and through time – as if through the mediation of a medium of propagation – such defined unities as individuals, œuvres, notions, or theories. There are the notions of development and evolution: they make it possible to group a succession of dispersed events, to link them to one and the same organizing principle, to subject them to the exemplary power of life (with its adaptations, its capacity for innovation, the incessant correlation of its different elements, its systems of assimilation and exchange), to discover, already at work in each beginning, a principle of coherence and the outline of a future unity, to master time through a perpetually reversible relation between an origin and a term that are never given, but are always at work. There is the notion of 'spirit', which enables us to establish between the simultaneous or successive phenomena of a given period a community of meanings, symbolic links, an interplay of resemblance and reflexion, or which allows the sovereignty of collective consciousness to emerge as the principle of unity and explanation. We must question those ready-made syntheses, those groupings that we normally accept before any examination, those links whose validity is recognized from the outset; we must oust those forms and obscure forces by which we usually link the discourse of one man with that of another; they must be driven out from the darkness in which they reign. And instead of according them unqualified, spontaneous value, we must accept, in the name of methodological rigour, that, in the first instance, they concern only a population of dispersed events.

We must also question those divisions or groupings with which we have become so familiar. Can one accept, as such, the distinction between the major types of discourse, or that between such forms or genres as science, literature, philosophy, religion, history, fiction, etc., and which tend to create certain great historical individualities? We are not even sure of ourselves when we use these distinctions in our own world of discourse, let alone when we are analysing groups of statements which, when first formulated, were distributed, divided, and characterized in a quite different way: after all, 'literature' and 'politics' are recent categories, which can be applied to medieval culture, or even classical culture, only by a retrospective hypothesis, and by an interplay of formal analogies or semantic resemblances; but neither literature, nor politics, nor philosophy and the sciences articulated the field of discourse, in the seventeenth or eighteenth century, as they did in the nineteenth century. In any case, these divisions – whether our own, or those contemporary with the discourse under examination – are always themselves reflexive categories, principles of classification, normative rules, institutionalized types: they, in turn, are facts of discourse that deserve to be analysed beside others; of course, they also have complex relations with each other, but they are not intrinsic, autochthonous, and universally recognizable characteristics.

But the unities that must be suspended above all are those that emerge in the most immediate way: those of the book and the *œuvre*. At first sight, it would seem that one could not abandon these unities without extreme artificiality. Are they not given in the most definite way? There is the material individualization of the book, which occupies a determined space, which has an economic value, and which itself indicates, by a number of signs, the limits of its beginning and its end; and there is the establishment of an *œuvre*, which we recognize and delimit by attributing a certain number of texts to an author. And yet as soon as one looks at the matter a little more closely the difficulties begin. The material unity of the book? Is this the same in the case of an anthology of poems, a collection of posthumous fragments, Desargues' *Traité des Coniques*, or a volume of Michelet's *Histoire de France*? Is it the same in the case of Mallarmé's *Un Coup de dés*, the trial of Gilles de Rais, Butor's *San Marco*, or a Catholic missal? In other words, is not the material unity of the volume a weak, accessory unity in relation to the discursive unity of which it is the support? But is this discursive unity itself homogeneous and uniformly applicable? A novel by Stendhal and a novel by Dostoevsky do not have the same relation of individuality as that between two novels belonging to Balzac's cycle *La Comédie humaine*; and the relation between Balzac's novels is not the same as that existing between Joyce's *Ulysses* and the *Odyssey*. The frontiers of a book are never clear-cut: beyond the title, the first lines, and the last full stop, beyond its internal configuration and its autonomous form, it is caught up in a system of references to other books, other texts, other sentences: it is a node within a network. And this network of references is not the same in the case of a mathematical treatise, a textual commentary, a historical account, and an episode in a novel cycle; the unity of the book, even in the sense of a group of relations, cannot be regarded as identical in each case. The book is not simply the object that one holds in one's hands; and it cannot remain within the little parallelepiped that contains it: its unity is variable and relative. As soon as one questions that unity, it loses its self-evidence; it indicates itself, constructs itself, only on the basis of a complex field of discourse.

The problems raised by the *œuvre* are even more difficult. Yet, at first sight, what could be more simple? A collection of texts that can be designated by the sign of a proper name. But this designation (even leaving to one side problems of attribution) is not a homogeneous function: does the name of an author designate in the same way a text that he has published under his name, a text that he has presented under a pseudonym, another found after his death in the form of an unfinished draft, and another that is merely a collection of jottings, a notebook? The establishment of a complete *œuvre* presupposes a number of choices that are difficult to justify or even to formulate: is it enough to add to the texts published by the author those that he intended for publication but which remained unfinished by the fact of his death? Should one also include all his sketches and first drafts, with all their corrections and crossings out? Should one add sketches that he himself abandoned? And what status should be given to letters, notes, reported conversations, transcriptions of what he said made by those present at the time, in short, to that vast mass of verbal traces left by an individual at his death, and which speak in an endless confusion so many different languages (*langages*)?[1] In any case, the name 'Mallarmé' does not refer in the same way to his *thèmes* (translation exercises from French into English), his translations of Edgar Allan Poe, his poems, and his replies to questionnaires; similarly, the same relation does not exist between the name Nietzsche on the one hand and the youthful autobiographies, the scholastic dissertations, the philological articles, *Zarathustra*, *Ecce Homo*, the letters, the last postcards signed 'Dionysos' or 'Kaiser Nietzsche', and the innumerable notebooks with their jumble of laundry bills and sketches for aphorisms. In fact, if one speaks, so undiscriminately and unreflectingly of an author's *œuvre*, it is because one imagines it to be defined by a certain expressive function. One is admitting that there must be a level (as deep as it is necessary to imagine it) at which the *œuvre* emerges, in all its fragments, even the smallest, most inessential ones, as the expression of the thought, the experience, the imagination, or the unconscious of the author, or, indeed, of the historical determinations that operated upon him. But it is at once apparent that such a unity, far from being given immediately, is the result of an operation; that this operation is interpretative (since it deciphers, in the text, the transcription of something that it both conceals and manifests); and that the operation that determines the *opus*, in its unity, and consequently the *œuvre* itself, will not be the same in the case of the author of *Le Théâtre et son Double* (Artaud) and the author of the *Tractatus* (Wittgenstein), and therefore when one speaks of an *œuvre* in each case one is using the word in a different sense. The *œuvre* can be regarded neither as an immediate unity, nor as a certain unity, nor as a homogeneous unity.

---

[1] The English word 'language' translates the French '*langue*' (meaning the 'natural' languages: French, English, etc.) and '*langage*' (meaning either 'language in general' or 'kinds of language': philosophical, medical language, etc.). Where the meaning would otherwise be unclear, I have added the original French word in brackets. (Tr.)

One last precaution must be taken to disconnect the unquestioned continuities by which we organize, in advance, the discourse that we are to analyse: we must renounce two linked, but opposite themes. The first involves a wish that it should never be possible to assign, in the order of discourse, the irruption of a real event; that beyond any apparent beginning, there is always a secret origin – so secret and so fundamental that it can never be quite grasped in itself. Thus one is led inevitably, through the naïvety of chronologies, towards an ever-receding point that is never itself present in any history; this point is merely its own void; and from that point all beginnings can never be more than recommencements or occultation (in one and the same gesture, this *and* that). To this theme is connected another according to which all manifest discourse is secretly based on an 'already-said'; and that this 'already-said' is not merely a phrase that has already been spoken, or a text that has already been written, but a 'never-said', an incorporeal discourse, a voice as silent as a breath, a writing that is merely the hollow of its own mark. It is supposed therefore that everything that is formulated in discourse was already articulated in that semi-silence that precedes it, which continues to run obstinately beneath it, but which it covers and silences. The manifest discourse, therefore, is really no more than the repressive presence of what it does not say; and this 'not-said' is a hollow that undermines from within all that is said. The first theme sees the historical analysis of discourse as the quest for and the repetition of an origin that eludes all historical determination; the second sees it as the interpretation of 'hearing' of an 'already-said' that is at the same time a 'not-said'. We must renounce all those themes whose function is to ensure the infinite continuity of discourse and its secret presence to itself in the interplay of a constantly recurring absence. We must be ready to receive every moment of discourse in its sudden irruption; in that punctuality in which it appears, and in that temporal dispersion that enables it to be repeated, known, forgotten, transformed, utterly erased, and hidden, far from all view, in the dust of books. Discourse must not be referred to the distant presence of the origin, but treated as and when it occurs.

These pre-existing forms of continuity, all these syntheses that are accepted without question, must remain in suspense. They must not be rejected definitively of course, but the tranquillity with which they are accepted must be disturbed; we must show that they do not come about of themselves, but are always the result of a construction the rules of which must be known, and the justifications of which must be scrutinized: we must define in what conditions and in view of which analyses certain of them are legitimate; and we must indicate which of them can never be accepted in any circumstances. It may be, for example, that the notions of 'influence' or 'evolution' belong to a criticism that puts them – for the foreseeable future – out of use. But need we dispense for ever with the '*œuvre*', the 'book', or even such unities as 'science' or 'literature'? Should we regard them as illusions, illegitimate constructions, or ill-acquired results? Should we never make use of them, even as a temporary support, and never provide them with a definition? What we must do, in fact, is to tear away from them their virtual self-evidence, and to free the problems that they pose; to recognize that they are not the tranquil locus on the basis of which other questions (concerning their structure, coherence, systematicity, transformations) may be posed, but that they themselves pose a whole cluster of questions (What are they? How can they be defined or limited? What distinct types of laws can they obey? What articulation are they capable of? What sub-groups can they give rise to? What specific phenomena do they reveal in the field of discourse?). We must recognize that they may not, in the last resort, be what they seem at first sight. In short, that they require a theory, and that this theory cannot be constructed unless the *field* of the facts of discourse on the basis of which those facts are built up appears in its non-synthetic purity.

And I, in turn, will do no more than this: of course, I shall take as my starting-point whatever unities are already given (such as psychopathology, medicine, or political economy); but I shall not place myself inside these dubious unities in order to study their internal configuration or their secret contradictions. I shall make use of them just long enough to ask myself what unities they form; by what right they can claim a field that specifies them in space and a continuity that individualizes them in time; according to what laws they are formed; against the background of which discursive events they stand out; and whether they are not, in their accepted and quasi-institutional individuality, ultimately the surface effect of more firmly grounded unities. I shall accept the groupings that history suggests only to subject them at once to interrogation; to break them up and then to see whether they can be legitimately reformed; or whether other groupings should be made; to replace them in a more general space which, while dissipating their apparent familiarity, makes it possible to construct a theory of them.

Once these immediate forms of continuity are suspended, an entire field is set free. A vast field, but one that can be defined nonetheless: this field is made up of the totality of all effective statements (whether spoken or written), in their dispersion as events and in the occurrence that is proper to them. Before approaching, with any degree of certainty, a science, or novels, or political speeches, or the *œuvre* of an author, or even a single book, the material with which one is dealing is, in its raw, neutral state, a population of events in the space of discourse in general. One is led therefore to the project of a *pure description of discursive events* as the horizon for the search for the unities that form within it. This description is easily distinguishable from an analysis of the language. Of course, a linguistic system can be established (unless it is constructed artificially) only by using a corpus of statements, or a collection of discursive facts; but we must then define, on the basis of this grouping, which has value as a sample, rules that may make it possible to construct other statements than these: even if it has long since disappeared, even if it is no longer spoken, and can be reconstructed only on the basis of rare fragments, a language (*langue*) is still a system for possible statements, a finite body of rules that authorizes an infinite number of performances. The field of discursive events, on the other hand, is a grouping that is always finite and limited at any moment to the linguistic sequences that have been formulated; they may be innumerable, they may, in sheer size, exceed the capacities of recording, memory, or reading: nevertheless they form a finite grouping. The question posed by language analysis of some discursive fact or other is always: according to what rules has a particular statement been made, and consequently according to what rules could other similar statements be made? The description of the events of discourse poses a quite different question: how is it that one particular statement appeared rather than another?

It is also clear that this description of discourses is in opposition to the history of thought. There too a system of thought can be reconstituted only on the basis of a definite discursive totality. But this totality is treated in such a way that one tries to rediscover beyond the statements themselves the intention of the speaking subject, his conscious activity, what he meant, or, again, the unconscious activity that took place, despite himself, in what he said or in the almost imperceptible fracture of his actual words; in any case, we must reconstitute another discourse, rediscover the silent murmuring, the inexhaustible speech that animates from within the voice that one hears, re-establish the tiny, invisible text that runs between and sometimes collides with them. The analysis of thought is always *allegorical* in relation to the discourse that it employs. Its question is unfailingly: what was being said in what was said? The analysis of the discursive field is orientated in a quite different way; we must grasp the statement in the exact specificity of its occurrence; determine its conditions of existence, fix at least its limits, establish its correlations with other statements that may be connected with it, and show what other forms of statement it excludes. We do not seek below what is manifest the half silent murmur of another discourse; we must show why it could not be other than it was, in what respect it is exclusive of any other, how it assumes, in the midst of others and in relation to them, a place that no other could occupy. The question proper to such an analysis might be formulated in this way: what is this specific existence that emerges from what is said and nowhere else?

We must ask ourselves what purpose is ultimately served by this suspension of all the accepted unities, if, in the end, we return to the unities that we pretended to question at the outset. In fact, the systematic erasure of all given unities enables us first of all to restore to the statement the specificity of its occurrence, and to show that discontinuity is one of those great accidents that create cracks not only in the geology of history, but also in the simple fact of the statement; it emerges in its historical irruption; what we try to examine is the incision that it makes, that irreducible – and very often tiny – emergence. However banal it may be, however unimportant its consequences may appear to be, however quickly it may be forgotten after its appearance, however little heard or however badly deciphered we may suppose it to be, a statement is always an event that neither the language (*langue*) nor the meaning can quite exhaust. It is certainly a strange event: first, because on the one hand it is linked to the gesture of writing or to the articulation of speech, and also on the other hand it opens up to itself a residual existence in the field of a memory, or in the materiality of manuscripts, books, or any other form of recording; secondly, because, like every event, it is unique, yet subject to repetition, transformation, and reactivation; thirdly, because it is linked not only to the situations that provoke it, and to the consequences that it gives rise to, but at the same time, and in accordance with a quite different modality, to the statements that precede and follow it.

But if we isolate, in relation to the language and to thought, the occurrence of the statement/event, it is not in order to spread over everything a dust of facts. It is in order to be sure that this occurrence is not linked with synthesizing operations of a purely psychological kind (the intention of the author, the form of his mind, the rigour of his thought, the themes that obsess him, the project that traverses his existence and gives it meaning) and to be able to grasp other forms of regularity, other types of relations. Relations between statements (even if the author is unaware of them; even if the statements do not have the same author; even if the authors were unaware of each other's existence); relations between groups of statements thus established (even if these groups do not concern the same, or even adjacent, fields; even if they do not possess the same formal level; even if they are not the locus of assignable exchanges); relations between statements and groups of statements and events of a quite different kind (technical, economic, social, political). To reveal in all its purity the space in which discursive events are deployed is not to undertake to re-establish it in an isolation that nothing could overcome; it is not to close it upon itself; it is to leave oneself free to describe the interplay of relations within it and outside it.

The third purpose of such a description of the facts of discourse is that by freeing them of all the groupings that purport to be natural, immediate, universal unities, one is able to describe other unities, but this time by means of a group of controlled decisions. Providing one defines the conditions clearly, it might be legitimate to constitute, on the basis of correctly described relations, discursive groups that are not arbitrary, and yet remain invisible. Of course, these relations would never be formulated for themselves in the statements in question (unlike, for example, those explicit relations that are posed and spoken in discourse itself, as in the form of the novel, or a series of mathematical theorems). But in no way would they constitute a sort of secret discourse, animating the manifest discourse from within; it is not therefore an interpretation of the facts of the statement that might reveal them, but the analysis of their coexistence, their succession, their mutual functioning, their reciprocal determination, and their independent or correlative transformation.

However, it is not possible to describe all the relations that may emerge in this way without some guide-lines. A provisional division must be adopted as an initial approximation: an initial region that analysis will subsequently demolish and, if necessary, reorganize. But how is such a region to be circumscribed? On the one hand, we must choose, empirically, a field in which the relations are likely to be numerous, dense, and relatively easy to describe: and in what other region do discursive events appear to be more closely linked to one another, to occur in accordance with more easily decipherable relations, than in the region usually known as science? But, on the other hand, what better way of grasping in a statement, not the moment of its formal structure and laws of construction, but that of its existence and the rules that govern its appearance, if not by dealing with relatively unformalized groups of discourses, in which the statements do not seem necessarily to be built on the rules of pure syntax? How can we be sure of avoiding such divisions as the *œuvre*, or such categories as 'influence', unless, from the very outset, we adopt sufficiently broad fields and scales that are chronologically vast enough? Lastly, how can we be sure that we will not find ourselves in the grip of all those over-hasty unities or syntheses concerning the speaking subject, or the author of the text, in short, all anthropological categories? Unless, perhaps, we consider all the statements out of which these categories are constituted – all the statements that have chosen the subject of discourse (their own subject) as their 'object' and have undertaken to deploy it as their field of knowledge?

This explains the *de facto* privilege that I have accorded to those discourses that, to put it very schematically, define the 'sciences of man'. But it is only a provisional privilege. Two facts must be constantly borne in mind: that the analysis of discursive events is in no way limited to such a field; and that the division of this field itself cannot be regarded either as definitive or as absolutely valid; it is no more than an initial approximation that must allow relations to appear that may erase the limits of this initial outline.

CHAPTER 2

Discursive Formations

I have undertaken, then, to describe the relations between statements. I have been careful to accept as valid none of the unities that would normally present themselves to anyone embarking on such a task. I have decided to ignore no form of discontinuity, break, threshold, or limit. I have decided to describe statements in the field of discourse and the relations of which they are capable. As I see it, two series of problems arise at the outset: the first, which I shall leave to one side for the time being and shall return to later, concerns the indiscriminate use that I have made of the terms statement, event, and discourse; the second concerns the relations that may legitimately be described between the statements that have been left in their provisional, visible grouping.

There are statements, for example, that are quite obviously concerned – and have been from a date that is easy enough to determine – with political economy, or biology, or psychopathology; there are others that equally obviously belong to those age-old continuities known as grammar or medicine. But what are these unities? How can we say that the analysis of headaches carried out by Willis or Charcot belong to the same order of discourse? That Petty's inventions are in continuity with Neumann's econometry? That the analysis of judgement by the Port-Royal grammarians belongs to the same domain as the discovery of vowel gradations in the Indo-European languages? What, in fact, are *medicine*, *grammar*, or *political economy*? Are they merely a retrospective regrouping by which the contemporary sciences deceive themselves as to their own past? Are they forms that have become established once and for all and have gone on developing through time? Do they conceal other unities? And what sort of links can validly be recognized between all these statements that form, in such a familiar and insistent way, such an enigmatic mass?

First hypothesis – and the one that, at first sight, struck me as being the most likely and the most easily proved: statements different in form, and dispersed in time, form a group if they refer to one and the same object. Thus, statements belonging to psychopathology all seem to refer to an object that emerges in various ways in individual or social experience and which may be called madness. But I soon realized that the unity of the object 'madness' does not enable one to individualize a group of statements, and to establish between them a relation that is both constant and describable. There are two reasons for this. It would certainly be a mistake to try to discover what could have been said of madness at a particular time by interrogating the being of madness itself, its secret content, its silent, self-enclosed truth; mental illness was constituted by all that was said in all the statements that named it, divided it up, described it, explained it, traced its developments, indicated its various correlations, judged it, and possibly gave it speech by articulating, in its name, discourses that were to be taken as its own. Moreover, this group of statements is far from referring to a single object, formed once and for all, and to preserving it indefinitely as its horizon of inexhaustible ideality; the object presented as their correlative by medical statements of the seventeenth or eighteenth century is not identical with the object that emerges in legal sentences or police action; similarly, all the objects of psychopathological discourses were modified from Pinel or Esquirol to Bleuler: it is not the same illnesses that are at issue in each of these cases; we are not dealing with the same madmen.

One might, perhaps one should, conclude from this multiplicity of objects that it is not possible to accept, as a valid unity forming a group of statements, a 'discourse, concerning madness'. Perhaps one should confine one's attention to those groups of statements that have one and the same object: the discourses on melancholia, or neurosis, for example. But one would soon realize that each of these discourses in turn constituted its object and worked it to the point of transforming it altogether. So that the problem arises of knowing whether the unity of a discourse is based not so much on the permanence and uniqueness of an object as on the space in which various objects emerge and are continuously transformed. Would not the typical relation that would enable us to individualize a group of statements concerning madness then be: the rule of simultaneous or successive emergence of the various objects that are named, described, analysed, appreciated, or judged in that relation? The unity of discourses on madness would not be based upon the existence of the object 'madness', or the constitution of a single horizon of objectivity; it would be the interplay of the rules that make possible the appearance of objects during a given period of time: objects that are shaped by measures of discrimination and repression, objects that are differentiated in daily practice, in law, in religious casuistry, in medical diagnosis, objects that are manifested in pathological descriptions, objects that are circumscribed by medical codes, practices, treatment, and care. Moreover, the unity of the discourses on madness would be the interplay of the rules that define the transformations of these different objects, their non-identity through time, the break produced in them, the internal discontinuity that suspends their permanence. Paradoxically, to define a group of statements in terms of its individuality would be to define the dispersion of these objects, to grasp all the interstices that separate them, to measure the distances that reign between them – in other words, to formulate their law of division.

Second hypothesis to define a group of relations between statements: their form and type of connexion. It seemed to me, for example, that from the nineteenth century medical science was characterized not so much by its objects or concepts as by a certain *style*, a certain constant manner of statement. For the first time, medicine no longer consisted of a group of traditions, observations, and heterogeneous practices, but of a corpus of knowledge that presupposed the same way of looking at things, the same division of the perceptual field, the same analysis of the pathological fact in accordance with the visible space of the body, the same system of transcribing what one perceived in what one said (same vocabulary, same play of metaphor); in short, it seemed to me that medicine was organized as a series of descriptive statements. But, there again, I had to abandon this hypothesis at the outset and recognize that clinical discourse was just as much a group of hypotheses about life and death, of ethical choices, of therapeutic decisions, of institutional regulations, of teaching models, as a group of descriptions; that the descriptions could not, in any case, be abstracted from the hypotheses, and that the descriptive statement was only one of the formulations present in medical discourse. I also had to recognize that this description has constantly been displaced: either because, from Bichat to cell pathology, the scales and guide-lines have been displaced; or because from visual inspection, auscultation and palpation to the use of the microscope and biological tests, the information system has been modified; or, again, because, from simple anatomo-clinical correlation to the delicate analysis of physiopathological processes, the lexicon of signs and their decipherment has been entirely reconstituted; or, finally, because the doctor has gradually ceased to be himself the locus of the registering and interpretation of information, and because, beside him, outside him, there have appeared masses of documentation, instruments of correlation, and techniques of analysis, which, of course, he makes use of, but which modify his position as an observing subject in relation to the patient.

All these alterations, which may now lead to the threshold of a new medicine, gradually appeared in medical discourse throughout the nineteenth century. If one wished to define this discourse by a codified and normative system of statement, one would have to recognize that this medicine disintegrated as soon as it appeared and that it really found its formulation only in Bichat and Laennec. If there is a unity, its principle is not therefore a determined form of statements; is it not rather the group of rules, which, simultaneously or in turn, have made possible purely perceptual descriptions, together with observations mediated through instruments, the procedures used in laboratory experiments, statistical calculations, epidemiological or demographic observations, institutional regulations, and therapeutic practice? What one must characterize and individualize is the coexistence of these dispersed and heterogeneous statements; the system that governs their division, the degree to which they depend upon one another, the way in which they interlock or exclude one another, the transformation that they undergo, and the play of their location, arrangement, and replacement.

Another direction of research, another hypothesis: might it not be possible to establish groups of statements, by determining the system of permanent and coherent concepts involved? For example, does not the Classical analysis of language and grammatical facts (from Lancelot to the end of the eighteenth century) rest on a definite number of concepts whose content and usage had been established once and for all: the concept of *judgement* defined as the general, normative form of any sentence, the concepts of *subject* and *predicate* regrouped under the more general category of *noun*, the concept of *verb* used as the equivalent of that of *logical copula*, the concept of *word* defined as the sign of a representation, etc.? In this way, one might reconstitute the conceptual architecture of Classical grammar. But there too one would soon come up against limitations: no sooner would one have succeeded in describing with such elements the analyses carried out by the Port-Royal authors than one would no doubt be forced to acknowledge the appearance of new concepts; some of these may be derived from the first, but the others are heterogeneous and a few even incompatible with them. The notion of natural or inverted syntactical order, that of complement (introduced in the eighteenth century by Beauzée), may still no doubt be integrated into the conceptual system of the Port-Royal grammar. But neither the idea of an originally expressive value of sounds, nor that of a primitive body of knowledge enveloped in words and conveyed in some obscure way by them, nor that of regularity in the mutation of consonants, nor the notion of the verb as a mere name capable of designating an action or operation, is compatible with the group of concepts used by Lancelot or Duclos. Must we admit therefore that grammar only appears to form a coherent figure; and that this group of statements, analyses, descriptions, principles and consequences, deductions that has been perpetrated under this name for over a century is no more than a false unity? But perhaps one might discover a discursive unity if one sought it not in the coherence of concepts, but in their simultaneous or successive emergence, in the distance that separates them and even in their incompatibility. One would no longer seek an architecture of concepts sufficiently general and abstract to embrace all others and to introduce them into the same deductive structure; one would try to analyse the interplay of their appearances and dispersion.

Lastly, a fourth hypothesis to regroup the statements, describe their interconnexion and account for the unitary forms under which they are presented: the identity and persistence of themes. In 'sciences' like economics or biology, which are so controversial in character, so open to philosophical or ethical options, so exposed in certain cases to political manipulation, it is legitimate in the first instance to suppose that a certain thematic is capable of linking, and animating a group of discourses, like an organism with its own needs, its own internal force, and its own capacity for survival. Could one not, for example, constitute as a unity everything that has constituted the evolutionist theme from Buffon to Darwin? A theme that in the first instance was more philosophical, closer to cosmology than to biology; a theme that directed research from afar rather than named, regrouped, and explained results; a theme that always presupposed more than one was aware of, but which, on the basis of this fundamental choice, forcibly transformed into discursive knowledge what had been outlined as a hypothesis or as a necessity. Could one not speak of the Physiocratic theme in the same way? An idea that postulated, beyond all demonstration and prior to all analysis, the natural character of the three ground rents; which consequently presupposed the economic and political primacy of agrarian property; which excluded all analysis of the

35

mechanisms of industrial production; which implied, on the other hand, the description of the circulation of money within a state, of its distribution between different social categories, and of the channels by which it flowed back into production; which finally led Ricardo to consider those cases in which this triple rent did not appear, the conditions in which it could form, and consequently to denounce the arbitrariness of the Physiocratic theme?

But on the basis of such an attempt, one is led to make two inverse and complementary observations. In one case, the same thematic is articulated on the basis of two sets of concepts, two types of analysis, two perfectly different fields of objects: in its most general formulation, the evolutionist idea is perhaps the same in the work of Benoît de Maillet, Bordeu or Diderot, and in that of Darwin; but, in fact, what makes it possible and coherent is not at all the same thing in either case. In the eighteenth century, the evolutionist idea is defined on the basis of a kinship of species forming a continuum laid down at the outset (interrupted only by natural catastrophes) or gradually built up by the passing of time. In the nineteenth century the evolutionist theme concerns not so much the constitution of a continuous table of species, as the description of discontinuous groups and the analysis of the modes of interaction between an organism whose elements are interdependent and an environment that provides its real conditions of life. A single theme, but based on two types of discourse. In the case of Physiocracy, on the other hand, Quesnay's choice rests exactly on the same system of concepts as the opposite opinion held by those that might be called utilitarists. At this period the analysis of wealth involved a relatively limited set of concepts that was accepted by all (coinage was given the same definition; prices were given the same explanation; and labour costs were calculated in the same way). But, on the basis of this single set of concepts, there were two ways of explaining the formation of value, according to whether it was analysed on the basis of exchange, or on that of remuneration for the day's work. These two possibilities contained within economic theory, and in the rules of its set of concepts, resulted, on the basis of the same elements, in two different options.

It would probably be wrong therefore to seek in the existence of these themes the principles of the individualization of a discourse. Should they not be sought rather in the dispersion of the points of choice that the discourse leaves free? In the different possibilities that it opens of reanimating already existing themes, of arousing opposed strategies, of giving way to irreconcilable interests, of making it possible, with a particular set of concepts, to play different games? Rather than seeking the permanence of themes, images, and opinions through time, rather than retracing the dialectic of their conflicts in order to individualize groups of statements, could one not rather mark out the dispersion of the points of choice, and define prior to any option, to any thematic preference, a field of strategic possibilities?

I am presented therefore with four attempts, four failures – and four successive hypotheses. They must now be put to the test. Concerning those large groups of statements with which we are so familiar – and which we call *medicine, economics,* or *grammar* – I have asked myself on what their unity could be based. On a full, tightly packed, continuous, geographically well-defined field of objects? What appeared to me were rather series full of gaps, intertwined with one another, interplays of differences, distances, substitutions, transformations. On a definite, normative type of statement? I found formulations of levels that were much too different and functions that were much too heterogeneous to be linked together and arranged in a single figure, and to simulate, from one period to another, beyond in-dividual *œuvres,* a sort of great uninterrupted text. On a well-defined alphabet of notions? One is confronted with concepts that differ in struc-ture and in the rules governing their use, which ignore or exclude one another, and which cannot enter the unity of a logical architecture. On the permanence of a thematic? What one finds are rather various strategic possibilities that permit the activation of incompatible themes, or, again, the establishment of the same theme in different groups of statement. Hence the idea of describing these dispersions themselves; of discovering whether, between these elements, which are certainly not organized as a progressively deductive structure, nor as an enormous book that is being gradually and continuously written, nor as the *œuvre* of a collective subject, one cannot discern a regularity: an order in their successive appearance, correlations in their simultaneity, assignable positions in a common space, a reciprocal functioning, linked and hierar-chized transformations. Such an analysis would not try to isolate small islands of coherence in order to describe their internal structure; it would not try to suspect and to reveal latent conflicts; it would study forms of division. Or again: instead of reconstituting *chains of inference* (as one often does in the history of the sciences or of philosophy), instead of drawing up *tables of differences* (as the linguists do), it would describe *systems of dispersion.*

Whenever one can describe, between a number of statements, such a system of dispersion, whenever, between objects, types of statement, concepts, or thematic choices, one can define a regularity (an order, correlations, positions and functionings, transformations), we will say, for the sake of convenience, that we are dealing with a *discursive formation* – thus avoiding words that are already overladen with conditions and consequences, and in any case inadequate to the task of designating such a dispersion, such as 'science', 'ideology', 'theory', or 'domain of objectivity'. The conditions to which the elements of this division (objects, mode of statement, concepts, thematic choices) are subjected we shall call the *rules of formation*. The rules of formation are conditions of existence (but also of coexistence, maintenance, modification, and disappearance) in a given discursive division.

This, then, is the field to be covered; these the notions that we must put to the test and the analyses that we must carry out. I am well aware that the risks are considerable. For an initial probe, I made use of certain fairly loose, but familiar, groups of statement: I have no proof that I shall find them again at the end of the analysis, nor that I shall discover the principle of their delimitation and individualization; I am not sure that the discursive formations that I shall isolate will define medicine in its overall unity, or economics and grammar in the overall curve of their historical destination; they may even introduce unexpected boundaries and divisions. Similarly, I have no proof that such a description will be able to take account of the scientificity (or non-scientificity) of the discursive groups that I have taken as an attack point and which presented themselves at the outset with a certain pretension to scientific rationality; I have no proof that my analysis will not be situated at a quite different level, constituting a description that is irreducible to epistemology or to the history of the sciences. Moreover, at the end of such an enterprise, one may not recover those unities that, out of methodological rigour, one initially held in suspense: one may be compelled to dissociate certain *œuvres*, ignore influences and traditions, abandon definitively the question of origin, allow the commanding presence of authors to fade into the background; and thus everything that was thought to be proper to the history of ideas may disappear from view. The danger, in short, is that instead of providing a basis for what already exists, instead of going over with bold strokes lines that have already been sketched, instead of finding reassurance in this return and final confirmation, instead of completing the blessed circle that announces, after innumerable stratagems and as many nights, that all is saved, one is forced to advance beyond familiar territory, far from the certainties to which one is accustomed, towards an as yet uncharted land and unforeseeable conclusion. Is there not a danger that everything that has so far protected the historian in his daily journey and accompanied him until nightfall (the destiny of rationality and the teleology of the sciences, the long, continuous labour of thought from period to period, the awakening and the progress of consciousness, its perpetual resumption of itself, the uncompleted, but uninterrupted movement of totalizations, the return to an ever-open source, and finally the historico-transcendental thematic) may disappear, leaving for analysis a blank, indifferent space, lacking in both interiority and promise?

CHAPTER 3

The Formation of Objects

We must now list the various directions that lie open to us, and see whether this notion of 'rules of formation' – of which little more than a rough sketch has so far been provided – can be given real content. Let us look first at the formation of objects. And in order to facilitate our analysis, let us take as an example the discourse of psychopathology from the nineteenth century onwards – a chronological break that is easy enough to accept in a first approach to the subject. There are enough signs to indicate it, but let us take just two of these: the establishment at the beginning of the century of a new mode of exclusion and confinement of the madman in a psychiatric hospital; and the possibility of tracing certain present-day notions back to Esquirol, Heinroth, or Pinel (paranoia can be traced back to monomania, the intelligence quotient to the initial notion of imbecility, general paralysis to chronic encephalitis, character neurosis to non-delirious madness); whereas if we try to trace the development of psycho-pathology beyond the nineteenth century, we soon lose our way, the path becomes confused, and the projection of Du Laurens or even Van Swieten on the pathology of Kraepelin or Bleuler provides no more than chance coincidences. The objects with which psychopathology has dealt since this break in time are very numerous, mostly very new, but also very precarious, subject to change and, in some cases, to rapid disappearance: in addition to motor disturbances, hallucinations, and speech disorders (which were already regarded as manifestations of madness, although they were recognized, delimited, described, and analysed in a different way), objects appeared that belonged to hitherto unused registers: minor behavioural disorders, sexual aberrations and disturbances, the pheno-mena of suggestion and hypnosis, lesions of the central nervous system, deficiencies of intellectual or motor adaptation, criminality. And on the basis of each of these registers a variety of objects were named, circumscribed, analysed, then rectified, re-defined, challenged, erased. Is it possible to lay down the rule to which their appearance was subject? Is it possible to discover according to which non-deductive system these objects could be juxtaposed and placed in succession to form the fragmented field – showing at certain points great gaps, at others a plethora of information – of psychopathology? What has ruled their existence as objects of discourse?

(a) First we must map the first *surfaces* of their *emergence*: show where these individual differences, which, according to the degrees of rationalization, conceptual codes, and types of theory, will be accorded the status of disease, alienation, anomaly, dementia, neurosis or psychosis, degeneration, etc., may emerge, and then be designated and analysed. These surfaces of emergence are not the same for different societies, at different periods, and in different forms of discourse. In the case of nineteenth-century psychopathology, they were probably constituted by the family, the immediate social group, the work situation, the religious community (which are all normative, which are all susceptible to deviation, which all have a margin of tolerance and a threshold beyond which exclusion is demanded, which all have a mode of designation and a mode of rejecting madness, which all transfer to medicine if not the responsibility for treatment and cure, at least the burden of explanation); although organized according to a specific mode, these surfaces of emergence were not new in the nineteenth century. On the other hand, it was no doubt at this period that new surfaces of appearance began to function: art with its own normativity, sexuality (its deviations in relation to customary prohibitions become for the first time an object of observation, description, and analysis for psychiatric discourse), penality (whereas in previous periods madness was carefully distinguished from criminal conduct and was regarded as an excuse, criminality itself becomes – and subsequent to the celebrated 'homicidal monomanias' – a form of deviance more or less related to madness). In these fields of initial differentiation, in the distances, the discontinuities, and the thresholds that appear within it, psychiatric discourse finds a way of limiting its domain, of defining what it is talking about, of giving it the status of an object – and therefore of making it manifest, nameable, and describable.

(b) We must also describe the authorities of delimitation: in the nineteenth century, medicine (as an institution possessing its own rules, as a group of individuals constituting the medical profession, as a body of knowledge and practice, as an authority recognized by public opinion, the law, and government) became the major authority in society that delimited, designated, named, and established madness as an object; but it was not alone in this: the law and penal law in particular (with the definitions of excuse, non-responsibility, extenuating circumstances, and with the application of such notions as the *crime passionel*, heredity, danger to society), the religious authority (in so far as it set itself up as the authority that divided the mystical from the pathological, the spiritual from the corporeal, the supernatural from the abnormal, and in so far as it practised the direction of conscience with a view to understanding individuals rather than carrying out a casuistical classification of actions and circumstances), literary and art criticism (which in the nineteenth century treated the work less and less as an object of taste that had to be judged, and more and more as a language that had to be interpreted and in which the author's tricks of expression had to be recognized).

(c) Lastly, we must analyse the *grids of specification*: these are the systems according to which the different 'kinds of madness' are divided, contrasted, related, regrouped, classified, derived from one another as objects of psychiatric discourse (in the nineteenth century, these grids of differentiation were: the soul, as a group of hierarchized, related, and more or less interpenetrable faculties; the body, as a three-dimensional volume of organs linked together by networks of dependence and communication; the life and history of individuals, as a linear succession of phases, a tangle of traces, a group of potential reactivations, cyclical repetitions; the interplays of neuropsychological correlations as systems of reciprocal projections, and as a field of circular causality).

Such a description is still in itself inadequate. And for two reasons. These planes of emergence, authorities of delimitation, or forms of specification do not provide objects, fully formed and armed, that the discourse of psychopathology has then merely to list, classify, name, select, and cover with a network of words and sentences: it is not the families – with their norms, their prohibitions, their sensitivity thresholds – that decide who is mad, and present the 'patients' to the psychiatrists for analysis and judgement; it is not the legal system itself that hands over certain criminals to psychiatry, that sees paranoia beyond a particular murder, or a neurosis behind a sexual offence. It would be quite wrong to see discourse as a place where previously established objects are laid one after another like words on a page. But the above enumeration is inadequate for a second reason. It has located, one after another, several planes of differentiation in which the objects of discourse may appear. But what relations exist between them? Why this enumeration rather than another? What defined and closed group does one imagine one is circumscribing in this way? And how can one speak of a 'system of formation' if one knows only a series of different, heterogeneous determinations, lacking attributable links and relations?

In fact, these two series of questions refer back to the same point. In order to locate that point, let us re-examine the previous example. In the sphere with which psychopathology dealt in the nineteenth century, one sees the very early appearance (as early as Esquirol) of a whole series of objects belonging to the category of delinquency: homicide (and suicide), *crimes passionels*, sexual offences, certain forms of theft, vagrancy – and then, through them, heredity, the neurogenic environment, aggressive or self-punishing behaviour, perversions, criminal impulses, suggestibility, etc. It would be inadequate to say that one was dealing here with the consequences of a discovery: of the sudden discovery by a psychiatrist of a resemblance between criminal and pathological behaviour, a discovery of the presence in certain delinquents of the classical signs of alienation, or mental derangement. Such facts lie beyond the grasp of contemporary research: indeed, the problem is how to decide what made them possible, and how these 'discoveries' could lead to others that took them up, rectified them, modified them, or even disproved them. Similarly, it would be irrelevant to attribute the appearance of these new objects to the norms of nineteenth-century bourgeois society, to a reinforced police and penal framework, to the establishment of a new code of criminal justice, to the introduction and use of extenuating circumstances, to the increase in crime. No doubt, all these processes were at work; but they could not of themselves form objects for psychiatric discourse; to pursue the description at this level one would fall short of what one was seeking.

If, in a particular period in the history of our society, the delinquent was psychologized and pathologized, if criminal behaviour could give rise to a whole series of objects of knowledge, this was because a group of particular relations was adopted for use in psychiatric discourse. The relation between planes of specification like penal categories and degrees of diminished responsibility, and planes of psychological characterization (faculties, aptitudes, degrees of development or involution, different ways of reacting to the environment, character types, whether acquired, innate, or hereditary). The relation between the authority of medical decision and the authority of judicial decision (a really complex relation since medical decision recognizes absolutely the authority of the judiciary to define crime, to determine the circumstances in which it is committed, and the punishment that it deserves; but reserves the right to analyse its origin and to determine the degree of responsibility involved). The relation between the filter formed by judicial interrogation, police information, investigation, and the whole machinery of judicial information, and the filter formed by the medical questionnaire, clinical examinations, the search for antecedents, and biographical accounts. The relation between the family, sexual and penal norms of the behaviour of individuals, and the table of pathological symptoms and diseases of which they are the signs. The relation between therapeutic confinement in hospital (with its own thresholds, its criteria of cure, its way of distinguishing the normal from the pathological) and punitive confinement in prison (with its system of punishment and pedagogy, its criteria of good conduct, improvement, and freedom). These are the relations that, operating in psychiatric discourse, have made possible the formation of a whole group of various objects.

Let us generalize: in the nineteenth century, psychiatric discourse is characterized not by privileged objects, but by the way in which it forms objects that are in fact highly dispersed. This formation is made possible by a group of relations established between authorities of emergence, delimitation, and specification. One might say, then, that a discursive formation is defined (as far as its objects are concerned, at least) if one can establish such a group; if one can show how any particular object of discourse finds in it its place and law of emergence; if one can show that it may give birth simultaneously or successively to mutually exclusive objects, without having to modify itself.

Hence a certain number of remarks and consequences.

1. The conditions necessary for the appearance of an object of discourse, the historical conditions required if one is to 'say anything' about it, and if several people are to say different things about it, the conditions necessary if it is to exist in relation to other objects, if it is to establish with them relations of resemblance, proximity, distance, difference, transformation – as we can see, these conditions are many and imposing. Which means that one cannot speak of anything at any time; it is not easy to say something new; it is not enough for us to open our eyes, to

pay attention, or to be aware, for new objects suddenly to light up and emerge out of the ground. But this difficulty is not only a negative one; it must not be attached to some obstacle whose power appears to be, exclusively, to blind, to hinder, to prevent discovery, to conceal the purity of the evidence or the dumb obstinacy of the things themselves; the object does not await in limbo the order that will free it and enable it to become embodied in a visible and prolix objectivity; it does not pre-exist itself, held back by some obstacle at the first edges of light. It exists under the positive conditions of a complex group of relations.

2. These relations are established between institutions, economic and social processes, behavioural patterns, systems of norms, techniques, types of classification, modes of characterization; and these relations are not present in the object; it is not they that are deployed when the object is being analysed; they do not indicate the web, the immanent rationality, that ideal nervure that reappears totally or in part when one conceives of the object in the truth of its concept. They do not define its internal constitution, but what enables it to appear, to juxtapose itself with other objects, to situate itself in relation to them, to define its difference, its irreducibility, and even perhaps its heterogeneity, in short, to be placed in a field of exteriority.

3. These relations must be distinguished first from what we might call 'primary' relations, and which, independently of all discourse or all object of discourse, may be described between institutions, techniques, social forms, etc. After all, we know very well that relations existed between the bourgeois family and the functioning of judicial authorities and categories in the nineteenth century that can be analysed in their own right. They cannot always be superposed upon the relations that go to form objects: the relations of dependence that may be assigned to this primary level are not necessarily expressed in the formation of relations that makes discursive objects possible. But we must also distinguish the secondary relations that are formulated in discourse itself: what, for example, the psychiatrists of the nineteenth century could say about the relations between the family and criminality does not reproduce, as we know, the interplay of real dependencies; but neither does it reproduce the interplay of relations that make possible and sustain the objects of psychiatric discourse. Thus a space unfolds articulated with possible discourses: a system of *real* or *primary relations*, a system of *reflexive* or *secondary relations*, and a system of relations that might properly be called *discursive*. The problem is to

45

reveal the specificity of these discursive relations, and their interplay with the other two kinds.

4. Discursive relations are not, as we can see, internal to discourse: they do not connect concepts or words with one another; they do not establish a deductive or rhetorical structure between propositions or sentences. Yet they are not relations exterior to discourse, relations that might limit it, or impose certain forms upon it, or force it, in certain circumstances, to state certain things. They are, in a sense, at the limit of discourse: they offer it objects of which it can speak, or rather (for this image of offering presupposes that objects are formed independently of discourse), they determine the group of relations that discourse must establish in order to speak of this or that object, in order to deal with them, name them, analyse them, classify them, explain them, etc. These relations characterize not the language (*langue*) used by discourse, nor the circumstances in which it is deployed, but discourse itself as a practice.

We can now complete the analysis and see to what extent it fulfils, and to what extent it modifies, the initial project.

Taking those group figures which, in an insistent but confused way, presented themselves as *psychology, economics, grammar, medicine,* we asked on what kind of unity they could be based: were they simply a reconstruction after the event, based on particular works, successive theories, notions and themes some of which had been abandoned, others maintained by tradition, and again others fated to fall into oblivion only to be revived at a later date? Were they simply a series of linked enterprises?

We sought the unity of discourse in the objects themselves, in their distribution, in the interplay of their differences, in their proximity or distance – in short, in what is given to the speaking subject; and, in the end, we are sent back to a setting-up of relations that characterizes discursive practice itself; and what we discover is neither a configuration, nor a form, but a group of *rules* that are immanent in a practice, and define it in its specificity. We also used, as a point of reference, a unity like *psychopathology*: if we had wanted to provide it with a date of birth and precise limits, it would no doubt have been necessary to discover when the word was first used, to what kind of analysis it could be applied, and how it achieved its separation from neurology on the one hand and psychology on the other. What has emerged is a unity of another type, which does not appear to have the same dates, or the same surface, or the same articulations, but which may take account of a group of objects for which the term psychopathology was merely a reflexive, secondary, classificatory rubric. Psychopathology finally emerged as a discipline in a constant state of renewal, subject to constant discoveries, criticisms, and corrected errors; the system of formation that we have defined remains stable. But let there be no misunderstanding: it is not the objects that remain constant, nor the domain that they form; it is not even their point of emergence or their mode of characterization; but the relation between the surfaces on which they appear, on which they can be delimited, on which they can be analysed and specified.

In the descriptions for which I have attempted to provide a theory, there can be no question of interpreting discourse with a view to writing a history of the referent. In the example chosen, we are not trying to find out who was mad at a particular period, or in what his madness consisted, or whether his disturbances were identical with those known to us today. We are not asking ourselves whether witches were unrecognized and persecuted madmen and madwomen, or whether, at a different period, a mystical or aesthetic experience was not unduly medicalized. We are not trying to reconstitute what madness itself might be, in the form in which it first presented itself to some primitive, fundamental, deaf, scarcely articulated[1] experience, and in the form in which it was later organized (translated, deformed, travestied, perhaps even repressed) by discourses, and the oblique, often twisted play of their operations. Such a history of the referent is no doubt possible; and I have no wish at the outset to exclude any effort to uncover and free these 'prediscursive' experiences from the tyranny of the text. But what we are concerned with here is not to neutralize discourse, to make it the sign of something else, and to pierce through its density in order to reach what remains silently anterior to it, but on the contrary to maintain it in its consistency, to make it emerge in its own complexity. What, in short, we wish to do is to dispense with 'things'. To 'depresentify' them. To conjure up their rich, heavy, immediate plenitude, which we usually regard as the primitive law of a discourse that has become divorced from it through error, oblivion, illusion, ignorance, or the inertia of beliefs and traditions, or even the perhaps unconscious desire not to see and not to speak. To substitute for the enigmatic treasure of 'things' anterior to discourse, the regular formation of objects that emerge only in discourse. To define these *objects*

---

[1] This is written against an explicit theme of my book *Madness and Civilization*, and one that recurs particularly in the Preface.

without reference to the *ground*, the *foundation of things*, but by relating them to the body of rules that enable them to form as objects of a discourse and thus constitute the conditions of their historical appearance. To write a history of discursive objects that does not plunge them into the common depth of a primal soil, but deploys the nexus of regularities that govern their dispersion.

However, to suppress the stage of 'things themselves' is not necessarily to return to the linguistic analysis of meaning. When one describes the formation of the objects of a discourse, one tries to locate the relations that characterize a discursive practice, one determines neither a lexical organization, nor the scansions of a semantic field: one does not question the meaning given at a particular period to such words as 'melancholia' or 'madness without delirium', nor the opposition of content between 'psychosis' and 'neurosis'. Not, I repeat, that such analyses are regarded as illegitimate or impossible; but they are not relevant when we are trying to discover, for example, how criminality could become an object of medical expertise, or sexual deviation a possible object of psychiatric discourse. The analysis of lexical contents defines either the elements of meaning at the disposal of speaking subjects in a given period, or the semantic structure that appears on the surface of a discourse that has already been spoken; it does not concern discursive practice as a place in which a tangled plurality – at once superposed and incomplete – of objects is formed and deformed, appears and disappears.

The sagacity of the commentators is not mistaken: from the kind of analysis that I have undertaken, *words* are as deliberately absent as *things* themselves; any description of a vocabulary is as lacking as any reference to the living plenitude of experience. We shall not return to the state anterior to discourse – in which nothing has yet been said, and in which things are only just beginning to emerge out of the grey light; and we shall not pass beyond discourse in order to rediscover the forms that it has created and left behind it; we shall remain, or try to remain, at the level of discourse itself. Since it is sometimes necessary to dot the 'i's of even the most obvious absences, I will say that in all these searches, in which I have still progressed so little, I would like to show that 'discourses', in the form in which they can be heard or read, are not, as one might expect, a mere intersection of things and words: an obscure web of things, and a manifest, visible, coloured chain of words; I would like to show that discourse is not a slender surface of contact, or confrontation, between a reality and a language (*langue*), the intrication of a lexicon and an experience; I would like to show with precise examples that in analysing discourses themselves, one sees the loosening of the embrace, apparently so tight, of words and things, and the emergence of a group of rules proper to discursive practice. These rules define not the dumb existence of a reality, nor the canonical use of a vocabulary, but the ordering of objects. 'Words and things' is the entirely serious title of a problem; it is the ironic title of a work that modifies its own form, displaces its own data, and reveals, at the end of the day, a quite different task. A task that consists of not – of no longer – treating discourses as groups of signs (signifying elements referring to contents or representations) but as practices that systematically form the objects of which they speak. Of course, discourses are composed of signs; but what they do is more than use these signs to designate things. It is this *more* that renders them irreducible to the language (*langue*) and to speech. It is this 'more' that we must reveal and describe.

CHAPTER 4

The Formation of
Enunciative Modalities

Qualitative descriptions, biographical accounts, the location, interpretation, and cross-checking of signs, reasonings by analogy, deduction, statistical calculations, experimental verifications, and many other forms of statement are to be found in the discourse of nineteenth-century doctors. What is it that links them together? What necessity binds them together? Why these and not others? Before attempting an answer to such questions, we must first discover the law operating behind all these diverse statements, and the place from which they come.

(a) First question: who is speaking? Who, among the totality of speaking individuals, is accorded the right to use this sort of language (*langage*)? Who is qualified to do so? Who derives from it his own special quality, his prestige, and from whom, in return, does he receive if not the assurance, at least the presumption that what he says is true? What is the status of the individuals who – alone – have the right, sanctioned by law or tradition, juridically defined or spontaneously accepted, to proffer such a discourse? The status of doctor involves criteria of competence and knowledge; institutions, systems, pedagogic norms; legal conditions that give the right – though not without laying down certain limitations – to practise and to extend one's knowledge. It also involves a system of differentiation and relations (the division of attributions, hierarchical subordination, functional complementarity, the request for and the provision and exchange of information) with other individuals or other groups that also possess their own status (with the state and its representatives, with the judiciary, with different professional bodies, with religious groups and, at times, with priests). It also involves a number of characteristics that define its functioning in relation to society as a whole (the role that is attributed to the doctor according to whether he is consulted by a private person or summoned, more or less under compulsion, by society, according to whether he practises a profession or carries out a function; the right to intervene or make decisions that is accorded him in these different cases; what is required of him as the supervisor, guardian, and guarantor of the health of a population, a group, a family, an individual; the payment that he receives from the community or from individuals; the form of contract, explicit or implicit, that he negotiates either with the group in which he practises, or with the authority that entrusts him with a task, or with the patient who requests advice, treatment, or cure). This status of the doctor is generally a rather special one in all forms of society and civilization: he is hardly ever an undifferentiated or interchangeable person. Medical statements cannot come from anybody; their value, efficacy, even their therapeutic powers, and, generally speaking, their existence as medical statements cannot be dissociated from the statutorily defined person who has the right to make them, and to claim for them the power to overcome suffering and death. But we also know that this status in western civilization was profoundly modified at the end of the eighteenth century when the health of the population became one of the economic norms required by industrial societies.

(b) We must also describe the institutional *sites* from which the doctor makes his discourse, and from which this discourse derives its legitimate source and point of application (its specific objects and instruments of verification). In our societies, these sites are: the hospital, a place of constant, coded, systematic observation, run by a differentiated and hierarchized medical staff, thus constituting a quantifiable field of frequencies; private practice, which offers a field of less systematic, less complete, and far less numerous observations, but which sometimes facilitates observations that are more far-reaching in their effects, with a better knowledge of the background and environment; the laboratory, an autonomous place, long distinct from the hospital, where certain truths of a general kind, concerning the human body, life, disease, lesions, etc., which provide certain elements of the diagnosis, certain signs of the developing condition, certain criteria of cure, and which makes therapeutic experiment possible; lastly, what might be called the 'library' or documentary field, which includes not only the books and treatises traditionally recognized as valid, but also all the observations and case-histories published and transmitted, and the mass of statistical information (concerning the social environment, climate, epidemics, mortality rates, the incidence of diseases, the centres of contagion, occupational diseases) that can be supplied to the doctor by public bodies, by other doctors, by sociologists, and by geographers. In this respect, too, these various 'sites' of medical discourse were profoundly modified in the nineteenth century: the importance of the document continues to increase (proportionately diminishing the authority of the book or tradition); the hospital, which had been merely a subsidiary site for discourse on diseases, and which took second place in importance and value to private practice (in which diseases left in their natural environment were, in the eighteenth century, to reveal themselves in their vegetal truth), then becomes the site of systematic, homogeneous observations, large-scale confrontations, the establishment of frequencies and probabilities, the annulation of individual variants, in short, the site of the appearance of disease, not as a particular species, deploying its essential features beneath the doctor's gaze, but as an average process, with its significant guide-lines, boundaries, and potential development. Similarly, it was in the nineteenth century that daily medical practice integrated the laboratory as the site of a discourse that has the same experimental norms as physics, chemistry, or biology.

(c) The positions of the subject are also defined by the situation that it is possible for him to occupy in relation to the various domains or groups of objects: according to a certain grid of explicit or implicit interrogations, he is the questioning subject and, according to a certain programme of information, he is the listening subject; according to a table of characteristic features, he is the seeing subject, and, according to a descriptive type, the observing subject; he is situated at an optimal perceptual distance whose boundaries delimit the wheat of relevant information; he uses instrumental intermediaries that modify the scale of the information, shift the subject in relation to the average or immediate perceptual level, ensure his movement from a superficial to a deep level, make him circulate in the interior space of the body – from manifest symptoms to the organs, from the organs to the tissues, and finally from the tissues to the cells. To these perceptual situations should be added the positions that the subject can occupy in the information networks (in theoretical teaching or in hospital training; in the system of oral communication or of written document: as emitter and receiver of observations, case-histories, statistical data, general theoretical propositions, projects, and decisions). The various situations that the subject of medical discourse may occupy were redefined at the beginning of the nineteenth century with the organization of a quite different perceptual field (arranged in depth, manifested by successive recourse to instruments, deployed by surgical techniques or methods of autopsy, centred upon lesional sites), and with the establishment of new systems of registration, notation, description, classification, integration in numerical series and in statistics, with the introduction of new forms of teaching, the circulation of information, relations with other theoretical domains (sciences or philosophy) and with other institutions (whether administrative, political, or economic).

If, in clinical discourse, the doctor is in turn the sovereign, direct questioner, the observing eye, the touching finger, the organ that deciphers signs, the point at which previously formulated descriptions are integrated, the laboratory technician, it is because a whole group of relations is involved. Relations between the hospital space as a place of assistance, of purified, systematic observation, and of partially proved, partially experimental therapeutics, and a whole group of perceptual codes of the human body – as it is defined by morbid anatomy; relations between the field of immediate observations and the domain of acquired information; relations between the doctor's therapeutic role, his pedagogic role, his role as an intermediary in the diffusion of medical knowledge, and his role as a responsible representative of public health in the social space. Understood as a renewal of points of view, contents, the forms and even the style of description, the use of inductive or probabilistic reasoning, types of attribution of causality, in short, as a renewal of the modalities of enunciation, clinical medicine must not be regarded as the result of a new technique of observation – that of autopsy, which was practised long before the advent of the nineteenth century; nor as the result of the search for pathogenic causes in the depths of the organism – Morgagni was engaged in such a search in the middle of the eighteenth century; nor as the effect of that new institution, the teaching hospital – such institutions had already been in existence for some decades in Austria and Italy; nor as the result of the introduction of the concept of tissue in Bichat's *Traité des membranes*. But as the establishment of a relation, in medical discourse, between a number of distinct elements, some of which concerned the status of doctors, others the institutional and technical site from which they spoke, others their position as subjects perceiving, observing, describing, teaching, etc. It can be said that this relation between different elements (some of which are new, while others were already in existence) is effected by clinical discourse: it is this, as a practice, that establishes between them all a system of relations that is not 'really' given or constituted *a priori*; and if there is a unity, if the modalities of enunciation that it uses, or to which it gives place, are not simply juxtaposed by a series of historical contingencies, it is because it makes constant use of this group of relations.

One further remark. Having noted the disparity of the types of enunciation in clinical discourse, I have not tried to reduce it by uncovering the formal structures, categories, modes of logical succession, types of reasoning and induction, forms of analysis and synthesis that may have operated in a discourse; I did not wish to reveal the rational organization that may provide statements like those of medicine with their element of intrinsic necessity. Nor did I wish to reduce to a single founding act, or to a founding consciousness the general horizon of rationality against which the progress of medicine gradually emerged, its efforts to model itself upon the exact sciences, the contraction of its methods of observation, the slow, difficult expulsion of the images or fantasies that inhabit it, the purification of its system of reasoning. Lastly, I have not tried to describe the empirical genesis, nor the various component elements of the medical mentality: how this shift of interest on the part of the doctors came about, by what theoretical or experimental model they were influenced, what philosophy or moral thematics defined the climate of their reflexion, to what questions, to what demands, they had to reply, what efforts were required of them to free themselves from traditional prejudices, by what ways they were led towards a unification and coherence that were never achieved, never reached, by their knowledge. In short, I do not refer the various enunciative modalities to the unity of the subject – whether it concerns the subject regarded as the pure founding authority of rationality, or the subject regarded as an empirical function of synthesis. Neither the 'knowing' (*le 'connaître'*), nor the 'knowledge' (*les 'connaissances'*).

In the proposed analysis, instead of referring back to *the* synthesis or *the* unifying function of *a* subject, the various enunciative modalities manifest his dispersion.[1] To the various statuses, the various sites, the various positions that he can occupy or be given when making a discourse. To the discontinuity of the planes from which he speaks. And if these planes are linked by a system of relations, this system is not established by the synthetic activity of a consciousness identical with itself, dumb and an-

[1] In this respect, the term '*regard médical*' used in my *Naissance de la clinique* was not a very happy one.

terior to all speech, but by the specificity of a discursive practice. I shall abandon any attempt, therefore, to see discourse as a phenomenon of expression – the verbal translation of a previously established synthesis; instead, I shall look for a field of regularity for various positions of subjectivity. Thus conceived, discourse is not the majestically unfolding manifestation of a thinking, knowing, speaking subject, but, on the contrary, a totality, in which the dispersion of the subject and his discontinuity with himself may be determined. It is a space of exteriority in which a network of distinct sites is deployed. I showed earlier that it was neither by 'words' nor by 'things' that the regulation of the objects proper to a discursive formation should be defined; similarly, it must now be recognized that it is neither by recourse to a transcendental subject nor by recourse to a psychological subjectivity that the regulation of its enunciations should be defined.

CHAPTER 5

The Formation of Concepts

Perhaps the family of concepts that emerges in the work of Linnaeus (but also in that of Ricardo, and in the *Grammaire de Port-Royal*) may be organized into a coherent whole. Perhaps one might be able to restore the deductive architecture that it forms. In any case, the experiment is worth attempting – and it has been attempted several times. On the other hand, if one takes a broader scale, and chooses as guide-lines such disciplines as grammar, or economics, or the study of living beings, the set of concepts that emerges does not obey such rigorous conditions; their history is not the stone-by-stone construction of an edifice. Should this dispersion be left in its apparent disorder? Or should it be seen as a succession of conceptual systems, each possessing its own organization, and being articulated only against the permanence of problems, the continuity of tradition, or the mechanism of influences? Could a law not be found that would account for the successive or simultaneous emergence of disparate concepts? Could a system of occurrence not be found between them that was not a logical systematicity? Rather than wishing to replace concepts in a virtual deductive edifice, one would have to describe the organization of the field of statements where they appeared and circulated.

(a) This organization involves firstly forms of *succession*. And among them, the various *orderings of enunciative series* (whether the order of inferences, successive implications, and demonstrative reasonings; or the order of descriptions, the schemata of generalization or progressive specification to which they are subject, the spatial distributions that they cover; or the order of the descriptive accounts, and the way in which the events of the time are distributed in the linear succession of the statements); the various *types of dependence* of the statements (which are not always either identical or superposable on the manifest successions of the series of statements: this is the case in the dependences of hypothesis/verification, assertion/critique, general law/particular application; the various rhetorical *schemata* according to which groups of statements may be *combined*, (how descriptions, deductions, definitions, whose succession characterizes the architecture of a text, are linked together). Take, for example, the case of Natural History in the Classical period: it does not use the same concepts as in the sixteenth century; certain of the older concepts (genus, species, signs) are used in different ways; new concepts (like that of structure) appear; and others (like that of organism) are formed later. But what was altered in the seventeenth century, and was to govern the appearance and recurrence of concepts, for the whole of Natural History, was the general arrangement of the statements, their successive arrangement in particular wholes; it was the way in which one wrote down what one observed and, by means of a series of statements, recreated a perceptual process; it was the relation and interplay of subordinations between describing, articulating into distinctive features, characterizing, and classifying; it was the reciprocal position of particular observations and general principles; it was the system of dependence between what one learnt, what one saw, what one deduced, what one accepted as probable, and what one postulated. In the seventeenth and eighteenth centuries, Natural History was not simply a form of knowledge that gave a new definition to concepts like 'genus' or 'character', and which introduced new concepts like that of 'natural classification' or 'mammal'; above all, it was a set of rules for arranging statements in series, an obligatory set of schemata of dependence, of order, and of successions, in which the recurrent elements that may have value as concepts were distributed.

(b) The configuration of the enunciative field also involves forms of *coexistence*. These outline first a *field of presence* (by which is understood all statements formulated elsewhere and taken up in a discourse, acknowledged to be truthful, involving exact description, well-founded reasoning, or necessary presupposition); we must also give our attention to those that are criticized, discussed, and judged, as well as those that are rejected or excluded); in this field of presence, the relations established may be of the order of experimental verification, logical validation, mere repetition, acceptance justified by tradition and authority, commentary, a search for hidden meanings, the analysis of error; these relations may be explicit (and sometimes formulated in types of specialized statements: references, critical discussions), or implicit and present in ordinary statements. Again, it is easy to see that the field of presence of Natural History in the Classical period does not obey the same forms, or the same criteria of choice, or the same principles of exclusion, as in the period when Aldrovandi was collecting in one and the same text everything that had been seen, observed, recounted, passed on innumerable times by word of mouth, and even imagined by the poets, on the subject of monsters. Distinct from this field of presence one may also describe a *field of concomitance* (this includes statements that concern quite different domains of objects, and belong to quite different domains of objects, and belong to quite different types of discourse, but which are active among the statements studied here, either because they serve as analogical confirmation, or because they serve as a general principle and as premises accepted by a reasoning, or because they serve as models that can be transferred to other contents, or because they function as a higher authority than that to which at least certain propositions are presented and subjected): thus the field of concomitance of the Natural History of the period of Linnaeus and Buffon is defined by a number of relations with cosmology, the history of the earth, philosophy, theology, scripture and biblical exegesis, mathematics (in the very general form of a science of order); and all these relations distinguish it from both the discourse of the sixteenth-century naturalists and that of the nineteenth-century biologists. Lastly, the enunciative field involves what might be called a *field of memory* (statements that are no longer accepted or discussed, and which consequently no longer define either a body of truth or a domain of validity, but in relation to which relations of filiation, genesis, transformation, continuity, and historical discontinuity can be established): thus the field of memory of Natural History, since Tournefort, seems particularly restricted and impoverished in its forms when compared with the broad, cumulative, and very specific field of memory possessed by nineteenth- and twentieth-century biology; on the other hand, it seems much better defined and better articulated than the field of memory surrounding the history of plants and animals in the Renaissance: for at that time it could scarcely be distinguished from the field of presence; they had the same extension and the same form, and involved the same relations.

(c) Lastly, we may define the *procedures of intervention* that may be legitimately applied to statements. These procedures are not in fact the same for all discursive formations; those that are used (to the exclusion of all others), the relations that link them and the unity thus created make it possible to specify each one. These procedures may appear: in *techniques of rewriting* (like those, for example, that enabled the naturalists of the Classical period to rewrite linear descriptions in classificatory tables that have neither the same laws nor the same configuration as the lists and groups of kinship established in the Middle Ages and during the Renaissance); in *methods of transcribing* statements (articulated in the natural language) according to a more or less formalized and artificial language (the project, and to a certain extent the realization, of such a language is to be found in Linnaeus and Adanson); the *modes of translating* quantitative statements into qualitative formulations and vice versa (the establishment of relations between purely perceptual measurements and descriptions); the means used to increase the *approximation* of statements and to refine their exactitude (structural analysis according to the form, number, arrangement, and size of the elements has made it possible, since Tournefort, to achieve a closer and above all more constant approximation of descriptive statements); the way in which one *delimits* once again – by extension or restriction – the domain of validity of statements (the enunciation of structural characters was restricted in the period between Tournefort and Linnaeus, then enlarged in that between Buffon and Jussieu); the way in which one *transfers* a type of statement from one field of application to another (like the transference from vegetal characterization to animal taxonomy; or from the description of superficial characters to the internal elements of the organism); the methods of *systematizing* propositions that already exist, because they have been previously formulated, but in a separated state; or again the methods of redistributing statements that are already linked together, but which one rearranges in a new systematic whole (as Adanson takes up the natural characterizations that had been made before, either by himself or by others, and placed them in a group of artificial descriptions, the schema of which he had previously worked out on the basis of some abstract combinatory).

These elements that I am proposing to analyse are of rather different kinds. Some constitute rules of formal construction, others rhetorical practices; some define the internal configuration of a text, others the modes of relation and interference between different texts; some are characteristic of a particular period, others have a distant origin and far-reaching chronological import. But what properly belongs to a discursive formation and what makes it possible to delimit the group of concepts, disparate as they may be, that are specific to it, is the way in which these different elements are related to one another: the way in which, for example, the ordering of descriptions or accounts is linked to the techniques of rewriting; the way in which the field of memory is linked to the forms of hierarchy and subordination that govern the statements of a text; the way in which the modes of approximation and development of the statements are linked to the modes of criticism, commentary and interpretation of previously formulated statements, etc. It is this group of relations that constitutes a system of conceptual formation.

The description of such a system could not be valid for a direct, immediate description of the concepts themselves. My intention is not to carry out an exhaustive observation of them, to establish the characteristics that they may have in common, to undertake a classification of them, to measure their internal coherence, or to test their mutual compatibility; I do not wish to take as an object of analysis the conceptual architecture of an isolated text, an individual *œuvre*, or a science at a particular moment in time. One stands back in relation to this manifest set of concepts; and one tries to determine according to what schemata (of series, simultaneous groupings, linear or reciprocal modification) the statements may be linked to one another in a type of discourse; one tries in this way to discover how the recurrent elements of statements can reappear, dissociate, recompose, gain in extension or determination, be taken up into new logical structures, acquire, on the other hand, new semantic contents, and constitute partial organizations among themselves. These schemata make it possible to describe – not the laws of the internal construction of concepts, not their progressive and individual genesis in the mind of man – but their anonymous dispersion through texts, books, and *œuvres*. A dispersion that characterizes a type of discourse, and which defines, between concepts, forms of deduction, derivation, and coherence, but also of incompatibility, intersection, substitution, exclusion, mutual alteration, displacement, etc. Such an analysis, then, concerns, at a kind of *preconceptual* level, the field in which concepts can coexist and the rules to which this field is subjected.

In order to define more precisely what I mean by 'preconceptual', I shall take the example of the four 'theoretical schemata', studied in my book *The Order of Things*, and which characterize General Grammar in the seventeenth and eighteenth centuries. These four schemata – attribution, articulation, designation, and derivation – do not designate concepts that were in fact used by the Classical grammarians; nor do they make it possible to reconstitute, over and above different grammatical works, a sort of more general, more abstract, more impoverished system, but discover, by that very fact, the profound compatibility of these different, apparently opposed systems. They make it possible to describe:

1. How the different grammatical analyses can be ordered and deployed; and what forms of succession are possible between analyses of the noun, analyses of the verb, and analyses of the adjective, those that concern phonetics and those that concern syntax, those that concern the original language (*langue*), and those that project an artificial language (*langue*). These different orders are laid down by the relations of dependence that may be observed between the theories of attribution, articulation, designation, and derivation.

2. How General Grammar defines a domain of *validity* for itself (according to what criteria one may discuss the truth or falsehood of a proposition); how it constitutes a domain of *normativity* for itself (according to what criteria one may exclude certain statements as being irrelevant to the discourse, or as inessential and marginal, or as non-scientific); how it constitutes a domain of *actuality* for itself (comprising acquired solutions, defining present problems, situating concepts and affirmations that have fallen into disuse).

3. What relations General Grammar has with Mathesis (with Cartesian and post-Cartesian algebra, with the project of a general science of order), with the philosophical analysis of representation and the theory of signs, with Natural History, the problems of characterization and taxonomy, with the Analysis of Wealth and the problems of the arbitrary signs of measurement and exchange: by marking out these relations one may determine the ways by which the circulation, the transfer and the modification of concepts, the alteration of their form or changes in their field of application, are made possible between one domain and another. The network formed by the four theoretical segments does not define the logical architecture of all the concepts used by grammarians; it outlines the regular space of their formation.

4. How the various conceptions of the verb 'to be', of the copula, of the verbal radical and the flexional ending (for a theoretical schema of *attribution*) were simultaneously or successively possible (under the form of alternative choice, modification, or substitution); the various conceptions of the phonetic elements, of the alphabet, of the name, of substantives

and adjectives (for a theoretical schema of *articulation*); the various concepts of proper noun and common noun, demonstrative, nominal root, syllable or expressive sonority (for the theoretical segment of *designation*); the various concepts of original and derived language (*langage*), metaphor and figure, poetic language (*langage*) (for the theoretical segment of *derivation*).

The 'preconceptual' level that we have uncovered refers neither to a horizon of ideality nor to an empirical genesis of abstractions. On the one hand, it is not a horizon of ideality, placed, discovered, or established by a founding gesture – and one that is so original that it eludes all chronological insertion; it is not an inexhaustible *a priori* at the confines of history, set back both because it eludes all beginning, all genetic restitution, and because it could never be contemporary with itself in an explicit totality. In fact one does not pose the question at the level of discourse itself, which is not external translation, but the locus of emergence of concepts; one does not attach the constants of discourse to the ideal structures of the concept, but one describes the conceptual network on the basis of the intrinsic regularities of discourse; one does not subject the multiplicity of statements to the coherence of concepts, and this coherence to the silent recollection of a meta-historical ideality; one establishes the inverse series: one replaces the pure aims of non-contradiction in a complex network of conceptual compatibility and incompatibility; and one relates this complexity to the rules that characterize a particular discursive practice. By that very fact, it is no longer necessary to appeal to the themes of an endlessly withdrawing origin and an inexhaustible horizon: the organization of a group of rules in the practice of discourse, even if it does not constitute an event so easy to situate as a formulation or a discovery, may be determined, however, in the element of history; and if it is inexhaustible, it is by that very fact that the perfectly describable system that it constitutes takes account of a very considerable set of concepts and a very large number of transformations that affect both these concepts and their relations. Instead of outlining a horizon that rises from the depths of history and maintains itself through history, the 'preconceptual' thus described is, on the contrary, at the most 'superficial' level (at the level of discourse), the group of rules that in fact operate within it.

Nor is it a genesis of abstractions, trying to rediscover the series of operations that have made it possible to constitute them: overall intuitions, discoveries of particular cases, the disconnexion of imaginary themes, the encountering of theoretical or technical obstacles, successive borrowings from traditional models, definition of the adequate formal structure, etc. In the analysis proposed here, the rules of formation operate not only in the mind or consciousness of individuals, but in discourse itself; they operate therefore, according to a sort of uniform anonymity, on all individuals who undertake to speak in this discursive field. On the other hand, one does not suppose them to be universally valid for every domain; one always describes them in particular discursive fields, and one does not accord them at the outset indefinite possibilities of extension. The most one can do is to make a systematic comparison, from one region to another, of the rules for the formation of concepts: it is in this way that I have tried to uncover the identities and differences that may be presented by these groups of rules in the General Grammar, the Natural History, and the Analysis of Wealth of the Classical period. These groups of rules are specific enough in each of these domains to characterize a particular, well-individualized discursive formation; but they offer enough analogies for us to see these various formations form a wider discursive grouping at a higher level. In any case, the rules governing the formation of concepts, however generalized the concepts may be, are not the result, laid down in history and deposited in the depth of collective customs, of operations carried out by individuals; they do not constitute the bare schema of a whole obscure work, in the course of which concepts would be made to emerge through illusions, prejudices, errors, and traditions. The pre-conceptual field allows the emergence of the discursive regularities and constraints that have made possible the heterogeneous multiplicity of concepts, and, beyond these the profusion of the themes, beliefs, and representations with which one usually deals when one is writing the history of ideas.

In order to analyse the rules for the formation of objects, one must neither, as we have seen, embody them in things, nor relate them to the domain of words; in order to analyse the formation of enunciative types, one must relate them neither to the knowing subject, nor to a psychological individuality. Similarly, to analyse the formation of concepts, one must relate them neither to the horizon of *ideality*, nor to the empirical progress of *ideas*.

CHAPTER 6

The Formation of Strategies

Such discourses as economics, medicine, grammar, the science of living beings give rise to certain organizations of concepts, certain regroupings of objects, certain types of enunciation, which form, according to their degree of coherence, rigour, and stability, themes or theories: the theme, in eighteenth-century grammar, of an original language (*langue*) from which all others derive, and of which all others carry within themselves a sometimes decipherable memory; a theory, in nineteenth-century philology, of a kinship between all the Indo-European languages, and of an archaic idiom that served as a common starting-point; a theme, in the eighteenth century, of an evolution of the species deploying in time the continuity of nature, and explaining the present gaps in the taxonomic table; a theory, propounded by the Physiocrats, of a circulation of wealth on the basis of agricultural production. Whatever their formal level may be, I shall call these themes and theories 'strategies'. The problem is to discover how they are distributed in history. Is it necessity that links them together, makes them invisible, calls them to their right places one after another, and makes of them successive solutions to one and the same problem? Or chance encounters between ideas of different origin, influences, discoveries, speculative climates, theoretical models that the patience or genius of individuals arranges into more or less well-constituted wholes? Or can one find a regularity between them and define the common system of their formation?

As for the analysis of these strategies, I can hardly enter into great detail. The reason is simple enough: in the various discursive domains, which I have tried to sketch out – rather hesitantly no doubt, and, especially at the beginning, with inadequate methodological control – the problem was to describe in each case the discursive formation in all its dimensions, and according to its own characteristics: it was necessary therefore to describe each time the rules for the formation of objects, modalities of statement, concepts, and theoretical choices. But it turned out that the difficult point of the analysis, and the one that demanded greatest attention, was not the same in each case. In *Madness and Civilization*, I was dealing with a discursive formation whose theoretical points of choice were fairly easy to locate, whose conceptual systems were relatively uncomplex and few in number, and whose enunciative rules were fairly homogeneous and repetitive; on the other hand, the problem lay in the emergence of a whole group of highly complex, interwoven objects; it was necessary above all to describe the formation of these objects, in order to locate in its specificity the whole of psychiatric discourse. In *Naissance de la clinique*, the essential point of the research was the way in which, at the end of the eighteenth and the beginning of the nineteenth century, the enunciative forms of medical discourse had been modified; the analysis was concerned therefore less with the formation of conceptual systems, or the formation of theoretical choices, than with the status, the institutional siting, the situation, and the modes of insertion used by the discoursing subject. Lastly, in *The Order of Things*, my attention was concentrated mainly on the networks of concepts and their rules of formation (identical or different) as they could be located in General Grammar, Natural History, and the Analysis of Wealth. The place, and the implications, of the strategic choices were indicated (whether, for example, in the case of Linnaeus and Buffon, or the Physiocrats and the Utilitarists); but I did little more than locate them, and my analysis scarcely touched on their formation. Let us say that a fuller analysis of theoretical choices must be left until a later study, in which I shall be able to give it my whole attention.

For the moment, the most that I can do is to indicate the directions in which the research will proceed. These might be summarized thus:

1. Determine the possible *points of diffraction* of discourse. These points are characterized in the first instance as *points of incompatibility*: two objects, or two types of enunciation, or two concepts may appear, in the same discursive formation, without being able to enter – under pain of manifest contradiction or inconsequence – the same series of statements. They are then characterized as *points of equivalence*: the two incompatible elements are formed in the same way and on the basis of the same rules; the conditions of their appearance are identical; they are situated at the same level; and instead of constituting a mere defect of coherence, they form an alternative: even if, chronologically speaking, they do not appear at the

same time, even if they do not have the same importance, and if they were not equally represented in the population of effective statements, they appear in the form of 'either . . . or'. Lastly, they are characterized as *link points of systematization*: on the basis of each of these equivalent, yet incompatible elements, a coherent series of objects, forms of statement, and concepts has been derived (with, in each series, possible new points of incompatibility). In other words, the dispersions studied at previous levels do not simply constitute gaps, non-identities, discontinuous series; they come to form discursive sub-groups – those very sub-groups that are usually regarded as being of major importance, as if they were the immediate unity and raw material out of which larger discursive groups ('theories', 'conceptions', 'themes') are formed. For example, one does not consider, in an analysis of this kind, that the Analysis of Wealth, in the eighteenth century, was the result (by way of simultaneous composition or chronological succession) of several different conceptions of coinage, of the exchange of objects of need, of the formation of value and prices, or of ground rent; one does not consider that it is made up of the ideas of Cantillon, taking up from those of Petty, of Law's experience reflected by various theoreticians in turn, and of the Physiocratic system opposing Utilitarist conceptions. One describes it rather as a unity of distribution that opens a field of possible options, and enables various mutually exclusive architectures to appear side by side or in turn.

2. But all the possible alternatives are not in fact realized: there are a good many partial groups, regional compatibilities, and coherent architectures that might have emerged, yet did not do so. In order to account for the choices that were made out of all those that could have been made (and those alone), one must describe the specific authorities that guided one's choice. Well to the fore is the role played by the discourse being studied in relation to those that are contemporary with it or related to it. One must study therefore the *economy of the discursive constellation* to which it belongs. It may in fact play the role of a formal system of which other discourses are applications with various semantic fields; it may, on the other hand, be that of a concrete model that must be applied to other discourses at a higher level of abstraction (thus General Grammar, in the seventeenth and eighteenth centuries, appears as a particular model of the general theory of signs and representation). The discourse under study may also be in a relation of analogy, opposition, or complementarity with certain other discourses (there is, for example, a relation of analogy, in the

Classical period, between the Analysis of Wealth and Natural History; the first is to the representation of need and desire what the second is to the representation of perceptions and judgements; one may also note that Natural History and General Grammar are opposed to one another in the same way as a theory of natural characters and a theory of conventional signs; both, in turn, are opposed to the Analysis of Wealth just as the study of qualitative signs is opposed to that of the quantitative signs of measurement; each, in fact, develops one of the three complementary roles of the representative sign: designation, classification, exchange). Lastly, one may describe between several discourses relations of mutual delimitation, each giving the other the distinctive marks of its singularity by the differentiation of its domain of application (as in the case of psychiatry and organic medicine which were virtually not distinguished from one another before the end of the eighteenth century, and which established from that moment a gap that has since characterized them). This whole group of relations forms a principle of determination that permits or excludes, within a given discourse, a certain number of statements: these are conceptual systematizations, enunciative series, groups and organizations of objects that might have been possible (and of which nothing can justify the absence at the level of their own rules of formation), but which are excluded by a discursive constellation at a higher level and in a broader space. A discursive formation does not occupy therefore all the possible volume that is opened up to it of right by the systems of formation of its objects, its enunciations, and its concepts; it is essentially incomplete, owing to the system of formation of its strategic choices. Hence the fact that, taken up again, placed, and interpreted in a new constellation, a given discursive formation may reveal new possibilities (thus in the present distribution of scientific discourses, the Grammar of Port-Royal or the taxonomy of Linnaeus may free elements that, in relation to them, are both intrinsic and new); but we are not dealing with a silent content that has remained implicit, that has been said and yet not said, and which constitutes beneath manifest statements a sort of sub-discourse that is more fundamental, and which is now emerging at last into the light of day; what we are dealing with is a modification in the principle of exclusion and the principle of the possibility of choices; a modification that is due to an insertion in a new discursive constellation.

3. The determination of the theoretical choices that were actually made is also dependent upon another authority. This authority is characterized

67

first by the *function* that the discourse under study must carry out *in a field of non-discursive practices*. Thus General Grammar played a role in pedagogic practice; in a much more obvious, and much more important way, the Analysis of Wealth played a role not only in the political and economic decisions of governments, but in the scarcely conceptualized, scarcely theoretized, daily practice of emergent capitalism, and in the social and political struggles that characterized the Classical period. This authority also involves *the rules and processes of appropriation* of discourse: for in our societies (and no doubt in many others) the property of discourse – in the sense of the right to speak, ability to understand, licit and immediate access to the corpus of already formulated statements, and the capacity to invest this discourse in decisions, institutions, or practices – is in fact confined (sometimes with the addition of legal sanctions) to a particular group of individuals; in the bourgeois societies that we have known since the sixteenth century, economic discourse has never been a common discourse (no more than medical or literary discourse, though in a different way). Lastly, this authority is characterized by the *possible positions of desire in relation to discourse*: discourse may in fact be the place for a phantasmatic representation, an element of symbolization, a form of the forbidden, an instrument of derived satisfaction (this possibility of being in relation with desire is not simply the fact of the poetic, fictional, or imaginary practice of discourse: the discourses on wealth, on language (*langage*), on nature, on madness, on life and death, and many others, perhaps, that are much more abstract, may occupy very specific positions in relation to desire). In any case, the analysis of this authority must show that neither the relation of discourse to desire, nor the processes of its appropriation, nor its role among non-discursive practices is extrinsic to its unity, its characterization, and the laws of its formation. They are not disturbing elements which, superposing themselves upon its pure, neutral, atemporal, silent form, suppress its true voice and emit in its place a travestied discourse, but, on the contrary, its formative elements.

A discursive formation will be individualized if one can define the system of formation of the different strategies that are deployed in it; in other words, if one can show how they all derive (in spite of their sometimes extreme diversity, and in spite of their dispersion in time) from the same set of relations. For example, the Analysis of Wealth in the seventeenth and eighteenth centuries is characterized by the system that could form both Colbert's mercantilism and Cantillon's 'neo-mercantilism';

Law's strategy and that of Paris-Duverney; the Physiocratic option and the Utilitarist option. And one will have defined this system if one can describe how the points of diffraction of economic discourse derive from one another, regulate one another, and are involved with one another (how a point of choice about prices derives from a decision about the concept of value); how the choices made depend on the general constellation in which economic discourse figures (the choice in favour of coinage-sign is linked to the place occupied by the Analysis of Wealth, beside the theory of language (*langage*), the analysis of representations, mathesis, and the science of order); how these choices are linked to the function carried out by economic discourse in the practice of emergent capitalism, the process of appropriation of which it is the object on the part of the bourgeoisie, the role that it can play in the realization of interests and desires. Economic discourse, in the Classical period, is defined by a certain constant way of relating possibilities of systematization interior to a discourse, other discourses that are exterior to it, and a whole non-discursive field of practices, appropriation, interests, and desires.

It should be noted that the strategies thus described are not rooted, anterior to discourse, in the silent depths of a choice that is both preliminary and fundamental. All these groups of discourses that are to be described are not the expression of a world-view that has been coined in the form of words, nor the hypocritical translation of an interest masquerading under the pretext of a theory: the Natural History of the Classical period is more than a confrontation, in the limbo that precedes manifest history, between a (Linnaean) view of a static, ordered, compartmented universe that is subjected from its very beginnings to the classificatory table, and the still confused perception of a nature that is the heir to time, with all the weight of its accidents, and open to the possibility of an evolution; similarly, the Analysis of Wealth is more than the conflict of interest between a bourgeoisie that has become a land-owning class, expressing its economic or political demands through the Physiocrats, and a commercial bourgeoisie that demands protectionist or liberal measures through the Utilitarists. Neither the Analysis of Wealth, nor Natural History, if one questions them at the level of their existence, their unity, their permanence, and their transformations, may be regarded as the sum of these various options. On the contrary, these options must be described as systematically different ways of treating objects of discourse (of delimiting them, regrouping or separating them, linking them together and making them derive from one another), of arranging forms of enunciation (of choosing them, placing them, constituting series, composing them into great rhetorical unities), of manipulating concepts (of giving them rules for their use, inserting them into regional coherences, and thus constituting conceptual architectures). These options are not seeds of discourse (in which discourses are determined in advance and prefigured in a quasi-microscopic form); they are regulated ways (and describable as such) of practising the possibilities of discourse.

But these strategies must not be analysed either as secondary elements that are superposed on a discursive rationality that is, of right, independent of them. There is not (or, at least, as far as the historical description whose possibility we are tracing here is concerned) a sort of ideal discourse that is both ultimate and timeless, and which choices, extrinsic in origin, have perverted, disturbed, suppressed, or thrust towards a possibly distant future; one must not suppose for example that it holds on nature or on the economy two superposed and intermingled discourses: one that proceeds slowly, accumulating its acquisitions and gradually achieving completion (a true discourse, but one that exists in its pure state only at the teleological confines of history); the other forever disintegrating, recommenced, in perpetual rupture with itself, composed of heterogeneous fragments (a discourse of opinion that history, in the course of time, throws back into the past). There is no natural taxonomy that has been exact, fixism excepted; there is no economy of exchange and use that has been true, without the preferences and illusions of a mercantile bourgeoisie. Classical taxonomy or the Analysis of Wealth, in the form in which they actually existed, and constituted historical figures, involve, in an articulated but indissociable system, objects, statements, concepts, *and* theoretical choices. And just as one must not relate the formation of objects either to words or to things, nor that of statements either to the pure form of knowledge or to the psychological subject, nor that of concepts either to the structure of ideality or to the succession of ideas, one must not relate the formation of theoretical choices either to a fundamental *project* or to the secondary play of *opinions*.

CHAPTER 7

Remarks and Consequences

We must now take up once more a number of remarks to be found in the preceding analyses, reply to some of the questions that they inevitably raise, and above all examine the objection that threatens to present itself, for the paradox of the enterprise is now apparent.

At the outset I questioned those pre-established unities according to which one has traditionally divided up the indefinite, repetitive, prolific domain of discourse. My intention was not to deny all value to these unities or to try to forbid their use; it was to show that they required, in order to be defined exactly, a theoretical elaboration. However – and it is here that all the preceding analyses appear so problematic – was it necessary to superpose upon these unities, which may in fact have been rather uncertain, another category of less visible, more abstract, and certainly far more problematical unities? But in cases when their historical limits and the specificity of their organization are fairly easy to perceive (witness General Grammar or Natural History), these discursive formations present far more difficult problems of location than the book, or the *œuvre*. Why, then, proceed to such dubious regroupings at the very moment when one is challenging those that once seemed the most obvious? What new domain is one hoping to discover? What hitherto obscure or implicit relations? What transformations that have hitherto remained outside the reach of historians? In short, what descriptive efficacy can one accord to these new analyses? I shall try to answer all these questions later. But for the moment I must reply to a question that is primary in relation to these later analyses, and terminal in relation to the preceding ones: on the question of the discursive formations that I have tried to define, can one really speak of unities? Is the re-division that I am proposing capable of individualizing wholes? And what is the nature of the unity thus discovered or constructed?

We set out with an observation: with the unity of a discourse like that of clinical medicine, or political economy, or Natural History, we are dealing with a dispersion of elements. This dispersion itself – with its gaps, its discontinuities, its entanglements, its incompatibilities, its replacements, and its substitutions – can be described in its uniqueness if one is able to determine the specific rules in accordance with which its objects, statements, concepts, and theoretical options have been formed: if there really is a unity, it does not lie in the visible, horizontal coherence of the elements formed; it resides, well anterior to their formation, in the system that makes possible and governs that formation. But in what way can we speak of unities and systems? How can we affirm that we have properly individualized certain discursive groups or wholes? When in a highly random way we have uncovered, behind the apparently irreducible multiplicity of objects, statements, concepts, and choices, a mass of elements that were no less numerous or dispersed, but which were heterogeneous with one another? When we have divided these elements into four distinct groups whose mode of articulation has scarcely been defined? And in what sense can one say that all these elements that have been uncovered behind the objects, statements, concepts, and strategies of discourses guarantee the existence of no less individualizable wholes such as *œuvres* or books?

1. As we have seen – and there is probably no need to reiterate it – when one speaks of a system of formation, one does not only mean the juxtaposition, coexistence, or interaction of heterogeneous elements (institutions, techniques, social groups, perceptual organizations, relations between various discourses), but also the relation that is established between them – and in a well determined form – by discursive practice. But what is to be done with those four systems or rather those four groups of relations? How can they all define a single system of formation?

In fact, the different levels thus defined are not independent of one another. I have shown that the strategic choices do not emerge directly from a world-view or from a predominance of interests peculiar to this or that speaking subject; but that their very possibility is determined by points of divergence in the group of concepts; I have also shown that concepts were not formed directly against the approximative, confused, and living background of ideas, but on the basis of forms of coexistence between statements; and, as we have seen, the modalities of enunciation were described on the basis of the position occupied by the subject in relation to the domain of objects of which he is speaking. In this way, there exists a vertical system of dependences: not all the positions of the subject, all the types of coexistence between statements, all the discursive strategies, are equally possible, but only those authorized by anterior levels; given, for example, the system of formation that governed, in the eighteenth century, the objects of Natural History (as individualities possessing characters, and therefore classifiable; as structural elements capable of variation; as visible, analysable surfaces; as a field of continuous, regular differences), certain modalities of enunciation are excluded (for example, the decipherment of signs), others are implied (for example, description according to a particular code); given, too, the different positions that the discoursing subject may occupy (as an observing subject with instrumental mediation, as a subject selecting out of the perceptual plurality only the elements of the structure, as a subject transcribing these elements into a coded vocabulary, etc.), there are a number of coexistences between the statements that are excluded (as, for example, the erudite reactivation of the already-said, or the exegetic commentary of a sacralized text), others on the other hand that are possible or required (such as the integration of totally or partially analogous statements into a classificatory table). The levels are not free from one another therefore, and are not deployed according to an unlimited autonomy: between the primary differentiation of objects and the formation of discursive strategies there exists a whole hierarchy of relations.

But relations are also established in a reverse direction. The lower levels are not independent of those above them. Theoretical choices exclude or imply, in the statements in which they are made, the formation of certain concepts, that is, certain forms of coexistence between statements: thus in the texts of the Physiocrats, one will not find the same modes of integrating quantitative data and measurements as in the analyses of the Utilitarists. It is not that the Physiocratic option can modify the group of rules that govern the formation of economic concepts in the eighteenth century; but it can implement some of these rules and exclude others and consequently reveal certain concepts (like that, for example, of the net product) that appear nowhere else. It is not the theoretical choice that governs the formation of the concept; but the choice has produced the concept by the mediation of specific rules for the formation of concepts, and by the set of relations that it holds with this level.

2. These systems of formation must not be taken as blocks of immobility, static forms that are imposed on discourse from the outside, and

73

that define once and for all its characteristics and possibilities. They are not constraints whose origin is to be found in the thoughts of men, or in the play of their representations; but nor are they determinations which, formed at the level of institutions, or social or economic relations, transcribe themselves by force on the surface of discourses. These systems – I repeat – reside in discourse itself; or rather (since we are concerned not with its interiority and what it may contain, but with its specific existence and with its conditions) on its frontier, at that limit at which the specific rules that enable it to exist as such are defined. By system of formation, then, I mean a complex group of relations that function as a rule: it lays down what must be related, in a particular discursive practice, for such and such an enunciation to be made, for such and such a concept to be used, for such and such a strategy to be organized. To define a system of formation in its specific individuality is therefore to characterize a discourse or a group of statements by the regularity of a practice.

As a group of rules for a discursive practice, the system of formation is not a stranger to time. It does not concentrate everything that may appear through an age-old series of statements into an initial point that is, at the same time, beginning, origin, foundation, system of axioms, and on the basis of which the events of real history have merely to unfold in a quite necessary way. What it outlines is the system of rules that must be put into operation if such and such an object is to be transformed, such and such a new enumeration appear, such and such a concept be developed, whether metamorphosed or imported, and such and such a strategy be modified – without ever ceasing to belong to this same discourse; and what it also outlines is the system of rules that has to be put into operation if a change in other discourses (in other practices, in institutions, in social relations, and in economic processes) is to be transcribed within a given discourse, thus constituting a new object, giving rise to a new strategy, giving place to new enunciations or new concepts. A discursive formation, then, does not play the role of a figure that arrests time and freezes it for decades or centuries; it determines a regularity proper to temporal processes; it presents the principle of articulation between a series of discursive events and other series of events, transformations, mutations, and processes. It is not an atemporal form, but a schema of correspondence between several temporal series.

This mobility of the system of formation appears in two ways. First at the level of the elements that are being related to one another: these in fact may undergo a number of intrinsic mutations that are integrated into discursive practice without the general form of its regularity being altered; thus, throughout the nineteenth century, criminal jurisprudence, demographic pressure, the demand for labour, the forms of public assistance, the status and juridical conditions of internment, were continually changing; yet the discursive practice of psychiatry continued to establish the same group of relations between these elements; in this way, the system preserved the characteristics of its individuality; through the same laws of formation, new objects appear (new types of individuals, new classes of behaviour are characterized as pathological), new modalities of enunciation are put into operation (quantitative notations and statistical calculations), new concepts are outlined (such as those of degeneracy, perversion, neurosis), and of course new theoretical structures can be built. But, inversely, the discursive practices modify the domains that they relate to one another. It is no use establishing specific relations that can be analysed only at their own level – the effect of these relations is not confined to discourse alone: it is also felt in the elements that they articulate upon one another. The hospital field, for example, did not remain unaffected when clinical discourse was put into relation with the laboratory: the body of rules that governed its working, the status accorded the hospital doctor, the function of his observation, the level of analysis that can be carried out in it, were necessarily modified.

3. What are described as 'systems of formation' do not constitute the terminal stage of discourse, if by that term one means the texts (or words) as they appear, with their vocabulary, syntax, logical structure, or rhetorical organization. Analysis remains anterior to this manifest level, which is that of the completed construction: in defining the principle of distributing objects in a discourse, it does not take into account all their connexions, their delicate structure, or their internal sub-divisions; in seeking the law of the dispersion of concepts, it does not take into account all the processes of elaboration, or all the deductive series in which they may figure; if analysis studies the modalities of enunciation, it questions neither the style nor the succession of the sentences; in short, it leaves the final placing of the *text* in dotted outline. But we must be clear on one point: if analysis stands back in relation to this final construction, it is not to turn away from the discourse and to appeal to the silent work of thought; nor is it to turn away from the systematic and to reveal the 'living' disorder of attempts, trials, errors, and new beginnings.

✳   ✳   ✳

75

In this respect, the analysis of discursive formations is opposed to many customary descriptions. One is used, in fact, to consider that discourses and their systematic ordering are not only the ultimate state, the final result of a long and often sinuous development involving language (*langue*) and thought, empirical experience and categories, the lived and ideal necessities, the contingency of events and the play of formal constraints. Behind the visible façade of the system, one posits the rich uncertainty of disorder; and beneath the thin surface of discourse, the whole mass of a largely silent development (*devenir*): a 'presystematic' that is not of the order of the system; a 'prediscursive' that belongs to an essential silence. Discourse and system produce each other – and conjointly – only at the crest of this immense reserve. What are being analysed here are certainly not the terminal states of discourse; they are the *preterminal regularities* in relation to which the ultimate state, far from constituting the birth-place of a system, is defined by its variants. Behind the completed system, what is discovered by the analysis of formations is not the bubbling source of life itself, life in an as yet uncaptured state; it is an immense density of systematicities, a tight group of multiple relations. Moreover, these relations cannot be the very web of the text – they are not by nature foreign to discourse. They can certainly be qualified as 'prediscursive', but only if one admits that this prediscursive is still discursive, that is, that they do not specify a thought, or a consciousness, or a group of representations which, *a posteriori*, and in a way that is never quite necessary, are transcribed into a discourse, but that they characterize certain levels of discourse, that they define rules that are embodied as a particular practice by discourse. One is not seeking, therefore, to pass from the text to thought, from talk to silence, from the exterior to the interior, from spatial dispersion to the pure recollection of the moment, from superficial multiplicity to profound unity. One remains within the dimension of discourse.

PART III

The Statement and the Archive

CHAPTER I

Defining the Statement

I suppose that by now we have accepted the risk; that we are now willing, in order to articulate the great surface of discourse, to posit the existence of those somewhat strange, somewhat distant figures that I have called discursive formations; that we have put to one side, not in a definitive way, but for a time and out of methodological rigour, the traditional unities of the book and the *œuvre*; that we have ceased to accept as a principle of unity the laws of constructing discourse (with the formal organization that results), or the situation of the speaking subject (with the context and the psychological nucleus that characterize it); that we no longer relate discourse to the primary ground of experience, nor to the *a priori* authority of knowledge; but that we seek the rules of its formation in discourse itself. I suppose that we have agreed to undertake these long inquiries into the system of emergence of objects, the system of the appearance and distribution of enunciative modes, the system of the placing and dispersion of concepts, the system of the deployment of strategic choices. I suppose that we are willing to construct such abstract, problematic unities, instead of welcoming those that presented themselves as being more or less perceptually familiar, if not as self-evident realities.

But what, in fact, have I been speaking about so far? What has been the object of my inquiry? And what did I intend to describe? 'Statements' – both in that discontinuity that frees them from all the forms in which one was so ready to allow them to be caught, and in the general, unlimited, apparently formless field of discourse. But I refrained from providing a preliminary definition of the statement. Nor did I try to construct one as I proceeded in order to justify the naïvety of my starting-point. Moreover – and this no doubt is the reason for so much unconcern – I wonder whether I have not changed direction on the way; whether I have not replaced my first quest with another; whether, while analysing 'objects' or 'concepts', let alone 'strategies', I was in fact still speaking of statements; whether the four groups of rules by which I characterized a discursive formation really did define groups of statements. Lastly, instead of gradually reducing the rather fluctuating meaning of the word 'discourse', I believe that I have in fact added to its meanings: treating it sometimes as the general domain of all statements, sometimes as an individualizable group of statements, and sometimes as a regulated practice that accounts for a certain number of statements; and have I not allowed this same word 'discourse', which should have served as a boundary around the term 'statement', to vary as I shifted my analysis or its point of application, as the statement itself faded from view?

This, then, is the task that now confronts me: to take up the definition of the statement at its very root. And to see whether that definition really was present in my earlier descriptions; to see whether I really was dealing with the statement in my analysis of discursive formations.

On several occasions I have used the term 'statement', either to speak of a population of statements (as if I were dealing with individuals or isolated events), or in order to distinguish it from the groups that I called 'discourses' (as the part is distinguished from the whole). At first sight, the statement appears as an ultimate, undecomposable element that can be isolated and introduced into a set of relations with other similar elements. A point without a surface, but a point that can be located in planes of division and in specific forms of groupings. A seed that appears on the surface of a tissue of which it is the constituent element. The atom of discourse.

And the problem soon arises: if the statement really is the elementary unit of discourse, what does it consist of? What are its distinctive features? What boundaries must one accord to it? Is this unity identical with that to which logicians have given the term 'proposition', and that which grammarians call a 'sentence', or that which 'analysts' try to map by the term 'speech act'? What place does it occupy among all those unities that the investigation of language (*langage*) has already revealed? (Even though the theory of these unities is so often incomplete, on account of the difficulty of the problems that they present, and the difficulty in many cases of delimiting them with any degree of rigour.)

I do not think that the necessary and sufficient condition of a statement is the presence of a defined propositional structure, or that one can speak of a statement only when there is a proposition. In fact, one can have two perfectly distinct statements, referring to quite different discursive groupings, when one finds only one proposition, possessing only one value, obeying only one group of laws for its construction, and involving the same possibilities of use. 'No one heard' and 'It is true that no one heard' are indistinguishable from a logical point of view, and cannot be regarded as two different propositions. But in so many statements, these two formations are not equivalent or interchangeable. They cannot occupy the same place on the plane of discourse, nor can they belong to exactly the same group of statements. If one finds the formulation 'No one heard' in the first line of a novel, we know, until a new order emerges, that it is an observation made either by the author, or by a character (aloud or in the form of an interior monologue); if one finds the second formulation, 'It is true that no one heard', one can only be in a group of statements constituting an interior monologue, a silent discussion with oneself, or a fragment of dialogue, a group of questions and answers. In each case, there is the same propositional structure, but there are distinct enunciative characteristics. There may, on the other hand, be complex and doubled propositional forms, or, on the contrary, fragmentary, incomplete propositions, when one is quite obviously dealing with a simple, complete, autonomous statement (even if it is part of a group of other statements): the example 'The present king of France is bald' is well known (it can be analysed from a logical point of view only if one accepts, in the form of a single statement, two distinct propositions, each of which may be true or false on its own account), or again there is a proposition like 'I am lying', which can be true only in relation to an assertion on a lower level. The criteria by which one can define the identity of a proposition, distinguish several of them beneath the unity of a formulation, characterize its autonomy or its completion are not valid when one comes to describe the particular unity of a statement.

And what of the sentence? Should we not accept an equivalence between sentence and statement? Wherever there is a grammatically isolable sentence, one can recognize the existence of an independent statement; but, on the other hand, one cannot speak of statement when, beneath the sentence itself, one reaches the level of its constituents. It would be pointless to object, against such an equivalence, that some statements may be composed, outside the canonical form of subject-copula-predicate, of a simple nominal syntagma ('That man!') or an adverb ('Absolutely'), or a personal pronoun ('You!'). For the grammarians themselves recognize such formulations as independent sentences, even if those formulations have been obtained through a series of transformations on the basis of the subject-predicate schema. Moreover: they recognize as 'acceptable' sentences groups of linguistic elements that have not been correctly constructed, providing they are interpretable; on the other hand, they accord the status of grammatical sentences to interpretable groups on condition however that they are correctly formed. With so broad – and, in a sense, so lax – a definition of the sentence, it is difficult to see how one is to recognize sentences that are not statements, or statements that are not sentences.

Yet the equivalence is far from being a total one; and it is relatively easy to cite statements that do not correspond to the linguistic structure of sentences. When one finds in a Latin grammar a series of words arranged in a column: *amo, amas, amat*, one is dealing not with a sentence, but with the statement of the different personal inflexions of the present indicative of the verb *amare*. One may find this example debatable; one may say that it is a mere artifice of presentation, that this statement is an elliptical, abbreviated sentence, spatialized in a relatively unusual mode, that should be read as the sentence 'The present indicative of the verb *amare* is *amo* for the first person', etc. Other examples, in any case, are less ambiguous: a classificatory table of the botanical species is made up of statements, not sentences (Linnaeus's *Genera Plantarum*a is a whole book of statements, in which one can recognize only a small number of sentences); a genealogical tree, an accounts book, the calculations of a trade balance are statements; where are the sentences? One can go further: an equation of the nth degree, or the algebraic formula of the law of refraction must be regarded as statements: and although they possess a highly rigorous grammaticality (since they are made up of symbols whose meaning is determined by rules of usage, and whose succession is governed by laws of construction), this grammaticality cannot be judged by the same criteria that, in a natural language (*langue*), make it possible to define an acceptable, or interpretable sentence. Lastly, a graph, a growth curve, an age pyramid, a distribution cloud are all statements: any sentences that may accompany them are merely interpretation or commentary; they are in no way an equivalent: this is proved by the fact that, in a great many cases, only an infinite number of sentences could equal all the elements that are explicitly formulated in this sort of statement. It would not appear to be possible, therefore, to define a statement by the grammatical characteristics of the sentence.

One last possibility remains: at first sight, the most likely of all. Can one not say that there is a statement wherever one can recognize and isolate an act of formulation – something like the speech act referred to by the English analysts? This term does not, of course, refer to the material act of speaking (aloud or to oneself) or of writing (by hand or typewriter); nor does it refer to the intention of the individual who is speaking (the fact that he wants to convince someone else, to be obeyed, to discover the solution to a problem, or to communicate information); nor does it refer to the possible result of what he has said (whether he has convinced someone or aroused his suspicion; whether he was listened to and whether his orders were carried out; whether his prayer was heard); what one is referring to is the operation that has been carried out by the formula itself, in its emergence: promise, order, decree, contract, agreement, observation. The speech act is not what took place just prior to the moment when the statement was made (in the author's thought or intentions); it is not what might have happened, after the event itself, in its wake, and the consequences that it gave rise to; it is what occurred by the very fact that a statement was made – and precisely this statement (and no other) in specific circumstances. Presumably, therefore, one individualization of statements refers to the same criteria as the location of acts of formulation: each act is embodied in a statement and each statement contains one of those acts. They exist through one another in an exact reciprocal relationship.

Yet such a correlation does not stand up to examination. For one thing, more than a statement is often required to effect a speech act: an oath, a prayer, a contract, a promise, or a demonstration usually require a certain number of distinct formulas or separate sentences: it would be difficult to challenge the right of each of these formulas and sentences to be regarded as a statement on the pretext that they are all imbued with one and the same speech act. In that case, it might be said that the act itself does not remain the same throughout the series of statements; that in a prayer there are as many limited, successive, and juxtaposed acts of prayer as demands formulated by distinct statements; and that in a promise there are as many engagements as sequences that can be individualized into separate statements. But one cannot be satisfied with this answer: first because the act of formulation would no longer serve to define the statement, but, on the contrary, the act of formulation would be defined by the statement – which raises problems, and requires criteria of individualization. Moreover, certain speech acts can be regarded as complete in their particular unity only if several statements have been made, each in its proper place. These acts are not constituted, therefore, by the series or sum of these statements, by their necessary juxtaposition; they cannot be regarded as being present whole and entire in the least of them, and as renewing themselves with each one. So one cannot establish a bi-univocal relation between the group of statements and that of speech acts either.

When one wishes to individualize statements, one cannot therefore accept unreservedly any of the models borrowed from grammar, logic, or 'analysis'. In all three cases, one realizes that the criteria proposed are too numerous and too heavy, that they limit the extent of the statement, and that although the statement sometimes takes on the forms described and adjusts itself to them exactly, it does not always do so: one finds statements lacking in legitimate propositional structure; one finds statements where one cannot recognize a sentence; one finds more statements than one can isolate speech acts. As if the statement were more tenuous, less charged with determinations, less strongly structured, more omnipresent, too, than all these figures; as if it had fewer features, and ones less difficult to group together; but as if, by that very fact, it rejected all possibility of describing anything. And this is all the more so, in that it is difficult to see at what level it should be situated, and by what method it should be approached: for all the analyses mentioned above, there is never more than a support, or accidental substance: in logical analysis, it is what is left when the propositional structure has been extracted and defined; for grammatical analysis, it is the series of linguistic elements in which one may or may not recognize the form of a sentence; for the analysis of speech acts, it appears as the visible body in which they manifest themselves. In relation to all these descriptive approaches, it plays the role of a residual element, of a mere fact, of irrelevant raw material.

Must we admit in the end that the statement cannot possess a character of its own and that it cannot be adequately defined, in so far as it is, for all analyses of language (*langage*), the extrinsic material on the basis of which they determine their own object? Must we admit that any series of signs, figures, marks, or traces – whatever their organization or probability may be – is enough to constitute a statement; and that it is the role of grammar to say whether or not it is a sentence, the role of logic to decide whether or not it contains a propositional form, the role of Analysis to determine what speech act it may embody? In which case, we would have to admit that there is a statement whenever a number of signs are juxtaposed – or even, perhaps – when there is a single sign. The threshold of the statement is the threshold of the existence of signs. Yet even here, things are not so simple, and the meaning of a term like 'the existence of signs' requires elucidation. What does one mean when one says that there are signs, and that it is enough for there *to be* signs for there *to be* a statement? What special status should be given to that verb *to be*?

For it is obvious that statements do not exist in the same sense in which a language (*langue*) exists, and, with that language, a collection of signs defined by their contrasting characteristics and their rules of use; a language in fact is never given in itself, in its totality; it could only be so in a secondary way, in the oblique form of a description that would take it as its object; the signs that make up its elements are forms that are imposed upon statements and control them from within. If there were no statements, the language (*langue*) would not exist; but no statement is indispensable for a language to exist (and one can always posit, in place of any statement, another statement that would in no way modify the language). The language exists only as a system for constructing possible statements; but in another respect, it exists only as a (more or less exhaustive) description obtained from a collection of real statements. Language (*langue*) and statement are not at the same level of existence; and one cannot say that there are statements in the same way as one says that there are languages (*langues*). But is it enough, then, that the signs of a language constitute a statement, if they were produced (articulated, drawn, made, traced) in one way or another, if they appeared in a moment of time and in a point in space, if the voice that spoke them or the gesture that formed them gave them the dimensions of a material existence? Can the letters of the alphabet written by me haphazardly on to a sheet of paper, as an example of what is not a statement, can the lead characters used for printing books – and one cannot deny their materiality, which has space and volume – can these signs, spread out, visible, manipulable, be reasonably regarded as statements?

When looked at more closely, however, these two examples (the lead characters and the signs that I wrote down on the sheet of paper) are seen to be not quite superposable. This pile of printer's characters, which I can hold in my hand, or the letters marked on the keyboard of a typewriter are not statements: at most they are tools with which one can write statements. On the other hand, what are the letters that I write down haphazardly on to a sheet of paper, just as they come to mind, and to show that they cannot, in their disordered state, constitute a statement? What figure do they form? Are they not a table of letters chosen in a contingent way, the statement of an alphabetical series governed by other laws than those of chance? Similarly, the table of random numbers that statisticians sometimes use is a series of numerical symbols that are not linked together by any syntactical structure; and yet that series is a statement: that of a group of figures obtained by procedures that eliminate everything that might increase the probability of the succeeding issues. Let us look at the example again: the keyboard of a typewriter is not a statement; but the same series of letters, A, Z, E, R, T, listed in a typewriting manual, is the statement of the alphabetical order adopted by French typewriters. So we are presented with a number of negative consequences: a regular linguistic construction is not required in order to form a statement (this statement may be made up of a series possessing a minimal probability); but neither is it enough to have any material effectuation of linguistic elements, any emergence of signs in time and space, for a statement to appear and to begin to exist. The statement exists therefore neither in the same way as a language (*langue*) (although it is made up of signs that are definable in their individuality only within a natural or artificial linguistic system), nor in the same way as the objects presented to perception (although it is always endowed with a certain materiality, and can always be situated in accordance with spatio-temporal coordinates).

This is not the place to answer the general question of the statement, but the problem can be clarified: the statement is not the same kind of unit as the sentence, the proposition, or the speech act; it cannot be referred therefore to the same criteria; but neither is it the same kind of unit as a material object, with its limits and independence. In its way of being unique (neither entirely linguistic, nor exclusively material), it is indispensable if we want to say whether or not there is a sentence, proposition, or speech act; and whether the sentence is correct (or acceptable, or interpretable), whether the proposition is legitimate and well constructed, whether the speech act fulfils its requirements, and was in fact carried out. We must not seek in the statement a unit that is either long or short, strongly and weakly structured, but one that is caught up, like the others, in a logical, grammatical, locutory nexus. It is not so much one element among others, a division that can be located at a certain level of analysis, as a function that operates vertically in relation to these various units, and which enables one to say of a series of signs whether or not they are present in it. The statement is not therefore a structure (that is, a group of relations between variable elements, thus authorizing a possibly infinite number of concrete models); it is a function of existence that properly belongs to signs and on the basis of which one may then decide, through analysis or intuition, whether or not they 'make sense', according to what rule they follow one another or are juxtaposed, of what they are the sign, and what sort of act is carried out by their formulation (oral or written). One should not be surprised, then, if one has failed to find structural criteria of unity for the statement; this is because it is not in itself a unit, but a function that cuts across a domain of structures and possible unities, and which reveals them, with concrete contents, in time and space.

It is this function that we must now describe as such, that is, in its actual practice, its conditions, the rules that govern it, and the field in which it operates.

CHAPTER 2

The Enunciative Function

It is useless therefore to look for the statement among unitary groups of signs. The statement is neither a syntagma, nor a rule of construction, nor a canonic form of succession and permutation; it is that which enables such groups of signs to exist, and enables these rules or forms to become manifest. But although it enables them to exist, it does so in a special way – a way that must not be confused with the existence of signs as elements of a language (*langue*), or with the material existence of those marks that occupy a fragment of space or last for a variable length of time. It is this special mode of existence, characteristic of every series of signs, providing it is stated, that we must now examine.

(a) So let us take once again the example of those signs made or drawn in a defined materiality, and grouped in a particular way, which may or may not be arbitrary, but which, in any case, is not grammatical: the keyboard of a typewriter, or a handful of printer's characters. All that is required is that the signs be given, that I copy them on to a sheet of paper (in the same order in which they appear, but without producing a word) for a statement to emerge: the statement of the letters of the alphabet in an order that makes the typing of them easier, and the statement of a random group of letters. What has happened, then, that a statement should have been made? What can the second group possess that is not possessed by the first? Reduplication, the fact that it is a copy? Certainly not, since the keyboards of typewriters all copy a certain model and are not, by that very fact, statements. The intervention of a subject? This answer is inadequate for two reasons: it is not enough that the reiteration of a series be due to the initiative of an individual for it to be transformed, by that very fact, into a statement; and, in any case, the problem does not lie in the cause or origin of the reduplication, but in the special relation between the two identical series. The second series is not a statement because and only because a bi-univocal relation can be established between each of its elements in the first series (this relation characterizes either the fact of duplication if it is simply a copy, or the exactitude of the statement if one has in fact crossed the threshold of enunciation; but it does not allow us to define this threshold and the very fact of the statement). A series of signs will become a statement on condition that it possesses 'something else' (which may be strangely similar to it, and almost identical as in the example chosen), a specific relation that concerns itself – and not its cause, or its elements.

It may be objected that there is nothing enigmatic about this relation; that, on the contrary, it is a very familiar one, which is constantly being analysed: that, in fact, it concerns the relation of the signifier (*signifiant*) to the signified (*signifié*), of the name to what it designates; the relation of the sentence to its meaning; the relation of the proposition to its referent (*référent*). But I believe that one can show that the relation of the statement to what it states is not superposable on any of these relations.

The statement, even if reduced to a nominal syntagma ('The boat!'), even if it is reduced to a proper noun ('Peter!'), does not have the same relation with what it states as the name with what it designates or signifies. The name or noun is a linguistic element that may occupy different places in grammatical groups: its meaning is defined by its rules of use (whether these concern individuals who may be validly designated by it, or syntactical structures in which it may correctly participate); a noun is defined by its possibility of recurrence. A statement exists outside any possibility of reappearing; and the relation that it possesses with what it states is not identical with a group of rules of use. It is a very special relation: and if in these conditions an identical formulation reappears, with the same words, substantially the same names – in fact, exactly the same sentence – it is not necessarily the same statement.

Nor should the relation between a statement and what it states be confused with the relation between a proposition and its referent. We know that logicians say that a proposition like 'The golden mountain is in California' cannot be verified because it has no referent: its negation is therefore neither more nor less true than its affirmation. Should we say similarly that a statement refers to nothing if the proposition, to which it lends existence, has no referent? Rather the reverse. We should say not that the absence of a referent brings with it the absence of a correlate for the statement, but that it is the correlate of the statement – that to which it refers, not only what is said, but also what it speaks of, its 'theme' – which makes it possible to say whether or not the proposition has a referent: it alone decides this in a definitive way. Let us suppose in fact that the formulation 'The golden mountain is in California' is found not in a geography book, nor in a travel book, but in a novel, or in some fictional context or other, one could still accord it a value of truth or error (according to whether the imaginary world to which it refers does or does not authorize such a geological and geographical fantasy). We must know to what the statement refers, what is its space of correlations, if we are to say whether a proposition has or has not a referent. 'The present king of France is bald' lacks a referent only if one supposes that the statement refers to the world of contemporary historical information. The relation of the proposition to the referent cannot serve as a model or as a law for the relation of the statement to what it states. The latter relation not only does not belong to the same level as the former, but it is anterior to it.

Nor is it superposable to the relation that may exist between a sentence and its meaning. The gap between these two forms of relation appears clearly in the case of two famous sentences that are meaningless, in spite of their perfectly correct grammatical structure (as in the example: 'Colourless green ideas sleep furiously'). In fact, to say that a sentence like this is meaningless presupposes that one has already excluded a number of possibilities – that it describes a dream, that it is part of a poetic text, that it is a coded message, that it is spoken by a drug addict – and that one assumes it to be a certain type of statement that must refer, in a very definite way, to some visible reality. The relation of a sentence with its meaning resides within a specific, well-stabilized enunciative relation. Moreover, even if these sentences are taken at an enunciative level at which they are meaningless, they are not, as statements, deprived of correlations: there are those that enable one to say, for example, that ideas are never either coloured or colourless, and therefore that the sentence is meaningless (and these correlations concern a level of reality in which ideas are invisible, and in which colours can be seen, etc.); there are also those correlations that validate the sentence in question as a mention of a type of correct syntactical organization that was also meaningless (and these correlations concern the level of the language (*langue*), with its laws and properties). A sentence cannot be non-significant; it refers to something, by virtue of the fact that it is a statement.

How, then, can we define this relation that characterizes the statement as statement – a relation that seems to be implicitly presupposed by the sentence or the proposition, and which is anterior to it? How can we disentangle it from those relations of meaning or those values of truth, with which it is usually confused? Any statement, as simple a statement as one can imagine, does not have as its *correlate* an individual or a particular object that is designated by this or that word in the sentence: in the case of a statement like 'The golden mountain is in California', the *correlate* is not the formation, real or imaginary, possible or absurd, that is designated by the nominal syntagma that serves as the subject. But nor is the *correlate* of the statement a state of things or a relation capable of verifying the proposition (in the example chosen, this would be the spatial inclusion of a particular mountain in a particular region). On the other hand, what might be defined as the *correlate* of the statement is a group of domains in which such objects may appear and to which such relations may be assigned: it would, for example, be a domain of material objects possessing a certain number of observable physical properties, relations of perceptible size – or, on the contrary, it would be a domain of fictitious objects, endowed with arbitrary properties (even if they have a certain constancy and a certain coherence), without any authority of experimental or perceptive verification; it would be a domain of spatial and geographical localizations, with coordinates, distances, relations of proximity and of inclusion – or, on the contrary, a domain of symbolic appurtenances and secret kinships; it would be a domain of objects that exist at the same moment and on the same time-scale as the statement is formulated, or it would be a domain of objects that belongs to a quite different present – that indicated and constituted by the statement itself, and not that to which the statement also belongs. A statement is not confronted (face to face, as it were) by a *correlate* – or the absence of a *correlate* – as a proposition has (or has not) a referent, or as a proper noun designates someone (or no one). It is linked rather to a 'referential' that is made up not of 'things', 'facts', 'realities', or 'beings', but of laws of possibility, rules of existence for the objects that are named, designated, or described within it, and for the relations that are affirmed or denied in it. The referential of the statement forms the place, the condition, the field of emergence, the authority to differentiate between individuals or objects, states of things and relations that are brought into play by the statement itself; it defines the possibilities of appearance and delimitation of that which gives meaning to the sentence, a value as truth to the proposition. It is this group that characterizes the *enunciative* level of the formulation, in contrast to its grammatical and logical levels: through the relation with these various domains of possibility the statement makes of a syntagma, or a series of symbols, a sentence to which one may or may not ascribe a meaning, a proposition that may or may not be accorded a value as truth.

One can see in any case that the description of this enunciative level can be performed neither by a formal analysis, nor by a semantic investigation, nor by verification, but by the analysis of the relations between the statement and the spaces of differentiation, in which the statement itself reveals the differences.

(b) A statement also differs from any series of linguistic elements by virtue of the fact that it possesses a particular relation with a subject. We must now define the nature of this relation, and, above all, distinguish it from other relations with which it might be confused.

We must not, in fact, reduce the subject of the statement to the first-person grammatical elements that are present within the sentence. First because the subject of the sentence is not within the linguistic syntagma; secondly because a statement that does not involve a first person nevertheless has a subject; lastly and above all, all statements that have a fixed grammatical form (whether in the first or second person) do not have the same type of relation with the subject of the statement. It is easy to see that this relation is not the same in a statement of the type 'Night is falling', and 'Every effect has a cause'; while in the case of a statement of the type 'Longtemps, je me suis couché de bonne heure' ('For a long time I used to go to bed early'), the relation to the enunciating subject is not the same if one hears it spoken in the course of a conversation, and if one reads it at the beginning of Proust's *A la Recherche du temps perdu*.

Is not this subject exterior to the sentence quite simply the individual who spoke or wrote those words? As we know, there can be no signs without someone, or at least something, to emit them. For a series of signs to exist, there must – in accordance with the system of causality – be an 'author' or a transmitting authority. But this 'author' is not identical with the subject of the statement; and the relation of production that he has with the formulation is not superposable to the relation that unites the enunciating subject and what he states. Let us ignore the over-simple case of a group of signs that have been materially fashioned or traced: their production implies an author even though there is neither a statement nor a subject of a statement. One might also mention, by way of showing the dissociation between the transmitter of signs and the subject of a statement, the case of a text read by a third person, or that of an actor speaking his part. But these are extreme cases. Generally speaking, it would seem, at first sight at least, that the subject of the statement is precisely he who has produced the various elements, with the intention of conveying meaning. Yet things are not so simple. In a novel, we know that the author of the formulation is that real individual whose name appears on the title page of the book (we are still faced with the problem of the dialogue, and sentences purporting to express the thoughts of a character; we are still faced with the problem of texts published under a pseudonym: and we know all the difficulties that these duplications raise for practitioners of interpretative analysis when they wish to relate these formulations, *en bloc*, to the author of the text, to what he wanted to say, to what he thought, in short, to that great silent, hidden, uniform discourse on which they build that whole pyramid of different levels); but, even apart from those authorities of formulation that are not identical with the individual/author, the statements of the novel do not have the same subject when they provide, as if from the outside, the historical and spatial setting of the story, when they describe things as they would be seen by an anonymous, invisible, neutral individual who moves magically among the characters of the novel, or when they provide, as if by an immediate, internal decipherment, the verbal version of what is silently experienced by a character. Although the author is the same in each case, although he attributes them to no one other than himself, although he does not invent a supplementary link between what he is himself and the text that one is reading, these statements do not presuppose the same characteristics for the enunciating subject; they do not imply the same relation between this subject and what is being stated.

It might be said that the often quoted example of the fictional text has no conclusive validity; or rather that it questions the very essence of literature, and not the status of the subject of statements in general. According to this view, it is in the nature of literature that the author should appear to be absent, conceal himself within it, delegate his authority, or divide himself up; and one should not draw a general conclusion from this dissociation that the subject of the statement is distinct in everything – in nature, status, function, and identity – from the author of the formulation. Yet this gap is not confined to literature alone. It is absolutely general in so far as the subject of the statement is a particular function, but is not necessarily the same from one statement to another; in so far as it is an empty function, that can be filled by virtually any individual when he formulates the statement; and in so far as one and the same individual may occupy in turn, in the same series of statements, different positions, and assume the role of different subjects. Take the example of a mathematical treatise. In the sentence in the preface in which one explains why this treatise was written, in what circumstances, in response to what unsolved problems, or with what pedagogical aim in view, using what methods, after what attempts and failures, the position of the enunciative subject can be occupied only by the author, or authors, of the formulation: the conditions of individualization of the subject are in fact very strict, very numerous, and authorize in this case only one possible subject. On the other hand, if in the main body of the treatise, one meets a proposition like 'Two quantities equal to a third quantity are equal to each other', the subject of the statement is the absolutely neutral position, indifferent to time, space, and circumstances, identical in any linguistic system, and in any code of writing or symbolization, that any individual may occupy when affirming such a proposition. Moreover, sentences like 'We have already shown that . . .' necessarily involve statements of precise contextual conditions that were not implied by the preceding formulation: the position is then fixed within a domain constituted by a finite group of statements; it is localized in a series of enunciative events that must already have occurred; it is established in a demonstrative time whose earlier stages are never lost, and which do not need therefore to be begun again and repeated identically to be made present once more (a mention is enough to reactivate them in their original validity); it is determined by the prior existence of a number of effective operations that need not have been performed by one and the same individual (he who is speaking now), but which rightfully belong to the enunciating subject, which are at his disposal, and of which he may avail himself when necessary. The subject of such a statement will be defined by these requisites and possibilities taken together; and he will not be described as an individual who has really carried out certain operations, who lives in an unbroken, never forgotten time, who has interiorized, in the horizon of his consciousness, a whole group of true propositions, and who retains, in the living present of his thought, their potential reappearance (this is merely, in the case of individuals, the psychological, 'lived' aspect of their position as enunciating subjects).

Similarly, one might describe the specific position of the enunciating subject in sentences like 'I call straight any series of points that . . .' or 'Let there be a finite series of any elements'; in each case the position of the subject is linked to the existence of an operation that is both determined and present; in each case, the subject of the statement is also the subject of the operation (he who establishes the definition of a straight line is also he who states it; he who posits the existence of a finite series is also, and at the same time, he who states it); and in each case, the subject links, by means of this operation and the statement in which it is embodied, his future statements and operations (as an enunciating subject, he accepts this statement as his own law). There is a difference however: in the first case, what is stated is a convention of language (*langage*) – of that language that the enunciating subject must use, and within which he is defined: the enunciating subject and what is stated are therefore at the same level (whereas for a formal analysis a statement like this one implies the difference of level proper to metalanguage); in the second case, on the other hand, the enunciating subject brings into existence outside himself an object that belongs to a previously defined domain, whose laws of possibility have already been articulated, and whose characteristics precede the enunciation that posits it. We saw above that the position of the enunciating subject is not always identical in the affirmation of a true proposition; we now see that it is also not identical when an operation is carried out within the statement itself.

So the subject of the statement should not be regarded as identical with the author of the formulation – either in substance, or in function. He is not in fact the cause, origin, or starting-point of the phenomenon of the written or spoken articulation of a sentence; nor is it that meaningful intention which, silently anticipating words, orders them like the visible body of its intuition; it is not the constant, motionless, unchanging focus of a series of operations that are manifested, in turn, on the surface of discourse through the statements. It is a particular, vacant place that may in fact be filled by different individuals; but, instead of being defined once and for all, and maintaining itself as such throughout a text, a book, or an *œuvre*, this place varies – or rather it is variable enough to be able either to persevere, unchanging, through several sentences, or to alter with each one. It is a dimension that characterizes a whole formulation *qua* statement. It is one of the characteristics proper to the enunciative function and enables one to describe it. If a proposition, a sentence, a group of signs can be called 'statement', it is not therefore because, one day, someone happened to speak them or put them into some concrete form of writing; it is because the position of the subject can be assigned. To describe a formulation *qua* statement does not consist in analysing the relations between the author and what he says (or wanted to say, or said without wanting to);

but in determining what position can and must be occupied by any individual if he is to be the subject of it.

(c) The third characteristic of the enunciative function: it can operate without the existence of an associated domain. This makes the statement something other, something more, than a mere collection of signs, which, in order to exist, need only a material base – a writing surface, sound, malleable material, the hollowed incision of a trace. But this also, and above all, distinguishes it from the sentence and the proposition.

Take a group of words or symbols. In order to decide whether they constitute a grammatical unit like the sentence or a logical unit like the proposition, it is necessary, and enough, to determine the rules according to which it was constructed. 'Peter arrived yesterday' forms a sentence, but 'Yesterday arrived Peter' does not; $A + B = C + D$ constitutes a proposition, but $ABC + = D$ does not. Only an examination of the elements and of their distribution, in reference to the system – natural or artificial – of the language (*langue*) enables us to distinguish between what is and what is not a proposition, between what is a sentence and what is merely an accumulation of words. Moreover, this examination is enough to determine to what type of grammatical structure the sentence in question belongs (affirmative sentence, in the past tense, containing a nominal subject, etc.), or to what type of proposition the series of signs in question belongs (an equivalence between two additions). One can even conceive of a sentence or a proposition that is 'self-determining', that requires no other sentence or proposition to serve as a context, no other associated sentences or propositions: that such a sentence or proposition would, in such conditions, be useless and unusable, does not mean that one would not be able to recognize it, even in its singularity.

One could no doubt make a number of objections to this. One might say, for example, that a proposition can be established and individualized as such only if one knows the system of axioms that it obeys; do not those definitions, those rules, those conventions of writing form an associated field inseparable from the proposition (similarly, the rules of grammar, implicitly at work in the competence of the subject, are necessary if one is to recognize a sentence, and a sentence of a certain type)? It should be noted however that this group – actual or potential – does not belong to the same level as the proposition or the sentence: but that it has a bearing on their possible elements, succession, and distribution. The group is not associated with them: it is presupposed by them. One might also object that many (non-tautological) propositions cannot be verified on the basis of their rules of construction alone, and that recourse to the referent is needed if one is to decide whether they are true or false: but true or false, a proposition remains a proposition, and it is not recourse to the referent that decides whether or not it is a proposition. The same goes for sentences; in many cases, they can yield their meaning only in relation to the context (whether they contain 'deictic' elements that refer to a concrete situation; or make use of first- or second-person pronouns that designate the speaking subject and his interlocutors; or make use of pronominal elements or connecting particles that refer to earlier or later sentences); but the fact that its meaning cannot be completed does not prevent the sentence from being grammatically complete and autonomous. Certainly, one is not very sure what a group of words like 'I'll tell you that to-morrow' *means*; in any case, one can neither date this 'tomorrow', nor name the interlocutors, nor guess what is to be said. Nevertheless, it is a perfectly delimited sentence, obeying the rules of construction of the language (*langue*) in which it is written. Lastly, one might object that, without a context, it is sometimes difficult to define the structure of a sentence ('I shall never know if he is dead' may be construed: 'I shall never know whether or not he is dead' or 'I shall never be informed of his death when this event occurs'). But this ambiguity is perfectly definable, simultaneous possibilities can be posited that belong to the structure proper of the sentence. Generally speaking, one can say that a sentence or a proposition – even when isolated, even divorced from the natural context that could throw light on to its meaning, even freed or cut off from all the elements to which, implicitly or not, it refers – always remains a sentence or a proposition and can always be recognized as such.

On the other hand, the enunciative function – and this shows that it is not simply a construction of previously existing elements – cannot operate on a sentence or proposition in isolation. It is not enough to say a sentence, it is not even enough to say it in a particular relation to a field of objects or in a particular relation to a subject, for a statement to exist: it must be related to a whole adjacent field. Or rather, since this is not some additional relation that is superimposed on the others, one cannot say a sentence, one cannot transform it into a statement, unless a collateral space is brought into operation. A statement always has borders peopled by other statements. These borders are not what is usually meant by 'context' – real or verbal – that is, all the situational or linguistic elements, taken together, that motivate a formulation and determine its meaning.

They are distinct from such a 'context' precisely in so far as they make it possible: the contextual relation between one sentence and those before and after it is not the same in the case of a novel and in that of a treatise in physics; the contextual relation between a formulation and the objective environment is not the same in a conversation and in the account of an experiment. It is against the background of a more general relation between the formulations, against the background of a whole verbal network, that the effect of context may be determined. Nor are these borders identical with the various texts and sentences that the subject may be conscious of when he speaks; again they are more extensive than such a psychological setting; and to a certain extent they determine that setting, for according to the position, status, and role of one formulation among others – according to whether it belongs to the field of literature or as an isolated remark, whether it is part of a narrative or the account of a demonstration – the way in which other statements are present in the mind of the subject will not be the same: neither the same level, nor the same form of linguistic experience, of verbal memory, of reference to what has already been said, is operating in each case. The psychological halo of a formulation is controlled from afar by the arrangement of the enunciative field.

The associated field that turns a sentence or a series of signs into a statement, and which provides them with a particular context, a specific representative content, forms a complex web. It is made up first of all by the series of other formulations within which the statement appears and forms one element (the network of spoken formulations that make up a conversation, the architecture of a demonstration, bound on the one side by its premises and on the other by its conclusion, the series of affirmations that make up a narrative). The associated field is also made up of all the formulations to which the statement refers (implicitly or not), either by repeating them, modifying them, or adapting them, or by opposing them, or by commenting on them; there can be no statement that in one way or another does not reactualize others (ritual elements in a narrative; previously accepted propositions in a demonstration; conventional sentences in a conversation). The associated field is also made up of all the formulations whose subsequent possibility is determined by the statement, and which may follow the statement as its consequence, its natural successor, or its conversational retort (an order does not open up the same enunciative possibilities as the propositions of an axiomatic or the beginning of a narrative). Lastly, the associated field is made up of all the formulations whose status the statement in question shares, among which it takes its place without regard to linear order, with which it will fade away, or with which, on the contrary, it will be valued, preserved, sacralized, and offered, as a possible object, to a future discourse (a statement is not dissociable from the status that it may receive as 'literature', or as an unimportant remark that is barely worthy of being forgotten, or as a scientific truth valid for all time, or as prophetic words, etc.). Generally speaking, one can say that a sequence of linguistic elements is a statement only if it is immersed in an enunciative field, in which it then appears as a unique element.

The statement is not the direct projection on to the plane of language (*langage*) of a particular situation or a group of representations. It is not simply the manipulation by a speaking subject of a number of elements and linguistic rules. At the very outset, from the very root, the statement is divided up into an enunciative field in which it has a place and a status, which arranges for its possible relations with the past, and which opens up for it a possible future. Every statement is specified in this way: there is no statement in general, no free, neutral, independent statement; but a statement always belongs to a series or a whole, always plays a role among other statements, deriving support from them and distinguishing itself from them: it is always part of a network of statements, in which it has a role, however minimal it may be, to play. Whereas grammatical construction needs only elements and rules in order to operate; whereas one might just conceive of a language (*langue*) – an artificial one, of course – whose only purpose is the construction of a single sentence; whereas the alphabet, the rules of construction and transformation of a formal system being given, one can perfectly well define the first proposition of this language (*langage*), the same cannot be said of the statement. There is no statement that does not presuppose others; there is no statement that is not surrounded by a field of coexistences, effects of series and succession, a distribution of functions and roles. If one can speak of a statement, it is because a sentence (a proposition) figures at a definite point, with a specific position, in an enunciative network that extends beyond it.

Against this background of enunciative coexistence, there stand out, at an autonomous and describable level, the grammatical relations between sentences, the logical relations between propositions, the metalinguistic relations between an object language and one that defines the rules, the rhetorical relations between groups (or elements) of sentences. It is permissible, of course, to analyse all these relations without taking as one's theme the enunciative field itself, that is, the domain of coexistence in which the enunciative function operates. But they can exist and are analysable only to the extent that these sentences have been 'enunciated'; in other words, to the extent that they are deployed in an enunciative field that allows them to follow one another, order one another, coexist with one another, and play roles in relation to one another. Far from being the principle of individualization of groups of 'signifiers' (the meaningful 'atom', the minimum on the basis of which there is meaning), the statement is that which situates these meaningful units in a space in which they breed and multiply.

(d) Lastly, for a sequence of linguistic elements to be regarded and analysed as a statement, it must fulfil a fourth condition: it must have a material existence. Could one speak of a statement if a voice had not articulated it, if a surface did not bear its signs, if it had not become embodied in a sense-perceptible element, and if it had not left some trace – if only for an instant – in someone's memory or in some space? Could one speak of a statement as an ideal, silent figure? The statement is always given through some material medium, even if that medium is concealed, even if it is doomed to vanish as soon as it appears. And the statement not only needs this materiality; its materiality is not given to it, in addition, once all its determinations have been fixed: it is partly made up of this materiality. Even if a sentence is composed of the same words, bears exactly the same meaning, and preserves the same syntactical and semantic identity, it does not constitute the same statement if it is spoken by someone in the course of a conversation, or printed in a novel; if it was written one day centuries ago, and if it now reappears in an oral formulation. The coordinates and the material status of the statement are part of its intrinsic characteristics. That is an obvious fact. Or almost. For as soon as one examines it a little more closely, things begin to blur and the problems increase.

Of course, it is tempting to say that if a statement is characterized, partly at least, by its material status, and if its identity is susceptible to a modification of that status, the same can be said of sentences and propositions: the materiality of signs is not, in fact, entirely indifferent to grammar or even to logic. We know what theoretical problems are presented to logic by the material constancy of the symbols used (how to define the identity of a symbol through the various substances in which it may be embodied and the variations of form that it can tolerate? How to recognize it and make certain that it is the same, if it must be defined as 'a concrete physical form'?); we know too what problems are presented to logic by the very notion of a series of symbols (what do 'precede' and 'follow' mean? Come 'before' and 'after'? In what space is such an order situated?). Much better known still are the relations of materiality and the language (*langue*) – the role of writing and the alphabet, the fact that neither the same syntax, nor the same vocabulary operate in a written text and in a conversation, in a newspaper and in a book, in a letter and on a poster; moreover, there are series of words that form perfectly individualized and acceptable sentences if they feature as newspaper headlines, and which, nevertheless, in the course of a conversation, could never stand as meaningful sentences. Yet the materiality plays a much more important role in the statement: it is not simply a principle of variation, a modification of the criteria of recognition, or a determination of linguistic sub-groups. It is constitutive of the statement itself: a statement must have a substance, a support, a place, and a date. And when these requisites change, it too changes identity. At this point, a host of questions arises: Does the same sentence repeated very loudly and very softly form one or more statements? When one learns a text by heart, does each recitation constitute a statement, or should one regard it as a repetition of the same statement? A sentence is faithfully translated into a foreign language: two distinct statements or one? And in a collective recitation – a prayer or a lesson – how many statements are produced? How can one establish the identity of the statement through all these various forms, repetitions, and transcriptions?

The problem is no doubt obscured by the fact that there is often a confusion of different levels. To begin with, we must set aside the multiplicity of enunciations. We will say that an enunciation takes place whenever a group of signs is emitted. Each of these articulations has its spatio-temporal individuality. Two people may say the same thing at the same time, but since there are two people there will be two distinct enunciations. The same person may repeat the same sentence several times; this will produce the same number of enunciations distinct in time. The enunciation is an unrepeatable event; it has a situated and dated uniqueness that is irreducible. Yet this uniqueness allows of a number of constants – grammatical, semantic, logical – by which one can, by neutralizing the moment of enunciation and the coordinates that individualize it, recognize the general form of a sentence, a meaning, a proposition. The time and place of the enunciation, and the material support that it uses, then become, very largely at least, indifferent: and what stands out is a form that is endlessly repeatable, and which may give rise to the most dispersed enunciations. But the statement itself cannot be reduced to this pure event of enunciation, for, despite its materiality, it cannot be repeated: it would not be difficult to say that the same sentence spoken by two people in slightly different circumstances constitute only one statement. And yet the statement cannot be reduced to a grammatical or logical form because, to a greater degree than that form, and in a different way, it is susceptible to differences of material, substance, time, and place. What, then, is that materiality proper to the statement, and which permits certain special types of repetition? How is it that one can speak of the same statement when there are several distinct enunciations of it, yet must speak of several statements when one can recognize identical forms, structures, rules of construction, and intentions? What, then, is this rule of *repeatable materiality* that characterizes the statement?

This may not be a perceptible, qualitative materiality, expressed in the form of colour, sound, or solidity, and divided up by the same spatio-temporal observation as the perceptual space. Let us take a very simple example: a text reproduced several times, the successive editions of a book, or, better still, the different copies of the same printing, do not give rise to the same number of distinct statements: in all the editions of *Les Fleurs du mal* (variants and rejected versions apart), we find the same set of statements; yet neither the characters, nor the ink, nor the paper, nor even the placing of the text and the positions of the signs, are the same: the whole texture of the materiality has changed. But in this case these 'small' differences are not important enough to alter the identity of the statement and to bring about another: they are all neutralized in the general element – material, of course, but also institutional and economic – of the 'book': a book, however many copies or editions are made of it, however many different substances it may use, is a locus of exact equiv-alence for the statements – for them it is an authority that permits repeti-tion without any change of identity. We see from this first example that the materiality of the statement is not defined by the space occupied or the date of its formulation; but rather by its status as a thing or object. A status that is never definitive, but modifiable, relative, and always suscept-ible of being questioned: we know for example that, for literary histor-ians, the edition of a book published with the agreement of the author does not have the same status as posthumous editions, that the statements in it have a unique value, that they are not one of the manifestations of one and the same whole, that they are that by relation to which there is and must be repetition. Similarly, between the text of a Constitution, or a will, or a religious revelation, and all the manuscripts or printed copies that reproduce them exactly, with the same writing, in the same characters, and on similar substances, one cannot say that there is an equivalence: on the one hand there are the statements themselves, and on the other their reproduction. The statement cannot be identified with a fragment of matter; but its identity varies with a complex set of material institutions.

For a statement may be the same, whether written on a sheet of paper or published in a book; it may be the same spoken, printed on a poster, or reproduced on a tape-recorder; on the other hand, when a novelist speaks a sentence in daily life, then reproduces the same sentence in the manuscript that he is writing, attributing it to one of his characters, or even allowing it to be spoken by that anonymous voice that passes for that of the author, one cannot say that it is the same statement in each case. The rule of materiality that statements necessarily obey is therefore of the order of the institution rather than of the spatio-temporal localization; it defines *possibilities of reinscription and transcription* (but also thresholds and limits), rather than limited and perishable individualities.

The identity of a statement is subjected to a second group of conditions and limits: those that are imposed by all the other statements among which it figures, by the domain in which it can be used or applied, by the role and functions that it can perform. The affirmation that the earth is round or that species evolve does not constitute the same statement before and after Copernicus, before and after Darwin; it is not, for such simple formulations, that the meaning of the words has changed; what changed was the relation of these affirmations to other propositions, their conditions of use and reinvestment, the field of experience, of possible verifications, of problems to be resolved, to which they can be referred. The sentence 'dreams fulfil desires' may have been repeated throughout the centuries; it is not the same statement in Plato and in Freud. The schemata of use, the rules of application, the constellations in which they can play a part, their strategic potentialities constitute for statements a *field of stabilization* that makes it possible, despite all the differences of enunciation, to repeat them in their identity; but this same field may also, beneath the most manifest semantic, grammatical, or formal identities, define a threshold beyond which there can be no further equivalence, and the appearance of a new statement must be recognized. But it is possible, no doubt, to go further: there are cases in which one may consider that there is only one statement, even though the words, the syntax, and the language (*langue*) itself are not identical. Such cases are a speech and its simultaneous translation; a scientific text in English and its French version; a notice printed in three columns in three different languages: there are not, in such cases, the same number of statements as there are languages used, but a single group of statements in different linguistic forms. Better still: a given piece of information may be retransmitted with other words, with a simplified syntax, or in an agreed code; if the information content and the uses to which it could be put are the same, one can say that it is the same statement in each case.

Here too, we are concerned not with a criterion of individualization for the statement, but rather with its principle of variation: it is sometimes more diverse than the structure of the sentence (and its identity is then finer, more fragile, more easily modifiable than that of a semantic or grammatical whole), sometimes more constant than that structure (and its identity is then broader, more stable, more susceptible to variations). Moreover, not only can this identity of the statement not be situated once and for all in relation to that of the sentence, but it is itself relative and oscillates according to the use that is made of the statement and the way in which it is handled. When one uses a statement in such a way as to reveal its grammatical structure, its rhetorical configuration, or the connotations that it may carry, it is obvious that one cannot regard it as being identical in its original language (*langue*) and in a translation. On the other hand, if it is intended as part of a procedure of experimental verification, then text and translation constitute a single enunciative whole. Or again, at a certain scale of macro-history, one may consider that an affirmation like 'species evolve' forms the same statement in Darwin and in Simpson; at a finer level, and considering more limited fields of use ('neo-Darwinism' as opposed to the Darwinian system itself), we are presented with two different statements. The constancy of the statement, the preservation of its identity through the unique events of the enunciations, its duplications through the identity of the forms, constitute the function of the *field of use* in which it is placed.

The statement, then, must not be treated as an event that occurred in a particular time and place, and that the most one can do is recall it – and celebrate it from afar off – in an act of memory. But neither is it an ideal form that can be actualized in any body, at any time, in any circumstances, and in any material conditions. Too repeatable to be entirely identifiable with the spatio-temporal coordinates of its birth (it is more than the place and date of its appearance), too bound up with what surrounds it and supports it to be as free as a pure form (it is more than a law of construction governing a group of elements), it is endowed with a certain modifiable heaviness, a weight relative to the field in which it is placed, a constancy that allows of various uses, a temporal permanence that does not have the inertia of a mere trace or mark, and which does not sleep on its own past. Whereas an enunciation may be *begun again* or *re-evoked*, and a (linguistic or logical) form may be *reactualized*, the statement may be *repeated* – but always in strict conditions.

This repeatable materiality that characterizes the enunciative function reveals the statement as a specific and paradoxical object, but also as one of those objects that men produce, manipulate, use, transform, exchange, combine, decompose and recompose, and possibly destroy. Instead of being something said once and for all – and lost in the past like the result of a battle, a geological catastrophe, or the death of a king – the statement, as it emerges in its materiality, appears with a status, enters various networks and various fields of use, is subjected to transferences or modifications, is integrated into operations and strategies in which its identity is maintained or effaced. Thus the statement circulates, is used, disappears, allows or prevents the realization of a desire, serves or resists various interests, participates in challenge and struggle, and becomes a theme of appropriation or rivalry.

CHAPTER 3

The Description of Statements

I now find that the analysis has shifted its ground to a quite considerable extent; it was my intention to return to the definition of the statement, which, at the outset, I had left in suspense. It was as if I had regarded the statement as a unit that could be established without difficulty, and that all I had to do was describe its possibilities and laws of combination. I now realize that I could not define the statement as a unit of a linguistic type (superior to the phenomenon of the word, inferior to the text); but that I was dealing with an enunciative function that involved various units (these may sometimes be sentences, sometimes propositions; but they are sometimes made up of fragments of sentences, series or tables of signs, a set of propositions or equivalent formulations); and, instead of giving a 'meaning' to these units, this function relates them to a field of objects; instead of providing them with a subject, it opens up for them a number of possible subjective positions; instead of fixing their limits, it places them in a domain of coordination and coexistence; instead of determining their identity, it places them in a space in which they are used and repeated. In short, what has been discovered is not the atomic statement – with its apparent meaning, its origin, its limits, and its individuality – but the operational field of the enunciative function and the conditions according to which it reveals various units (which may be, but need not be, of a grammatical or logical order). But I now feel that I must answer two questions: what do I now understand by the task, which I originally set myself, of describing statements? How can this theory of the statement be adjusted to the analysis of discursive formations that I outlined previously?

I

1. First task: fix the vocabulary. If we agree to call *verbal performance*, or, better, *linguistic performance*, any group of signs produced on the basis of a natural (or artificial) language (*langue*), we could call *formulation* the individual (or possibly collective) act that reveals, on any material and according to a particular form, that group of signs: the formulation is an event that can always be located by its spatio-temporal coordinates, which can always be related to an author, and which may constitute in itself a specific act (a 'performative' act, as the British analysts call it); we can call *sentence* or *proposition* the units that grammar or logic may recognize in a group of signs: these units may always be characterized by the elements that figure in them, and by the rules of construction that unite them; in relation to the sentence and the proposition, the questions of origin, time and place, and context are merely subsidiary; the decisive question is that of their correctness (if only under the form of 'acceptability'). We will call *statement* the modality of existence proper to that group of signs: a modality that allows it to be something more than a series of traces, something more than a succession of marks on a substance, something more than a mere object made by a human being; a modality that allows it to be in relation with a domain of objects, to prescribe a definite position to any possible subject, to be situated among other verbal performances, and to be endowed with a repeatable materiality. We can now understand the reason for the equivocal meaning of the term *discourse*, which I have used and abused in many different senses: in the most general, and vaguest way, it denoted a group of verbal performances; and by discourse, then, I meant that which was produced (perhaps all that was produced) by the groups of signs. But I also meant a group of acts of formulation, a series of sentences or propositions. Lastly – and it is this meaning that was finally used (together with the first, which served in a provisional capacity) – discourse is constituted by a group of sequences of signs, in so far as they are statements, that is, in so far as they can be assigned particular modalities of existence. And if I succeed in showing, as I shall try to do shortly, that the law of such a series is precisely what I have so far called a *discursive formation*, if I succeed in showing that this discursive formation really is the principle of dispersion and redistribution, not of formulations, not of sentences, not of propositions, but of statements (in the sense in which I have used this word), the term discourse can be defined as the group of statements that belong to a single system of formation; thus I shall be able

to speak of clinical discourse, economic discourse, the discourse of natural history, psychiatric discourse.

I am well aware that most of these definitions do not conform with current usage: linguists usually give the word discourse a quite different meaning; logicians and analysts use the term statement in a different way. But my intention here is not to transfer to some hitherto benighted domain a set of concepts, a form of analysis, and a theory that have been formed elsewhere; and I do not intend to use a model by applying it, with its own efficacy, to new contents. Not, of course, that I wish to question the value of such a model; not that I wish, even before trying it, to limit its application, or to lay down the threshold that it must not cross. But I would like to reveal a descriptive possibility, outline the domain of which it is capable, define its limits and its autonomy. This descriptive possibility is articulated upon others; it does not derive from them.

In particular, then, the analysis of statements does not claim to be a total, exhaustive description of 'language' (*langage*), or of 'what was said'. In the whole density implied by verbal performances, it is situated at a particular level that must be distinguished from the others, characterized in relation to them, and abstract. In particular, it does not replace a logical analysis of propositions, a grammatical analysis of sentences, a psychological or contextual analysis of formulations: it is another way of attacking verbal performances, of dissociating their complexity, of isolating the terms that are entangled in its web, and of locating the various regularities that they obey. By confronting the statement with the sentence or the proposition, I am not trying to rediscover a lost totality, or to resuscitate, as many would nostalgically like to do, the plenitude of living speech, the richness of the Word, the profound unity of the Logos. The analysis of statements corresponds to a specific level of description.

2. The statement, then, is not an elementary unity that can be added to the unities described by grammar or logic. It cannot be isolated like a sentence, a proposition, or an act of formulation. To describe a statement is not a matter of isolating and characterizing a horizontal segment; but of defining the conditions in which the function that gave a series of signs (a series that is not necessarily grammatical or logically structured) an existence, and a specific existence, can operate. An existence that reveals such a series as more than a mere trace, but rather a relation to a domain of objects; as more than the result of an action or an individual operation, but rather a set of possible positions for a subject; as more than an organic,

autonomous whole, closed in upon itself and capable of forming meaning of its own accord, but rather an element in a field of coexistence; as more than a passing event or an inert object, but rather a repeatable materiality. The description of statements is concerned, in a sort of vertical dimension, with the conditions of existence of different groups of signifiers (*signifiants*). Hence a paradox: the description of statements does not attempt to evade verbal performances in order to discover behind them or below their apparent surface a hidden element, a secret meaning that lies buried within them, or which emerges through them without saying so; and yet the statement is not immediately visible; it is not given in such a manifest way as a grammatical or logical structure (even if such a structure is not entirely clear, or is very difficult to elucidate). The statement is neither visible nor hidden.

Not hidden, by definition, since it characterizes the modalities of existence proper to a group of effectively produced signs. The analysis of statements can never confine its attention to the things said, to the sentences that were actually spoken or written, to the 'signifying' elements that were traced or pronounced – and, more particularly, to that very uniqueness that gives them existence, offers them to the view of the reader, to a possible reactivation, to innumerable uses or possible transformations, among other things, but not like other things. It cannot concern only realized verbal performances since it analyses them at the level of their existence: it is a description of things said, precisely as they were said. The analysis of statements, then, is a historical analysis, but one that avoids all interpretation: it does not question things said as to what they are hiding, what they were 'really' saying, in spite of themselves, the unspoken element that they contain, the proliferation of thoughts, images, or fantasies that inhabit them; but, on the contrary, it questions them as to their mode of existence, what it means to them to have come into existence, to have left traces, and perhaps to remain there, awaiting the moment when they might be of use once more; what it means to them to have appeared when and where they did – they and no others. From this point of view, there is no such thing as a latent statement: for what one is concerned with is the fact of language (*langage*).

A difficult thesis to sustain. We know – and this has probably been the case ever since men began to speak – that one thing is often said in place of another; that one sentence may have two meanings at once; that an obvious meaning, understood without difficulty by everyone, may conceal a second esoteric or prophetic meaning that a more subtle deciphering, or perhaps only the erosion of time, will finally reveal; that beneath a visible formulation, there may reign another that controls it, disturbs it, and imposes on it an articulation of its own; in short, that in one way or another, things said say more than themselves. But, in fact, these apparent duplications, this unsaid that is nevertheless said, do not affect the statement, at least as it has been defined here. Polysemia – which justifies hermeneutics and the discovery of another meaning – concerns the sentence, and the semantic fields that it employs: the same group of words may give rise to several meanings, and to several possible constructions; there may be, therefore, interwoven or alternating, different meanings operating on the same enunciative base. Similarly, the suppression of one verbal performance by another, their substitution or interference, are phenomena that belong to the level of the formulation (even if they have incidences on the linguistic or logical structures); but the statement itself is not concerned with this duplication or this suppression: since it is the modality of existence of the verbal performance as it has taken place. The statement cannot be regarded as the cumulative result or the crystallization of several fluctuating, scarcely articulated, and mutually opposed statements. The statement is not haunted by the secret presence of the unsaid, of hidden meanings, of suppressions; on the contrary, the way in which these hidden elements function, and in which they can be restored, depends on the enunciative modality itself: we know that the 'unsaid', the 'suppressed', is not the same – either in its structure or in its effect – in the case of a mathematical statement, a statement in economics, an autobiography, or the account of a dream.

However, to all these various modalities of the *unsaid* that may be located against the background of the enunciative field, should no doubt be added a *lack*, which, instead of being inside seems to be correlative with this field and to play a role in the determination of its very existence. There may in fact be – and probably always are – in the conditions of emergence of statements, exclusions, limits, or gaps that divide up their referential, validate only one series of modalities, enclose groups of coexistence, and prevent certain forms of use. But one should not confuse, either in its status or in its effect, the lack that is characteristic of an enunciative regularity and the meanings concealed in what is formulated in it.

3. Although the statement cannot be hidden, it is not visible either; it is not presented to the perception as the manifest bearer of its limits and

characteristics. It requires a certain change of viewpoint and attitude to be recognized and examined in itself. Perhaps it is like the over-familiar that constantly eludes one; those familiar transparencies, which, although they conceal nothing in their density, are nevertheless not entirely clear. The enunciative level emerges in its very proximity.

There are several reasons for this. The first has already been given: the statement is not just another unity – above or below – sentences and propositions; it is always invested in unities of this kind, or even in sequences of signs that do not obey their laws (and which may be lists, chance series, tables); it characterizes not what is given in them, but the very fact that they are given, and the way in which they are given. It has this quasi-invisibility of the 'there is', which is effaced in the very thing of which one can say: 'there is this or that thing'.

Another reason: the 'signifying' structure of language (*langage*) always refers back to something else; objects are designated by it; meaning is intended by it; the subject is referred back to it by a number of signs even if he is not himself present in them. Language always seems to be inhabited by the other, the elsewhere, the distant; it is hollowed by absence. Is it not the locus in which something other than itself appears, does not its own existence seem to be dissipated in this function? But if one wishes to describe the enunciative level, one must consider that existence itself; question language, not in the direction to which it refers, but in the dimension that gives it; ignore its power to designate, to name, to show, to reveal, to be the place of meaning or truth, and, instead, turn one's attention to the moment – which is at once solidified, caught up in the play of the 'signifier' and the 'signified' – that determines its unique and limited existence. In the examination of language, one must suspend, not only the point of view of the 'signified' (we are used to this by now), but also that of the 'signifier', and so reveal the fact that, here and there, in relation to possible domains of objects and subjects, in relation to other possible formulations and re-uses, there is *language*.

The last reason for this quasi-invisibility of the statement: it is implied, but never made explicit, in all other analyses of language. If language is to be taken as an object, decomposed into distinct levels, described and analysed, an 'enunciative datum' must exist that will always be determined and not infinite: the analysis of a language (*langue*) always operates on a corpus of words and texts; the uncovering and interpretation of implicit meanings always rests on a limited group of sentences; the logical analysis of a system implies a given group of propositions in the rewriting, in a formal language (*langage*). The enunciative level is neutralized each time: either it is defined only as a representative sample that enables one to free endlessly applicable structures; or it disappears into a pure appearance behind which the truth of words is revealed; or it acts as a neutral substance that serves as a support for formal relations. The fact that, each time, it is indispensable if an analysis is to take place deprives it of all relevance for the analysis itself. If one adds to this that all these descriptions can be made only when they themselves form finite groups of statements, it will be clear why they are surrounded on all sides by the enunciative field, why they cannot free themselves from it, and why they cannot take it directly as its theme. In considering statements in themselves, we will not seek, beyond all these analyses and at a deeper level, some secret or some root of language (*langage*) that they have omitted. We shall try to render visible, and analysable, that immediate transparency that constitutes the element of their possibility.

Neither hidden, nor visible, the enunciative level is at the limit of language (*langage*): it is not, in itself, a group of characteristics that are presented, even in an unsystematic way, to immediate experience; but neither is it the enigmatic, silent remainder that it does not translate. It defines the modality of its appearance: its periphery rather than its internal organization, its surface rather than its content. But the fact that one can describe this enunciative surface proves that the 'given', the datum, of language is not the mere rending of a fundamental silence; that the words, sentences, meanings, affirmations, series of propositions do not back directly on to a primeval night of silence; but that the sudden appearance of a sentence, the flash of meaning, the brusque gesture of the index finger of designation, always emerge in the operational domain of an enunciative function; that between language as one reads and hears it, and also as one speaks it, and the absence of any formulation, there is not a profusion of things half said, sentences left unfinished, thoughts half expressed, an endless monologue of which only a few fragments emerge; but, before all – or in any case before it (for it depends on them) – the conditions according to which the enunciative function operates. This also proves that it is vain to seek, beyond structural, formal, or interpretative analyses of language, a domain that is at last freed from all positivity, in which the freedom of the subject, the labour of the human being, or the opening up of a transcendental destiny could be fulfilled. One should not object to linguistic methods or logical analyses: 'When you have said so much about the rules of its construction, what do you do with language itself, in the plenitude of its living body? What do you do with this free-dom, or with this meaning that is prior to all signification, without which individuals could not understand one another in the never-ending work of language? Are you not aware that as soon as one has crossed the finite systems that make possible the infinity of discourse, but which are in-capable of founding it and of accounting for it, what one finds is the mark of a transcendence, or the work of the human being? Do you know that you have described only a few of the characteristics of a language (*langage*) whose emergence and mode of being are entirely irreducible to your analyses?' Such objections must be set aside: for if it is true that there is a dimension there that belongs neither to logic nor to linguistics, it is not, for all that, a restored transcendence, nor a way that has been reopened in the direction of an inaccessible origin, nor a creation by the human being of his own meanings. Language, in its appearance and mode of being, is the statement; as such, it belongs to a description that is neither trans-cendental nor anthropological. The enunciative analysis does not lay down for linguistic or logical analyses the limit beyond which they must renounce their power and recognize their powerlessness; it does not mark the line that encloses their domain; it is deployed in another direction, which intersects them. The possibility of an enunciative analysis, if it is established, must make it possible to raise the transcendental obstacle that a certain form of philosophical discourse opposes to all analyses of lan-guage, in the name of the being of that language and of the ground from which it should derive its origin.

II

I must now turn to the second group of questions: how can the description of statements, thus defined, be adjusted to the analysis of discursive for-mations, the principles of which I outlined above? And inversely: to what extent can one say that the analysis of discursive formations really is a description of statements, in the sense in which I have used this word? It is important to answer these questions; for it is at this point that the enter-prise to which I have devoted myself for so many years, which I have developed in a somewhat blind way, but of which I am now trying – even if I readjust it, even if I rectify a number of errors or imprudences – to recapture the general outline, must close its circle. As has already become clear, I am not trying to say here what I once tried to say in this or that concrete analysis, or to describe the project that I had in mind, the obstacles that I encountered, the attempts that I was forced to abandon, the more or less satisfactory results that I managed to obtain; I am not describing an effective trajectory in order to indicate what should have been and what will be from now on: I am trying to elucidate in itself – in order to measure it and to determine its requirements – a possibility of description that I have used without being aware of its constraints and resources; rather than trying to discover what I said, and what I might have said, I shall try to reveal, in its own regularity – a regularity that I have not yet succeeded in mastering – what made it possible to say what I did. But one can also see that I am not developing here a theory, in the strict sense of the term: the deduction, on the basis of a number of axioms, of an abstract model applicable to an indefinite number of empirical descriptions. If such an edifice were ever possible, the time for it has certainly not yet arrived. I am not inferring the analysis of discursive formations from a definition of statements that would serve as a basis; nor am I inferring the nature of statements from what discursive formations are, as one was able to abstract them from this or that description; but I am trying to show how a domain can be organized, without flaw, without contradiction, without internal arbitrariness, in which statements, their principle of grouping, the great historical unities that they may form, and the methods that make it possible to describe them are all brought into question. I am not proceeding by linear deduction, but rather by concentric circles, moving sometimes towards the outer and sometimes towards the inner ones: beginning with the problem of discontinuity in discourse and of the uniqueness of the statement (the central theme), I have tried to analyse, on the periphery, certain forms of enigmatic groupings; but the principles of unification with which I was then presented, and which are neither grammatical, nor logical, nor psychological, and which consequently cannot refer either to sentences, propositions, or representations, forced me to return to the centre, to that problem of the statement; to try to elucidate what is meant by the term statement. And I will consider, not that I have constructed a rigorous theoretical model, but that I have freed a coherent domain of description, that I have, if not established the model, at least opened up and arranged the possibility of one, if I have been able to 'loop the loop', and show that the analysis of discursive formations really is centred on a description of the statement in its specificity. In short, if I have been able to show that they really are the proper dimensions of the statement that are at work in the mapping of discursive formations. Rather than *founding* a theory – and perhaps before being able to do so (I do not deny that I regret not yet having succeeded in doing so) – my present concern is to *establish* a possibility.

In examining the statement what we have discovered is a function that has a bearing on groups of signs, which is identified neither with grammatical 'acceptability' nor with logical correctness, and which requires if it is to operate: a referential (which is not exactly a fact, a state of things, or even an object, but a principle of differentiation); a subject (not the speaking consciousness, not the author of the formulation, but a position that may be filled in certain conditions by various individuals); an associated field (which is not the real context of the formulation, the situation in which it was articulated, but a domain of coexistence for other statements); a materiality (which is not only the substance or support of the articulation, but a status, rules of transcription, possibilities of use and re-use). Now, what has been described as discursive formations are, strictly speaking, groups of statements. That is, groups of verbal performances that are not linked to one another at the *sentence* level by grammatical (syntactical or semantic) links; which are not linked to one another at the *proposition* level by logical links (links of formal coherence or conceptual connexion); and which are not linked either at the *formulation* level by psychological links (either the identity of the forms of consciousness, the constancy of the mentalities, or the repetition of a project); but which are linked at the *statement* level. That which implies that one can define the general set of rules that govern their objects, the form of dispersion that regularly divides up what they say, the system of their referentials; that which implies that one defines the general set of rules that govern the different modes of enunciation, the possible distribution of the subjective positions, and the system that defines and prescribes them; that which implies that one defines the set of rules common to all their associated domains, the forms of succession, of simultaneity, of the repetition of which they are capable, and the system that links all these fields of coexistence together; lastly, that which implies that one can define the general set of rules that govern the status of these statements, the way in which they are institutionalized, received, used, re-used, combined together, the mode according to which they become objects of appropriation, instruments for desire or interest, elements for a strategy. To describe statements, to describe the enunciative function of which they are the bearers, to analyse the conditions in which this function operates, to cover the different domains that this function presupposes and the way in which those domains are articulated, is to undertake to uncover what might be called the discursive formation. Or again, which amounts to the same thing, but in the opposite direction; the discursive formation is the general enunciative system that governs a group of verbal performances – a system that is not alone in governing it, since it also obeys, and in accordance with its other dimensions, logical, linguistic, and psychological systems. What has been called 'discursive formation' divides up the general plane of things said at the specific level of statements. The four directions in which it is analysed (formation of objects, formation of the subjective positions, formation of concepts, formation of strategic choices) correspond to the four domains in which the enunciative function operates. And if the discursive formations are free in relation to the great rhetorical unities of the text or the book, if they are not governed by the rigour of a deductive architecture, if they are not identified with the *œuvre* of an author, it is because they bring into play the enunciative level, together with the regularities that characterize it, and not the grammatical level of sentences, or the logical level of propositions, or the psychological level of formulation.

On this basis, we can now advance a number of propositions that lie at the heart of these analyses:

1. It can be said that the mapping of discursive formations, independently of other principles of possible unification, reveals the specific level of the statement; but it can also be said that the description of statements and of the way in which the enunciative level is organized leads to the individualization of the discursive formations. The two approaches are equally justifiable and reversible. The analysis of the statement and that of the formation are established correlatively. When the time finally comes to found a theory, it will have to define a deductive order.

2. A statement belongs to a discursive formation as a sentence belongs to a text, and a proposition to a deductive whole. But whereas the regularity of a sentence is defined by the laws of a language (*langue*), and that of a proposition by the laws of logic, the regularity of statements is defined by the discursive formation itself. The fact of its belonging to a discursive formation and the laws that govern it are one and the same thing; this is not paradoxical since the discursive formation is characterized not by principles of construction but by a dispersion of fact, since for statements it is not a condition of possibility but a law of coexistence, and since statements are not interchangeable elements but groups characterized by their modality of existence.

3. So we can now give a full meaning to the definition of 'discourse' that we suggested above. We shall call discourse a group of statements in so far as they belong to the same discursive formation; it does not form a rhetorical or formal unity, endlessly repeatable, whose appearance or use in history might be indicated (and, if necessary, explained); it is made up of a limited number of statements for which a group of conditions of existence can be defined. Discourse in this sense is not an ideal, timeless form that also possesses a history; the problem is not therefore to ask oneself how and why it was able to emerge and become embodied at this point in time; it is, from beginning to end, historical – a fragment of history, a unity and discontinuity in history itself, posing the problem of its own limits, its divisions, its transformations, the specific modes of its temporality rather than its sudden irruption in the midst of the complicities of time.

4. Lastly, what we have called 'discursive practice' can now be defined more precisely. It must not be confused with the expressive operation by which an individual formulates an idea, a desire, an image; nor with the rational activity that may operate in a system of inference; nor with the 'competence' of a speaking subject when he constructs grammatical sentences; it is a body of anonymous, historical rules, always determined in the time and space that have defined a given period, and for a given social, economic, geographical, or linguistic area, the conditions of operation of the enunciative function.

It remains for me now to invert the analysis and, after referring discursive formations to the statements that they describe, to seek in another direction, this time towards the exterior, the legitimate use of these notions: what can be discovered through them, how they can take their place among other methods of description, to what extent they can modify and redistribute the domain of the history of ideas. But before operating this inversion, and in order to operate it more surely, I shall remain a little longer in the dimension that I have been exploring, and try to define what the analysis of the enunciative field and of the formation that divide it up require and exclude.

CHAPTER 4

Rarity, Exteriority, Accumulation

The enunciative analysis takes into consideration an element of rarity.

Generally speaking, the analysis of discourse operates between the twin poles of totality and plethora. One shows how the different texts with which one is dealing refer to one another, organize themselves into a single figure, converge with institutions and practices, and carry meanings that may be common to a whole period. Each element considered is taken as the expression of the totality to which it belongs and whose limits it exceeds. And in this way one substitutes for the diversity of the things said a sort of great, uniform text, which has never before been articulated, and which reveals for the first time what men 'really meant' not only in their words and texts, their discourses and their writings, but also in the institutions, practices, techniques, and objects that they produced. In relation to this implicit, sovereign, communal 'meaning', statements appear in superabundant proliferation, since it is to that meaning alone that they all refer and to it alone that they owe their truth: a plethora of signifying elements in relation to this single 'signified' (*signifié*). But this primary and ultimate meaning springs up through the manifest formulations, it hides beneath what appears, and secretly duplicates it, because each discourse contains the power to say something other than what it actually says, and thus to embrace a plurality of meanings: a plethora of the 'signified' in relation to a single 'signifier'. From this point of view, discourse is both plenitude and endless wealth.

The analysis of statements and discursive formations opens up a quite contrary direction: it wishes to determine the principle according to which only the 'signifying' groups that were enunciated could appear. It sets out to establish a law of rarity. This task involves several aspects:

—It is based on the principle that *everything* is never said; in relation to what might have been stated in a natural language (*langue*), in relation to

118

the unlimited combination of linguistic elements, statements (however numerous they may be) are always in deficit; on the basis of the grammar and of the wealth of vocabulary available at a given period, there are, in total, relatively few things that are said. We must look therefore for the principle of rarification or at least of non-filling of the field of possible formulations as it is opened up by the language (*langue*). Discursive formation appears both as a principle of division in the entangled mass of discourses and as a principle of vacuity in the field of language (*langage*).

—We are studying statements at the limit that separates them from what is not said, in the occurrence that allows them to emerge to the exclusion of all others. Our task is not to give voice to the silence that surrounds them, nor to rediscover all that, in them and beside them, had remained silent or had been reduced to silence. Nor is it to study the obstacles that have prevented a particular discovery, held back a particular formulation, repressed a particular form of enunciation, a particular unconscious meaning, or a particular rationality in the course of development; but to define a limited system of presences. The discursive formation is not therefore a developing totality, with its own dynamism or inertia, carrying with it, in an unformulated discourse, what it does not say, what it has not yet said, or what contradicts it at that moment; it is not a rich, difficult germination, it is a distribution of gaps, voids, absences, limits, divisions.

—However, we are not linking these 'exclusions' to a repression; we do not presuppose that beneath manifest statements something remains hidden and subjacent. We are analysing statements, not as being in the place of other statements that have fallen below the line of possible emergence, but as being always in their own place. They are put back into a space that is entirely deployed and involves no reduplication. There is no sub-text. And therefore no plethora. The enunciative domain is identical with its own surface. Each statement occupies in it a place that belongs to it alone. The description of a statement does not consist therefore in rediscovering the unsaid whose place it occupies; nor how one can reduce it to a silent, common text; but on the contrary in discovering what special place it occupies, what ramifications of the system of formations make it possible to map its localization, how it is isolated in the general dispersion of statements.

—This rarity of statements, the incomplete, fragmented form of the enunciative field, the fact that few things, in all, can be said, explain that statements are not, like the air we breathe, an infinite transparency; but things that are transmitted and preserved, that have value, and which one tries to appropriate; that are repeated, reproduced, and transformed; to which pre-established networks are adapted, and to which a status is given in the institution; things that are duplicated not only by copy or translation, but by exegesis, commentary, and the internal proliferation of meaning. Because statements are rare, they are collected in unifying totalities, and the meanings to be found in them are multiplied.

Unlike all those interpretations whose very existence is possible only through the actual rarity of statements, but which nevertheless ignore that rarity, and, on the contrary, take as their theme the compact richness of what is said, the analysis of discursive formations turns back towards that rarity itself; it takes that rarity as its explicit object; it tries to determine its unique system; and, at the same time, it takes account of the fact that there could have been interpretation. To interpret is a way of reacting to enunciative poverty, and to compensate for it by a multiplication of meaning; a way of speaking on the basis of that poverty, and yet despite it. But to analyse a discursive formation is to seek the law of that poverty, it is to weigh it up, and to determine its specific form. In one sense, therefore, it is to weigh the 'value' of statements. A value that is not defined by their truth, that is not gauged by the presence of a secret content; but which characterizes their place, their capacity for circulation and exchange, their possibility of transformation, not only in the economy of discourse, but, more generally, in the administration of scarce resources. In this sense, discourse ceases to be what it is for the exegetic attitude: an inexhaustible treasure from which one can always draw new, and always unpredictable riches; a providence that has always spoken in advance, and which enables one to hear, when one knows how to listen, retrospective oracles: it appears as an asset – finite, limited, desirable, useful – that has its own rules of appearance, but also its own conditions of appropriation and operation; an asset that consequently, from the moment of its existence (and not only in its 'practical applications'), poses the question of power; an asset that is, by nature, the object of a struggle, a political struggle.

Another characteristic feature: the analysis of statements treats them in the systematic form of exteriority. Usually, the historical description of things said is shot through with the opposition of interior and exterior; and wholly directed by a desire to move from the exterior – which may be no more than contingency or mere material necessity, a visible body or uncertain translation – towards the essential nucleus of interiority. To undertake the history of what has been said is to re-do, in the opposite direction, the work of expression: to go back from statements preserved through time and dispersed in space, towards that interior secret that preceded them, left its mark in them, and (in every sense of the term) is betrayed by them. Thus the nucleus of the initiating subjectivity is freed. A subjectivity that always lags behind manifest history; and which finds, beneath events, another, more serious, more secret, more fundamental history, closer to the origin, more firmly linked to its ultimate horizon (and consequently more in control of all its determinations). This other history, which runs beneath history, constantly anticipating it and endlessly recollecting the past, can be described – in a sociological or psychological way – as the evolution of mentalities; it can be given a philosophical status in the recollection of the Logos or the teleology of reason; lastly, it can be purified in the problematic of a trace, which, prior to all speech, is the opening of inscription, the gap of deferred time, it is always the historico-transcendental theme that is reinvested.

A theme whose enunciative analysis tries to free itself. In order to restore statements to their pure dispersion. In order to analyse them in an exteriority that may be paradoxical since it refers to no adverse form of interiority. In order to consider them in their discontinuity, without having to relate them, by one of those shifts that disconnect them and render them inessential, to a more fundamental opening or difference. In order to seize their very irruption, at the place and at the moment at which it occurred. In order to rediscover their occurrence as an event. Perhaps we should speak of 'neutrality' rather than exteriority; but even this word implies rather too easily a suspension of belief, an effacement or a 'placing in parentheses' of all position of existence, whereas it is a question of rediscovering that outside in which, in their relative rarity, in their incomplete proximity, in their deployed space, enunciative events are distributed.

—This task presupposes that the field of statements is not described as a 'translation' of operations or processes that take place elsewhere (in men's thought, in their consciousness or unconscious, in the sphere of transcendental constitutions); but that it is accepted, in its empirical modesty, as the locus of particular events, regularities, relationships, modifications and systematic transformations; in short, that it is treated not as the result or trace of something else, but as a practical domain that is autonomous (although dependent), and which can be described at its own level (although it must be articulated on something other than itself).

—It also presupposes that this enunciative domain refers neither to an individual subject, nor to some kind of collective consciousness, nor to a transcendental subjectivity; but that it is described as an anonymous field whose configuration defines the possible position of speaking subjects. Statements should no longer be situated in relation to a sovereign subjectivity, but recognize in the different forms of the speaking subjectivity effects proper to the enunciative field.

—As a result, it presupposes that, in its transformations, in its successive series, in its derivations, the field of statements does not obey the temporality of the consciousness as its necessary model. One must not hope – at least at this level and in this form of description – to be able to write a history of things said that is legitimately, in its form, in its regularity and in its nature, the history of an individual or anonymous consciousness, of a project, of a system of intentions, of a set of aims. The time of discourse is not the translation, in a visible chronology, of the obscure time of thought.

The analysis of statements operates therefore without reference to a cogito. It does not pose the question of the speaking subject, who reveals or who conceals himself in what he says, who, in speaking, exercises his sovereign freedom, or who, without realizing it, subjects himself to constraints of which he is only dimly aware. In fact, it is situated at the level of the 'it is said' – and we must not understand by this a sort of communal opinion, a collective representation that is imposed on every individual; we must not understand by it a great, anonymous voice that must, of necessity, speak through the discourses of everyone; but we must understand by it the totality of things said, the relations, the regularities, and the transformations that may be observed in them, the domain of which certain figures, certain intersections indicate the unique place of a speaking subject and may be given the name of author. 'Anyone who speaks', but what he says is not said from anywhere. It is necessarily caught up in the play of an exteriority.

The third feature of enunciative analysis: it is addressed to specific forms of accumulation that can be identified neither with an interiorization in the form of memory nor with an undiscriminating totalization of documents. Usually, when one analyses already existing discourses, one regards them as having sprung from an essential inertia: they have survived through chance, or through the care with which men have treated them, and the illusions that they have entertained as to their value and the immortal dignity of their words; but now they are nothing more than written symbols piling up in dusty libraries, slumbering in a sleep towards which they have never ceased to glide since the day they were pronounced, since they were forgotten and their visible effect lost in time. At most they may be lucky enough to be picked up and examined in some chance reading; at most they can discover that they bear the marks that refer back to the moment of their enunciation; at most, once these marks have been deciphered they can, by a sort of memory that moves across time, free meanings, thoughts, desires, buried fantasies. These four terms: reading – trace – decipherment – memory (however much importance one may accord to one or another of them, and whatever the metaphorical extent that one may accord it, and which enables it to embrace the other three) define the system that usually makes it possible to snatch past discourse from its inertia and, for a moment, to rediscover something of its lost vitality.

Now, the function of enunciative analysis is not to awaken texts from their present sleep, and, by reciting the marks still legible on their surface, to rediscover the flash of their birth; on the contrary, its function is to follow them through their sleep, or rather to take up the related themes of sleep, oblivion, and lost origin, and to discover what mode of existence may characterize statements, independently of their enunciation, in the density of time in which they are preserved, in which they are reactivated, and used, in which they are also – but this was not their original destiny – forgotten, and possibly even destroyed.

—This analysis presupposes that statements are considered in the *remanence* (*rémanence*) that is proper to them, and which is not that of an ever-realizable reference back to the past event of the formulation. To say that statements are residual (*rémanent*) is not to say that they remain in the field of memory, or that it is possible to rediscover what they meant; but it means that they are preserved by virtue of a number of supports and material techniques (of which the book is, of course, only one example), in accordance with certain types of institutions (of which the library is one), and with certain statutory modalities (which are not the same in the case of a religious text, a law, or a scientific truth). This also means that they are invested in techniques that put them into operation, in practices that derive from them, in the social relations that they form, or, through those relations, modify. Lastly, it means that things do not have quite the same mode of existence, the same system of relations with their environment, the same schemata of use, the same possibilities of transformation once they have been said. This survival in time is far from being the accidental or fortunate prolongation of an existence originally intended only for the moment; on the contrary, this remanence is of the nature of the statement; oblivion and destruction are in a sense only the zero degree of this remanence. And against the background that it constitutes, the operations of memory can be deployed.

—This analysis also presupposes that statements are treated in the form of *additivity* that is specific to them. In fact, the types of grouping between successive statements are not always the same, and they never proceed by a simple piling-up or juxtaposition of successive elements. Mathematical statements are not added to one another in the same way as religious texts or laws (they each have their own way of merging together, annulling one another, excluding one another, complementing one another, forming groups that are in varying degrees indissociable and endowed with unique properties). Moreover, these forms of additivity are not given once and for all, and for a particular category of statements: medical case-history today forms a corpus of knowledge that does not obey the same laws of composition as medical case-history in the eighteenth century; modern mathematics does not accumulate its statements according to the same model as Euclidean geometry.

—Lastly, enunciative analysis presupposes that one takes phenomena of *recurrence* into account. Every statement involves a field of antecedent elements in relation to which it is situated, but which it is able to reorganize and redistribute according to new relations. It constitutes its own past, defines, in what precedes it, its own filiation, redefines what makes it possible or necessary, excludes what cannot be compatible with it. And it poses this enunciative past as an acquired truth, as an event that has occurred, as a form that can be modified, as material to be transformed, or as an object that can be spoken about, etc. In relation to all these possibilities of recurrence, memory and oblivion, the rediscovery of meaning or its repression, far from being fundamental, are merely unique figures.

The description of statements and discursive formations must therefore free itself from the widespread and persistent image of return. It does not claim to go back, beyond a time that is no more than a falling off, a latency, an oblivion, a covering up or a wandering, towards that moment of foundation when speech was not yet caught up in any form of materiality, when it had no chances of survival, and when it was confined to the non-determined dimension of the opening. It does not try to constitute for the already said the paradoxical instant of the second birth; it does not invoke a dawn about to return. On the contrary, it deals with statements in the density of the accumulation in which they are caught up and which nevertheless they never cease to modify, to disturb, to overthrow, and sometimes to destroy.

To describe a group of statements not as the closed, plethoric totality of a meaning, but as an incomplete, fragmented figure; to describe a group of statements not with reference to the interiority of an intention, a thought, or a subject, but in accordance with the dispersion of an exteriority; to describe a group of statements, in order to rediscover not the moment or the trace of their origin, but the specific forms of an accumulation, is certainly not to uncover an interpretation, to discover a foundation, or to free constituent acts; nor is it to decide on a rationality, or to embrace a teleology. It is to establish what I am quite willing to call a *positivity*. To analyse a discursive formation therefore is to deal with a group of verbal performances at the level of the statements and of the form of positivity that characterizes them; or, more briefly, it is to define the type of positivity of a discourse. If, by substituting the analysis of rarity for the search for totalities, the description of relations of exteriority for the theme of the transcendental foundation, the analysis of accumulations for the quest of the origin, one is a positivist, then I am quite happy to be one. Similarly, I am not in the least unhappy about the fact that several times (though still in a rather blind way) I have used the term positivity to designate from afar the tangled mass that I was trying to unravel.

CHAPTER 5

The Historical *a priori* and the Archive

The positivity of a discourse – like that of Natural History, political economy, or clinical medicine – characterizes its unity throughout time, and well beyond individual *œuvres*, books, and texts. This unity certainly does not enable us to say of Linnaeus or Buffon, Quesnay or Turgot, Broussais or Bichat, who told the truth, who reasoned with rigour, who most conformed to his own postulates; nor does it enable us to say which of these *œuvres* was closest to a primary, or ultimate, destination, which would formulate most radically the general project of a science. But what it does reveal is the extent to which Buffon and Linnaeus (or Turgot and Quesnay, Broussais and Bichat) were talking about 'the same thing', by placing themselves at 'the same level' or at 'the same distance', by deploying 'the same conceptual field', by opposing one another on 'the same field of battle'; and it reveals, on the other hand, why one cannot say that Darwin is talking about the same thing as Diderot, that Laennec continues the work of Van Swieten, or that Jevons answers the Physiocrats. It defines a limited space of communication. A relatively small space, since it is far from possessing the breadth of a science with all its historical development, from its most distant origin to its present stage; but a more extensive space than the play of influences that have operated from one author to another, or than the domain of explicit polemics. Different *œuvres*, dispersed books, that whole mass of texts that belong to a single discursive formation – and so many authors who know or do not know one another, criticize one another, invalidate one another, pillage one another, meet without knowing it and obstinately intersect their unique discourses in a web of which they are not the masters, of which they cannot see the whole, and of whose breadth they have a very inadequate idea – all these various figures and individuals do not communicate solely by the logical succession of propositions that they advance, nor by the recurrence of themes, nor by the obstinacy of a meaning transmitted, forgotten, and rediscovered; they communicate by the form of positivity of their discourse, or more exactly, this form of positivity (and the conditions of operation of the enunciative function) defines a field in which formal identities, thematic continuities, translations of concepts, and polemical interchanges may be deployed. Thus positivity plays the role of what might be called a *historical a priori*.

Juxtaposed these two words produce a rather startling effect; what I mean by the term is an *a priori* that is not a condition of validity for judgements, but a condition of reality for statements. It is not a question of rediscovering what might legitimize an assertion, but of freeing the conditions of emergence of statements, the law of their coexistence with others, the specific form of their mode of being, the principles according to which they survive, become transformed, and disappear. An *a priori* not of truths that might never be said, or really given to experience; but the *a priori* of a history that is given, since it is that of things actually said. The reason for using this rather barbarous term is that this *a priori* must take account of statements in their dispersion, in all the flaws opened up by their non-coherence, in their overlapping and mutual replacement, in their simultaneity, which is not unifiable, and in their succession, which is not deductible; in short, it has to take account of the fact that discourse has not only a meaning or a truth, but a history, and a specific history that does not refer it back to the laws of an alien development. It must show, for example, that the history of grammar is not the projection into the field of language and its problems of a history that is generally that of reason or of a particular mentality, a history in any case that it shares with medicine, mechanical sciences, or theology; but that it involves a type of history – a form of dispersion in time, a mode of succession, of stability, and of reactivation, a speed of deployment or rotation – that belongs to it alone, even if it is not entirely unrelated to other types of history. Moreover, this *a priori* does not elude historicity: it does not constitute, above events, and in an unmoving heaven, an atemporal structure; it is defined as the group of rules that characterize a discursive practice: but these rules are not imposed from the outside on the elements that they relate together; they are caught up in the very things that they connect; and if they are not modified with the least of them, they modify them, and are transformed with them into certain decisive thresholds. The *a priori* of positivities is not only the system of a temporal dispersion; it is itself a transformable group.

Opposed to formal *a prioris* whose jurisdiction extends without contingence, there is a purely empirical figure; but on the other hand, since it makes it possible to grasp discourses in the law of their actual development, it must be able to take account of the fact that such a discourse, at a given moment, may accept or put into operation, or, on the contrary, exclude, forget, or ignore this or that formal structure. It cannot take account (by some kind of psychological or cultural genesis) of the formal *a prioris*; but it enables us to understand how the formal *a prioris* may have in history points of contact, places of insertion, irruption, or emergence, domains or occasions of operation, and to understand how this history may be not an absolutely extrinsic contingence, not a necessity of form deploying its own dialectic, but a specific regularity. Nothing, therefore, would be more pleasant, or more inexact, than to conceive of this historical *a priori* as a formal *a priori* that is also endowed with a history: a great, unmoving, empty figure that irrupted one day on the surface of time, that exercised over men's thought a tyranny that none could escape, and which then suddenly disappeared in a totally unexpected, totally unprecedented eclipse: a transcendental syncopation, a play of intermittent forms. The formal *a priori* and the historical *a priori* neither belong to the same level nor share the same nature: if they intersect, it is because they occupy two different dimensions.

The domain of statements thus articulated in accordance with historical *a prioris*, thus characterized by different types of positivity, and divided up by distinct discursive formations, no longer has that appearance of a monotonous, endless plain that I attributed to it at the outset when I spoke of 'the surface of discourse'; it also ceases to appear as the inert, smooth, neutral element in which there arise, each according to its own movement, or driven by some obscure dynamic, themes, ideas, concepts, knowledge. We are now dealing with a complex volume, in which heterogeneous regions are differentiated or deployed, in accordance with specific rules and practices that cannot be superposed. Instead of seeing, on the great mythical book of history, lines of words that translate in visible characters thoughts that were formed in some other time and place, we have in the density of discursive practices, systems that establish statements as events (with their own conditions and domain of appearance) and things (with their own possibility and field of use). They are all these systems of statements (whether events or things) that I propose to call *archive*.

By this term I do not mean the sum of all the texts that a culture has kept upon its person as documents attesting to its own past, or as evidence of a continuing identity; nor do I mean the institutions, which, in a given society, make it possible to record and preserve those discourses that one wishes to remember and keep in circulation. On the contrary, it is rather the reason why so many things, said by so many men, for so long, have not emerged in accordance with the same laws of thought, or the same set of circumstances, why they are not simply the signalization, at the level of verbal performances, of what could be deployed in the order of the mind or in the order of things; but they appeared by virtue of a whole set of relations that are peculiar to the discursive level; why, instead of being adventitious figures, grafted, as it were, in a rather haphazard way, on to silent processes, they are born in accordance with specific regularities; in short, why, if there are things said – and those only – one should seek the immediate reason for them in the things that were said not in them, nor in the men that said them, but in the system of discursivity, in the enunciative possibilities and impossibilities that it lays down. The archive is first the law of what can be said, the system that governs the appearance of statements as unique events. But the archive is also that which determines that all these things said do not accumulate endlessly in an amorphous mass, nor are they inscribed in an unbroken linearity, nor do they disappear at the mercy of chance external accidents; but they are grouped together in distinct figures, composed together in accordance with multiple relations, maintained or blurred in accordance with specific regularities; that which determines that they do not withdraw at the same pace in time, but shine, as it were, like stars, some that seem close to us shining brightly from afar off, while others that are in fact close to us are already growing pale. The archive is not that which, despite its immediate escape, safeguards the event of the statement, and preserves, for future memories, its status as an escapee; it is that which, at the very root of the statement–event, and in that which embodies it, defines at the outset *the system of its enunciability*. Nor is the archive that which collects the dust of statements that have become inert once more, and which may make possible the miracle of their resurrection; it is that which defines the mode of occurrence of the statement–thing; it is *the system of its functioning*. Far from being that which unifies everything that has been said in the great confused murmur of a discourse, far from being only that which ensures that we exist in the midst of preserved discourse, it is that which differentiates discourses in their multiple existence and specifies them in their own duration.

Between the *language* (*langue*) that defines the system of constructing possible sentences, and the *corpus* that passively collects the words that are spoken, the *archive* defines a particular level: that of a practice that causes a multiplicity of statements to emerge as so many regular events, as so many things to be dealt with and manipulated. It does not have the weight of tradition; and it does not constitute the library of all libraries, outside time and place; nor is it the welcoming oblivion that opens up to all new speech the operational field of its freedom; between tradition and oblivion, it reveals the rules of a practice that enables statements both to survive and to undergo regular modification. It is *the general system of the formation and transformation of statements.*

It is obvious that the archive of a society, a culture, or a civilization cannot be described exhaustively; or even, no doubt, the archive of a whole period. On the other hand, it is not possible for us to describe our own archive, since it is from within these rules that we speak, since it is that which gives to what we can say – and to itself, the object of our discourse – its modes of appearance, its forms of existence and coexistence, its system of accumulation, historicity, and disappearance. The archive cannot be described in its totality; and in its presence it is unavoidable. It emerges in fragments, regions, and levels, more fully, no doubt, and with greater sharpness, the greater the time that separates us from it: at most, were it not for the rarity of the documents, the greater chronological distance would be necessary to analyse it. And yet could this description of the archive be justified, could it elucidate that which makes it possible, map out the place where it speaks, control its rights and duties, test and develop its concepts – at least at this stage of the search, when it can define its possibilities only in the moment of their realization – if it persisted in describing only the most distant horizons? Should it not approach as close as possible to the positivity that governs it and the archive system that makes it possible today to speak of the archive in general? Should it not illuminate, if only in an oblique way, that enunciative field of which it is itself a part? The analysis of the archive, then, involves a privileged region: at once close to us, and different from our present existence, it is the border of time that surrounds our presence, which overhangs it, and which indicates it in its otherness; it is that which, outside ourselves, delimits us. The description of the archive deploys its possibilities (and the mastery of its possibilities) on the basis of the very discourses that have just ceased to be ours; its threshold of existence is established by the discontinuity that separates us from what we can no longer say, and from that which falls outside our discursive practice; it begins with the outside of our own language (*langage*); its locus is the gap between our own discursive practices. In this sense, it is valid for our diagnosis. Not because it would enable us to draw up a table of our distinctive features, and to sketch out in advance the face that we will have in the future. But it deprives us of our continuities; it dissipates that temporal identity in which we are pleased to look at ourselves when we wish to exorcise the discontinuities of history; it breaks the thread of transcendental teleologies; and where anthropological thought once questioned man's being or subjectivity, it now bursts open the other, and the outside. In this sense, the diagnosis does not establish the fact of our identity by the play of distinctions. It establishes that we are difference, that our reason is the difference of discourses, our history the difference of times, our selves the difference of masks. That difference, far from being the forgotten and recovered origin, is this dispersion that we are and make.

The never completed, never wholly achieved uncovering of the archive forms the general horizon to which the description of discursive formations, the analysis of positivities, the mapping of the enunciative field belong. The right of words – which is not that of the philologists – authorizes, therefore, the use of the term *archaeology* to describe all these searches. This term does not imply the search for a beginning; it does not relate analysis to geological excavation. It designates the general theme of a description that questions the already-said at the level of its existence: of the enunciative function that operates within it, of the discursive formation, and the general archive system to which it belongs. Archaeology describes discourses as practices specified in the element of the archive.

PART IV

Archaeological Description

CHAPTER I

Archaeology and the History of Ideas

We can now reverse the procedure; we can go downstream, and, once we have covered the domain of discursive formations and statements, once we have outlined their general theory, we can proceed to possible domains of application. We can examine what use is served by this analysis that I have rather solemnly called 'archaeology'. Indeed, we must: for, to be frank, as they are at the moment, things are rather disturbing. I set out with a relatively simple problem: the division of discourse into great unities that were not those of *œuvres*, authors, books, or themes. And with the sole purpose of establishing them, I have set about constructing a whole series of notions (discursive formations, positivity, archive), I have defined a domain (statements, the enunciative field, discursive practices), I have tried to reveal the specificity of a method that is neither formalizing nor interpretative; in short, I have appealed to a whole apparatus, whose sheer weight and, no doubt, somewhat bizarre machinery are a source of embarrassment. For two or three reasons: there exist already enough methods for describing and analysing language (*langage*) for it not to be presumptuous to wish to add another. And, anyway, I was suspicious of such unities of discourse as the 'book' and the '*œuvre*' because I suspected them of not being as immediate and self-evident as they appeared: is it reasonable to replace them by unities that one has established with so much effort, after so much groping, and in accordance with principles so obscure that it has taken hundreds of pages to elucidate them? And are the things that all these instruments finally delimit, those 'discourses' whose identity they map out, the same as those figures (called 'psychiatry', or 'political economy', or 'Natural History') for which I empirically set out, and which have provided me with a pretext for developing this strange arsenal? It is now of the utmost importance that I should measure the descriptive efficacy of the notions that I have tried to define. I must discover whether the machine works, and what it can produce. What, then, can this 'archaeology' offer that other descriptions are unable to provide? What are the rewards for such a heavy enterprise?

And now a suspicion occurs to me. I have behaved as if I were discovering a new domain, as if, in order to chart it, I needed new measurements and guide-lines. But, in fact, was I not all the time in that very space that has long been known as 'the history of ideas'? Was it not to that space that I was implicitly referring, even when on two or three occasions I tried to keep my distance? And if I had not forced myself to turn away from it, would I not have found in it, already prepared, already analysed, all that I was looking for? Perhaps I am a historian of ideas after all. But an ashamed, or, if you prefer, a presumptuous historian of ideas. One who set out to renew his discipline from top to bottom; who wanted, no doubt, to achieve a rigour that so many other, similar descriptions have recently acquired; but who, unable to modify in any real way that old form of analysis, to make it cross the threshold of scientificity (or finding that such a metamorphosis is always impossible, or that he did not have the strength to effect that transformation himself), declares that he had been doing, and wanted to do, something quite different. All this new fog just to hide what remained in the same landscape, fixed to an old patch of ground cultivated to the point of exhaustion. I cannot be satisfied until I have cut myself off from ' the history of ideas', until I have shown in what way archaeological analysis differs from the descriptions of 'the history of ideas'.

It is not easy to characterize a discipline like the history of ideas: it is an uncertain object, with badly drawn frontiers, methods borrowed from here and there, and an approach lacking in rigour and stability. And it seems to possess two roles. On the one hand, it recounts the by-ways and margins of history. Not the history of the sciences, but that of imperfect, ill-based knowledge, which could never in the whole of its long, persistent life attain the form of scientificity (the history of alchemy rather than chemistry, of animal spirits or phrenology rather than physiology, the history of atomistic themes rather than physics). The history of those shady philosophies that haunt literature, art, the sciences, law, ethics, and even man's daily life; the history of those age-old themes that are never crystallized in a rigorous and individual system, but which have formed the spontaneous philosophy of those who did not philosophize. The history not of literature but of that tangential rumour, that everyday, transient writing that never acquires the status of an *œuvre*, or is immediately lost: the analysis of sub-literatures, almanacs, reviews and newpapers, temporary successes, anonymous authors. Thus defined – but one can see at once how difficult it is to fix precise limits for it – the history of ideas is concerned with all that insidious thought, that whole interplay of representations that flow anonymously between men; in the interstices of the great discursive monuments, it reveals the crumbling soil on which they are based. It is the discipline of fluctuating languages (*langages*), of shapeless works, of unrelated themes. The analysis of opinions rather than of knowledge, of errors rather than of truth, of types of mentality rather than of forms of thought.

But on the other hand the history of ideas sets out to cross the boundaries of existing disciplines, to deal with them from the outside, and to re-interpret them. Rather than a marginal domain, then, it constitutes a style of analysis, a putting into perspective. It takes account of the historical field of the sciences, of literature, of philosophy: but it describes the knowledge that has served as an empirical, unreflective basis for subsequent formalizations; it tries to rediscover the immediate experience that dis-course transcribes; it follows the genesis, which, on the basis of received or acquired representations, gives birth to systems and *œuvres*. It shows, on the other hand, how the great figures that are built up in this way gradually decompose: how the themes fall apart, pursue their isolated lives, fall into disuse, or are recomposed in a new way. The history of ideas, then, is the discipline of beginnings and ends, the description of obscure continuities and returns, the reconstitution of developments in the linear form of history. But it can also, by that very fact, describe, from one domain to another, the whole interplay of exchanges and intermediaries: it shows how scientific knowledge is diffused, gives rise to philosophical concepts, and takes form perhaps in literary works; it shows how problems, notions, themes may emigrate from the philosophical field where they were formulated to scientific or political discourses; it relates work with institu-tions, social customs or behaviour, techniques, and unrecorded needs and practices; it tries to revive the most elaborate forms of discourse in the concrete landscape, in the midst of the growth and development that witnessed their birth. It becomes therefore the discipline of interferences, the description of the concentric circles that surround works, underline them, relate them to one another, and insert them into whatever they are not.

It is clear how these two roles of the history of ideas are articulated one upon the other. In its most general form, it can be said that it continually describes – and in all the directions in which it operates – the transition from non-philosophy to philosophy, from non-scientificity to science, from non-literature to the *œuvre* itself. It is the analysis of silent births, or distant correspondences, of permanences that persist beneath apparent changes, of slow formations that profit from innumerable blind complicities, of those total figures that gradually come together and suddenly condense into the fine point of the work. Genesis, continuity, totalization: these are the great themes of the history of ideas, and that by which it is attached to a certain, now traditional, form of historical analysis. In these conditions, it is normal that anyone who still practises history, its methods, its requirements and possibilities – this now rather shop-soiled idea – cannot conceive that a discipline like the history of ideas should be abandoned; or rather, considers that any other form of analysing discourses is a betrayal of history itself. But archaeological description is precisely such an abandonment of the history of ideas, a systematic rejection of its postulates and procedures, an attempt to practise a quite different history of what men have said. That some people do not recognize in this enterprise the history of their childhood, that they mourn its passing, and continue to invoke, in an age that is no longer made for it, that great shade of former times, certainly proves their fidelity. But such conservative zeal confirms me in my purpose and gives me the confidence to do what I set out to do.

Between archaeological analysis and the history of ideas there are a great many points of divergence. I shall try shortly to establish four differences that seem to me to be of the utmost importance. They concern the attribution of innovation, the analysis of contradictions, comparative descriptions, and the mapping of transformations. I hope that by examining these different points we will be able to grasp the specific qualities of archaeological analysis, and that we may be able to measure its descriptive capacity. For the moment, however, I should like to lay down a few principles.

1. Archaeology tries to define not the thoughts, representations, images, themes, preoccupations that are concealed or revealed in discourses; but those discourses themselves, those discourses as practices obeying certain rules. It does not treat discourse as *document*, as a sign of something else, as an element that ought to be transparent, but whose unfortunate opacity must often be pierced if one is to reach at last the depth of the essential in the place in which it is held in reserve; it is concerned with discourse in

its own volume, as a *monument*. It is not an interpretative discipline: it does not seek another, better-hidden discourse. It refuses to be 'allegorical'.

2. Archaeology does not seek to rediscover the continuous, insensible transition that relates discourses, on a gentle slope, to what precedes them, surrounds them, or follows them. It does not await the moment when, on the basis of what they were not yet, they became what they are; nor the moment when, the solidity of their figure crumbling away, they will gradually lose their identity. On the contrary, its problem is to define discourses in their specificity; to show in what way the set of rules that they put into operation is irreducible to any other; to follow them the whole length of their exterior ridges, in order to underline them the better. It does not proceed, in slow progression, from the confused field of opinion to the uniqueness of the system or the definitive stability of science; it is not a 'doxology'; but a differential analysis of the modalities of discourse.

3. Archaeology is not ordered in accordance with the sovereign figure of the *œuvres;* it does not try to grasp the moment in which the *œuvre* emerges on the anonymous horizon. It does not wish to rediscover the enigmatic point at which the individual and the social are inverted into one another. It is neither a psychology, nor a sociology, nor more generally an anthropology of creation. The *œuvre* is not for archaeology a relevant division, even if it is a matter of replacing it in its total context or in the network of causalities that support it. It defines types of rules for discursive practices that run through individual *œuvres*, sometimes govern them entirely, and dominate them to such an extent that nothing eludes them; but which sometimes, too, govern only part of it. The authority of the creative subject, as the *raison d'être* of an *œuvre* and the principle of its unity, is quite alien to it.

4. Lastly, archaeology does not try to restore what has been thought, wished, aimed at, experienced, desired by men in the very moment at which they expressed it in discourse; it does not set out to recapture that elusive nucleus in which the author and the *œuvre* exchange identities; in which thought still remains nearest to oneself, in the as yet unaltered form of the same, and in which language (*langage*) has not yet been deployed in the spatial, successive dispersion of discourse. In other words, it does not try to repeat what has been said by reaching it in its very identity. It does not claim to efface itself in the ambiguous modesty of a reading that would

bring back, in all its purity, the distant, precarious, almost effaced light of the origin. It is nothing more than a rewriting: that is, in the preserved form of exteriority, a regulated transformation of what has already been written. It is not a return to the innermost secret of the origin; it is the systematic description of a discourse-object.

CHAPTER 2

The Original and the Regular

In general, the history of ideas deals with the field of discourses as a domain with two values; any element located there may be characterized as old or new; traditional or original; conforming to an average type or deviant. One can distinguish therefore between two categories of formulation: those that are highly valued and relatively rare, which appear for the first time, which have no similar antecedents, which may serve as models for others, and which to this extent deserve to be regarded as creations; and those, ordinary, everyday, solid, that are not responsible for themselves, and which derive, sometimes going so far as to repeat it word for word, from what has already been said. To each of these two groups the history of ideas gives a status; and it does not subject them to the same analysis: in describing the first, it recounts the history of inventions, changes, transformations, it shows how truth freed itself from error, how consciousness awoke from its successive slumbers, how new forms rose up in turn to produce the landscape that we know today; it is the task of the historian to rediscover on the basis of these isolated points, these successive ruptures, the continuous line of an evolution. The second group, on the other hand, reveals history as inertia and weight, as a slow accumulation of the past, a silent sedimentation of things said; in this second group, statements must be treated by weight and in accordance with what they have in common; their unique occurrence may be neutralized; the importance of their author's identity, the time and place of their appearance are also diminished; on the other hand, it is their extent that must be measured; the extent of their repetition in time and place, the channels by which they are diffused, the groups in which they circulate; the general horizon that they outline for men's thought, the limits that they impose on it; and how, in characterizing a period, they make it possible to distinguish it from others; one then describes a series of overall figures. In the first case, the history of ideas describes a succession of events in thought; in the second, there are uninterrupted expanses of effects; in the first, one reconstitutes the emergence of truths or forms; in the second, one re-establishes forgotten solidities, and refers discourses to their relativity.

It is true that, between these two authorities, the history of ideas is continuously determining relations; neither analysis is ever found in its pure state: it describes conflicts between the old and the new, the resistance of the acquired, the repression that it exercises over what has so far never been said, the coverings by which it masks it, the oblivion to which it sometimes succeeds in confining it; but it also describes the conditions, which, obscurely and at a distance, will facilitate the emergence of future discourses; it describes the repercussions of discoveries, the speed and extent of their diffusion, the slow processes of replacement or the sudden upheavals that overthrow familiar language (*langage*); it describes the integration of the new in the already structured field of the acquired, the progressive fall from the original into the traditional, or, again, the reappearances of the already-said, and the uncovering of the original. But this intersection does not prevent it from always maintaining a bipolar analysis of the old and the new. An analysis that reinvests in the empirical element of history, and in each of its stages, the problematic of the origin: in every *œuvre*, in every book, in the smallest text, the problem is to rediscover the point of rupture, to establish, with the greatest possible precision, the division between the implicit density of the already-said, a perhaps involuntary fidelity to acquired opinion, the law of discursive fatalities, and the vivacity of creation, the leap into irreducible difference. Although this description of originalities may seem obvious enough, it poses two very different methodological problems: that of resemblance and that of procession. It presupposes, in effect, that one can establish a sort of single, great series in which every formulation would assume a date in accordance with homogeneous chronological guide-lines. But, to examine the question more closely, does Grimm, with his law of vowel-gradations, precede Bopp (who quoted him, used him, applied and modified what he said) in the same way and on the same temporal line; and did Cœurdoux and Anquetil-Duperron (in observing analogies between Greek and Sanskrit) anticipate the definition of the Indo-European languages, and precede the founders of comparative grammar? Was Saussure 'preceded' by Peirce and his semiotics, by Arnauld and Lancelot with the Classical analysis of the sign, and by the Stoics and the theory of the 'signifier', in the same series and in accordance with the same mode of anteriority? Precession is not an irreducible and primary *donnée;* it cannot play the role of an absolute measure that makes it possible to gauge all discourse and to distinguish the original from the repetitive. The mapping of antecedents is not enough, in itself, to determine a discursive order; on the contrary, it is subordinated to the discourse that one is analysing, at the level that one chooses, on the scale that one establishes. By deploying discourse throughout a calendar, and by giving a date to each of its elements, one does not obtain a definitive hierarchy of precessions and originalities; this hierarchy is never more than relative to the systems of discourse that it sets out to evaluate.

Similarly, the resemblance between two or several successive formulations also poses a whole series of problems. In what sense and in accordance with what criteria can one affirm: 'this has been said'; 'the same thing can already be found in this or that text', etc.? What is identity, partial or total, in the order of discourse? The fact that two enunciations are exactly identical, that they are made up of the same words used with the same meaning, does not, as we know, mean that they are absolutely identical. Even when one finds, in the work of Diderot and Lamarck, or of Benoît de Maillet and Darwin, the same formulation of the principle of evolution, one cannot consider that one is dealing in each case with the same discursive event, which has been subjected at different times to a series of repetitions. Identity is not a criterion even when it is exhaustive; even less so when it is partial, when words are not used each time in the same sense, or when the same nucleus of meaning is apprehended through different words: to what extent can one affirm that it is the same organicist theme that emerges in the so very different discourses and vocabularies of Buffon, Jussieu, and Cuvier? And, inversely, can one say that the word 'organization' has the same meaning in the work of Daubenton, Blumenbach, and Geoffroy Saint-Hilaire? Generally speaking, does one find the same type of resemblance between Cuvier and Darwin, and between Cuvier and Linnaeus (or Aristotle)? There is no immediately recognizable resemblance between the formulations: their analogy is an effect of the discursive field in which it is mapped.

It is not legitimate, then, to demand, point-blank, of the texts that one is studying their title to originality, and whether they really possess those degrees of nobility that are measured here by the absence of ancestors. The question can have meaning only in very precisely defined series, in groups whose limits and domain have been established, between guide-lines that delimit sufficiently homogeneous discursive fields.[1] But to seek in the great accumulation of the already-said the text that resembles 'in advance' a later text, to ransack history in order to rediscover the play of anticipations or echoes, to go right back to the first seeds or to go forward to the last traces, to reveal in a work its fidelity to tradition or its irreducible uniqueness, to raise or lower its stock of originality, to say that the Port-Royal grammarians invented nothing, or to discover that Cuvier had more predecessors than one thought, these are harmless enough amusements for historians who refuse to grow up.

Archaeological description is concerned with those discursive practices to which the facts of succession must be referred if one is not to establish them in an unsystematic and naïve way, that is in terms of merit. At the level in which they are, the originality/banality opposition is therefore not relevant: between an initial formulation and the sentence, which, years, centuries later, repeats it more or less exactly, it establishes no hierarchy of value; it makes no radical difference. It tries only to establish the *regularity* of statements. In this sense, regularity is not in opposition to irregularity, which, in the margins of current opinion or the most frequent texts, characterizes the deviant statement (abnormal, prophetic, retarded, pathological, or the product of genius); it designates, for every verbal performance (extraordinary, or banal, unique in its own kind or endlessly repeated), the set of conditions in which the enunciative function operates, and which guarantees and defines its existence. In this sense, regularity does not characterize a certain central position between the ends of a statistical curve – it is not valid therefore as an index of frequency or probability; it specifies an effective field of appearance. Every statement bears a certain regularity and it cannot be dissociated from it. One must not therefore oppose the regularity of a statement with the irregularity of another (that may be less expected, more unique, richer in innovation), but to other regularities that characterize other statements.

Archaeology is not in search of inventions; and it remains unmoved at the moment (a very moving one, I admit) when for the first time someone was sure of some truth; it does not try to restore the light of those joyful mornings. But neither is it concerned with the average phenomena of opinion, with the dull grey of what everyone at a particular period might repeat. What it seeks in the texts of Linnaeus or Buffon, Petty or Ricardo, Pinel or Bichat, is not to draw up a list of founding saints; it is to uncover

[1] It was in this way that M. Canguilhem established the series of propositions which, from Willis to Prochaska, made possible the definition of the reflex.

the regularity of a discursive practice. A practice that is in operation, in the same way, in the work of their predecessors; a practice that takes account in their work not only of the most original affirmations (those that no one else dreamt of before them), but also of those that they borrowed, even copied, from their predecessors. A discovery is no less regular, from the enunciative point of view, than the text that repeats and diffuses it; regularity is no less operant, no less effective and active, in a banal as in a unique formation. In such a description one cannot admit a difference in nature between creative statements (which reveal something new, which emit hitherto unknown information, and which are 'active' in the same way) and imitative statements (which receive and repeat information, and remain, as it were, 'passive'). The field of statements is not a group of inert areas broken up by fecund moments; it is a domain that is active throughout.

This analysis of enunciative regularities opens up in several directions that one day perhaps will be explored with greater care.

1. A group of statements is characterized, then, by a certain form of regularity, without it being either necessary or possible to distinguish between what is new and what is not. But these regularities – we shall come back to them later – are not given once and for all; the same regularity is not to be found at work in Tournefort and Darwin, Lancelot and Saussure, Petty and Keynes. There are, then, homogeneous fields of enunciative regularities (they characterize a discursive formation), but these fields are different from one another. The movement from one field of enunciative regularities to another need not be accompanied by corresponding changes at all other levels of discourse. There are verbal performances that are identical from the point of view of grammar (vocabulary, syntax, and the language (*langue*) in general); that are also identical from the point of view of logic (from the point of view of propositional structure, or of the deductive system in which it is placed); but which are *enunciatively* different. Thus the formation of the quantitative relation between prices and monetary mass in circulation may be expressed in the same words – or synonymous words – and be obtained by the same reasoning; but it is not enunciatively identical in Gresham or Locke and the nineteenth-century marginalists; it does not belong in each case to the same system of formation of objects and concepts. We must distinguish, then, between *linguistic analogy* (or translatability), *logical identity* (or equivalence), and *enunciative homogeneity*. It is with these homogeneities

and these alone that archaeology is concerned. It can see the appearance of a new discursive practice through verbal formulations that remain linguistically analogous or logically equivalent (by taking up again, sometimes word for word, the old theory of sentence-attribution and verb–copula the Port-Royal grammarians opened up an enunciative regularity whose specificity it is the duty of archaeology to describe). Inversely, it may ignore differences of vocabulary, it may pass over semantic fields or different deductive organizations, if it is capable of recognizing in each case, despite their heterogeneity, a certain enunciative regularity (from this point of view, the theory of the language (*langage*) of action, the search for the origin of languages (*langues*), the establishment of primitive roots, as they are found in the eighteenth century, are not 'new' in relation to Lancelot's 'logical' analyses).

One can see the emergence therefore of a number of disconnexions and articulations. One can no longer say that a discovery, the formulation of a general principle, or the definition of a project, inaugurates, in a massive way, a new phase in the history of discourse. One no longer has to seek that point of absolute origin or total revolution on the basis of which everything is organized, everything becomes possible and necessary, everything is effaced in order to begin again. One is dealing with events of different types and levels, caught up in distinct historical webs; the establishment of an enunciative homogeneity in no way implies that, for decades or centuries to come, men will say and think the same thing; nor does it imply the definition, explicit or not, of a number of principles from which everything else would flow, as inevitable consequences. Enunciative homogeneities (and heterogeneities) intersect with linguistic continuities (and changes), with logical identities (and differences), without any of them proceeding at the same pace or necessarily affecting one another. But there must exist between them a number of relations and interdependences whose no doubt highly complex domain must be described.

2. Another direction of research: the interior hierarchies within enunciative regularities. We have seen that every statement belongs to a certain regularity – that consequently none can be regarded as pure creation, as the marvellous disorder of genius. But we have also seen that no statement can be regarded as inactive, and be valid as the scarcely real shadow or transfer of the initial statement. The whole enunciative field is both regular and alerted: it never sleeps; the least statement – the most

discreet or the most banal – puts into operation a whole set of rules in accordance with which its object, its modality, the concepts that it employs, and the strategy of which it is a part, are formed. These rules are never given in a formulation, they 'traverse' formulations, and set up for them a space of coexistence; one cannot therefore rediscover the unique statement that would articulate them for themselves. However, certain groups of statements put these rules into operation in their most general and most widely applicable form; using them as a starting-point, one can see how other objects, other concepts, other enunciative modalities, or other strategic choices may be formed on the basis of rules that are less general and whose domain of application is more specified. One can thus describe a tree of enunciative *derivation:* at its base are the statements that put into operation rules of formation in their most extended form; at its summit, and after a number of branchings, are the statements that put into operation the same regularity, but one more delicately articulated, more clearly delimited and localized in its extension.

Archaeology – and this is one of its principal themes – may thus constitute the tree of derivation of a discourse. That of Natural History, for example. It will place at the root, as *governing statements*, those that concern the definition of observable structures and the field of possible objects, those that prescribe the forms of description and the perceptual codes that it can use, those that reveal the most general possibilities of characterization, and thus open up a whole domain of concepts to be constructed, and, lastly, those that, while constituting a strategic choice, leave room for the greatest number of subsequent options. And it will find, at the ends of the branches, or at various places in the whole, a burgeoning of 'discoveries' (like that of fossil series), conceptual trans-formations (like the new definition of the genus), the emergence of new notions (like that of mammals or organism), technical improvements (principles for organizing collections, methods of classification and nomenclature). This derivation from governing statements must not be confused with a deduction that is made on the basis of axioms; nor must it be identified with the germination of a general idea, or a philosophical nucleus whose significance emerges gradually in experience or precise conceptualizations; lastly, it must not be taken as a psychological genesis based on a discovery whose consequences and possibilities gradually develop and unfold. It is different from all these courses, and it must be described in its autonomy. One can thus describe the archaeological derivations of Natural History without beginning with its undemonstrable axioms or its fundamental themes (the continuity of nature, for example), and without taking as one's starting-point and guiding-thread the first discoveries or the first approaches (those of Tournefort before those of Linnaeus, those of Jonston before those of Tournefort). The archaeological order is neither that of systematicities, nor that of chronological successions.

But one can see that a whole domain of possible questions is opening up here. For these different orders cannot be specific and autonomous; there must be relations and dependences between them. For certain discursive formations, the archaeological order is perhaps not very different from the systematic order, as in other cases it may follow the thread of chronological successions. These parallelisms (contrary to the distortions met with elsewhere) are worthy of analysis. In any case, it is important not to confuse these different orders, not to seek in an 'initial' discovery or in the originality of a formulation the principle from which everything can be deduced and derived; not to seek in a general principle the law of enunciative regularities or individual inventions; not to demand of archaeological derivation that it reproduce the order of time or reveal a deductive schema.

Nothing would be more false than to see in the analysis of discursive formations an attempt at totalitarian periodization, whereby from a certain moment and for a certain time, everyone would think in the same way, in spite of surface differences, say the same thing, through a polymorphous vocabulary, and produce a sort of great discourse that one could travel over in any direction. On the contrary, archaeology describes a level of enunciative homogeneity that has its own temporal articulations, and which does not carry with it all the other forms of identity and difference that are to be found in language; and at this level, it establishes an order, hierarchies, a whole burgeoning that excludes a massive, amorphous synchrony, given totally once and for all. In those confused unities that we call 'periods', it reveals, with all their specificity, 'enunciative periods' that are articulated, but without being confused with them, upon the time of concepts, on theoretical phases, on stages of formalization and of linguistic development.

CHAPTER 3

Contradictions

The history of ideas usually credits the discourse that it analyses with coherence. If it happens to notice an irregularity in the use of words, several incompatible propositions, a set of meanings that do not adjust to one another, concepts that cannot be systematized together, then it regards it as its duty to find, at a deeper level, a principle of cohesion that organizes the discourse and restores to it its hidden unity. This law of coherence is a heuristic rule, a procedural obligation, almost a moral constraint of research: not to multiply contradictions uselessly; not to be taken in by small differences; not to give too much weight to changes, disavowals, returns to the past, and polemics; not to suppose that men's discourse is perpetually undermined from within by the contradiction of their desires, the influences that they have been subjected to, or the conditions in which they live; but to admit that if they speak, and if they speak among themselves, it is rather to overcome these contradictions, and to find the point from which they will be able to be mastered. But this same coherence is also the result of research: it defines the terminal unities that complete the analysis; it discovers the internal organization of a text, the form of development of an individual *œuvre*, or the meeting-place of different discourses. In order to reconstitute it, it must first be presupposed, and one will only be sure of finding it if one has pursued it far enough and for long enough. It appears as an optimum: the greatest possible number of contradictions resolved by the simplest means.

But a great many means are used and, by that very fact, the coherences found may differ considerably. By analysing the truth of propositions and the relations that unite them, one can define a field of logical non-contradiction: one will then discover a systematicity; one will rise from the visible body of sentences to that pure, ideal architecture that the ambiguities of grammar and the overloading of words with meanings have probably concealed as much as expressed. But one can adopt the contrary course, and, by following the thread of analogies and symbols, rediscover a thematic that is more imaginary than discursive, more affective than rational, and less close to the concept than to desire; its force animates the most opposed figures, but only to melt them at once into a slowly transformable unity; what one then discovers is a plastic continuity, the movement of a meaning that is embodied in various representations, images, and metaphors. These coherences may be thematic or systematic, explicit or not: they can be sought at the level of representations that were conscious in the speaking subject, but which his discourse – for circumstantial reasons or because of an inadequacy in the very form of his language (*langage*) – failed to express; it can also be sought in structures that would have constrained the author the more he constructed them, and which would have imposed on him, without his realizing it, postulates, operational schemata, linguistic rules, a set of affirmations and fundamental beliefs, types of images, or a whole logic of the fantastic. Lastly, there are coherences that one establishes at the level of an individual – his biography, or the unique circumstances of his discourse – but one can also establish them in accordance with broader guide-lines, one can give them the collective, diachronic dimensions of a period, a general form of consciousness, a type of society, a set of traditions, an imaginary landscape common to a whole culture. In all these forms, a coherence discovered in this way always plays the same role: it shows that immediately visible contradictions are merely surface reflections; and that this play of dispersed light must be concentrated into a single focus. Contradiction is the illusion of a unity that hides itself or is hidden: it has its place only in the gap between consciousness and unconsciousness, thought and the text, the ideality and the contingent body of expression. In any case, analysis must suppress contradiction as best it can.

At the end of this work, only residual contradictions remain – accidents, defects, mistakes – or, on the contrary, as if the entire analysis had been carried out in secrecy and in spite of itself, the fundamental contradiction emerges: the bringing into play, at the very origin of.the system, of incompatible postulates, intersections of irreconcilable influences, the first diffraction of desire, the economic and political conflict that opposes a society to itself, all this, instead of appearing as so many superficial elements that must be reduced, is finally revealed as an organizing principle, as the founding, secret law that accounts for all minor contradictions and gives them a firm foundation: in short, a model for all the other oppositions. Such a contradiction, far from being an appearance or accident of discourse, far from being that from which it must be freed if its truth is at last to be revealed, constitutes the very law of its existence: it is on the basis of such a contradiction that discourse emerges, and it is in order both to translate it and to overcome it that discourse begins to speak; it is in order to escape that contradiction, whereas contradiction is ceaselessly reborn through discourse, that discourse endlessly pursues itself and endlessly begins again; it is because contradiction is always anterior to the discourse, and because it can never therefore entirely escape it, that discourse changes, undergoes transformation, and escapes of itself from its own continuity. Contradiction, then, functions throughout discourse, as the principle of its historicity.

The history of ideas recognizes, therefore, two levels of contradiction: that of appearances, which is resolved in the profound unity of discourse; and that of foundations, which gives rise to discourse itself. In relation to the first level of contradiction, discourse is the ideal figure that must be separated from their accidental presence, from their too visible body; in relation to the second, discourse is the empirical figure that contradictions may take up and whose apparent cohesion must be destroyed, in order to rediscover them at last in their irruption and violence. Discourse is the path from one contradiction to another: if it gives rise to those that can be seen, it is because it obeys that which it hides. To analyse discourse is to hide and reveal contradictions; it is to show the play that they set up within it; it is to manifest how it can express them, embody them, or give them a temporary appearance.

For archaeological analysis, contradictions are neither appearances to be overcome, nor secret principles to be uncovered. They are objects to be described for themselves, without any attempt being made to discover from what point of view they can be dissipated, or at what level they can be radicalized and effects become causes. Let us take a simple example, one that has already been mentioned several times: in the eighteenth century, Linnaeus's fixist principle was contradicted, not so much by the discovery of the *Peloria*, which changed only its modes of application, but by a number of 'evolutionist' affirmations that are to be found in the works of Buffon, Diderot, Bordeu, Maillet, and many others. Archaeological analysis does not consist in showing that beneath this opposition, at a more essential level, everyone accepted a number of fundamental theses (the continuity and plenitude of nature, the correlation between recent forms and climate, the almost imperceptible transition from the non-living to the living); nor does it consist in showing that such an opposition reflects, in the particular domain of Natural History, a more general conflict that divides all eighteenth-century knowledge and thought (the conflict between the theme of an ordered creation, acquired once and for all, deployed without irreducible secret, and the theme of a prolific nature, endowed with enigmatic powers, gradually deploying itself through history, and overturning all spatial orders in obedience to the onward thrust of time). Archaeology tries to show how the two affirmations, fixist and 'evolutionist', share a common locus in a certain description of species and genera: this description takes as its object the visible structure of organs (that is, their form, size, number, and arrangement in space); and it can limit that object in two ways (to the organism as a whole, or to certain elements, determined either by importance or by taxonomic convenience); one then reveals, in the second case, a regular table, containing a number of definite squares, that in a way constitutes the programme of all possible creation (so that, whether present, still to come, or already disappeared, the ordering of the species and genera is definitively fixed); and in the first case, groups of kinship that remain indefinite and open, that are separated from one another, and that tolerate an indeterminate number of new forms, however close they may be to preexisting forms. By deriving in this way the contradiction between two theses from a certain domain of objects, from its delimitations and divisions, one does not discover a point of conciliation. But neither does one transfer it to a more fundamental level; one defines the locus in which it takes place; it reveals the place where the two branches of the alternative join; it localizes the divergence and the place where the two discourses are juxtaposed. The theory of structure is not a common postulate, a basis of general belief shared by Linnaeus and Buffon, a solid, fundamental affirmation that throws back to the level of a subsidiary debate the conflict of evolutionism and fixism; it is the principle of their incompatibility, the law that governs their derivation and their coexistence. By taking contradictions as objects to be described, archaeological analysis does not try to discover in their place a common form or theme, it tries to determine the extent and form of the gap that separates them. In relation to a history of ideas that attempts to melt contradictions in the semi-nocturnal unity of an overall figure, or which attempts to transmute them into a general, abstract, uniform principle of interpretation or explanation, archaeology describes the different *spaces of dissension*.

It ceases, therefore, to treat contradictions as a general function operating, in the same way, at all levels of discourse, and which analysis should either suppress entirely or lead back to a primary, constitutive form: for the great game of *contradiction* – present under innumerable guises, then suppressed, and finally restored in the major conflict in which it culminates – it substitutes the analysis of different types of contradiction, different levels in accordance with which it can be mapped, different functions that it can exercise.

Different types first of all. Some contradictions are localized only at the level of propositions and assertions, without in any way affecting the body of enunciative rules that makes them possible: thus in the eighteenth century the thesis of the animal character of fossils was opposed by the more traditional thesis of their mineral nature; the consequences that can be drawn from these two theses are certainly very numerous and far-reaching; but it can be shown that they originated in the same discursive formation, at the same point, and in accordance with the same conditions of operation of the enunciative function; they are contradictions that are archaeologically *derived*, and which constitute a terminal state. Others, on the contrary, go beyond the bounds of a discursive formation, and they oppose theses that do not belong to the same conditions of enunciation: thus Linnaeus's fixism is contradicted by Darwin's evolutionism, but only to the extent that one neutralizes the difference between Natural History, to which the first belongs, and biology, to which the second belongs. They are *extrinsic* contradictions that reflect the opposition between distinct discursive formations. For archaeological description (ignoring, for the moment, any possible procedural differences), this opposition constitutes the *terminus a quo*, whereas derived contradictions constitute the *terminus ad quem* of analysis. Between these two extremes, archaeological description describes what might be called *intrinsic* contradictions: those that are deployed in the discursive formation itself, and which, originating at one point in the system of formations, reveal sub-systems: hence, to keep to the example of eighteenth-century Natural History, the contradiction between 'methodical' analyses and 'systematic' analyses. The opposition here is not a terminal one: they are not two contradictory propositions about the same object, they are not two incompatible uses of the same concept, but two ways of forming statements, both characterized by certain objects, certain positions of subjectivity, certain concepts, and certain strategic choices. Yet these systems are not primary ones: for it can be shown to what extent they both derive from a single positivity, that of Natural History. It is these *intrinsic oppositions* that are relevant to archaeological analysis.

Then different levels. An intrinsic archaeological contradiction is not a fact, purely and simply, that it is enough to state as a principle or explain as an effect. It is a complex phenomenon that is distributed over different levels of the discursive formation. Thus, for systematic Natural History and methodical Natural History, which were in constant opposition for a good part of the eighteenth century, one can recognize: an *inadequation* of the objects (in the one case one describes the general appearance of the plant; in the other certain predetermined variables; in the one case, one describes the totality of the plant, or at least its most important parts, in the other one describes a number of elements chosen arbitrarily for their taxonomic convenience; sometimes one takes account of the plant's different states of growth and maturity, at others one confines one's attention to a single moment, a stage of optimum visibility); a *divergence* of enunciative modalities (in the case of the systematic analysis of plants, one applies a rigorous perceptual and linguistic code, and in accordance with a constant scale; for methodical description, the codes are relatively free, and the scales of mapping may oscillate); an *incompatibility* of concepts (in the 'systems', the concept of generic character is an arbitrary, though misleading mark to designate the genera; in the methods this same concept must include the real definition of the genus); lastly, an *exclusion* of theoretical options (systematic taxonomy makes 'fixism' possible, even if it is rectified by the idea of a continuous creation in time, gradually unfolding the elements of the tables, or by the idea of natural catastrophes having disturbed by our present gaze the linear order of natural proximities, but excludes the possibility of a transformation that the method accepts without absolutely implying it).

Functions. These forms of opposition do not all play the same role in discursive practice: they are not, in a homogeneous way, obstacles to overcome or a principle of growth. In any case, it is not enough to seek in them the cause either of the deceleration or the acceleration of history; time is not introduced into the truth and ideality of discourse on the basis of the empty, general form of opposition. These oppositions are always particular functional stages. Some of them bring about an *additional development* of the enunciative field: they open up sequences of argumentation, experiment, verification, and various inferences; they make possible the determination of new objects, they arouse new enunciative modalities, they define new concepts or modify the field of application of those that already exist: but without anything being modified in the system of positivity of the discourse (this was the case in the discussions of the eighteenth-century naturalists on the frontier between the mineral and the vegetal, or on the boundaries of life or nature and the origin of fossils); such additive processes may remain decisively open or closed by a demonstration that refutes them or a discovery that puts them out of operation. Others induce a *reorganization* of the discursive field: they pose the question of the possible translation of one group of statements into another, of the point of coherence that might articulate one on another, of their integration in a more general space (thus the system/method opposition among eighteenth-century naturalists induces a series of attempts to recreate both of them in a single form of description, to give to the method the rigour and regularity of the system, to coincide the arbitrariness of the system with the concrete analyses of the method); they are not new objects, new concepts, new enunciative modalities that are added in a linear fashion to the old; but objects of another (more general or more particular) level, concepts that have another structure and another field of application, enunciations of another type, without, however, altering the rules of formation. Other oppositions play a *critical* role: they put into operation the existence of the 'acceptability' of the discursive practice; they define the point of its effective impossibility and of its historical reflexion (thus the description, in Natural History itself, of organic similarities and functions that operate, through anatomical variables, in definite conditions of existence, no longer permits, as an autonomous discursive formation at least, a Natural History that is a taxonomic science of beings on the basis of their visible characters).

A discursive formation is not, therefore, an ideal, continuous, smooth text that runs beneath the multiplicity of contradictions, and resolves them in the calm unity of coherent thought; nor is it the surface in which, in a thousand different aspects, a contradiction is reflected that is always in re-treat, but everywhere dominant. It is rather a space of multiple dissensions; a set of different oppositions whose levels and roles must be described. Archaeological analysis, then, erects the primacy of a contradiction that has its model in the simultaneous affirmation and negation of a single proposition. But the reason for this is not to even out oppositions in the general forms of thought and to pacify them by force, by a recourse to a constructing *a priori*. On the contrary, its purpose is to map, in a particular discursive practice, the point at which they are constituted, to define the form that they assume, the relations that they have with each other, and the domain that they govern. In short, its purpose is to maintain discourse in all its many irregularities; and consequently to suppress the theme of a contradiction uniformly lost and rediscovered, resolved and forever rising again, in the undifferentiated element of the Logos.

CHAPTER 4

The Comparative Facts

Archaeological analysis individualizes and describes discursive formations. That is, it must compare them, oppose them to one another in the simultaneity in which they are presented, distinguish them from those that do not belong to the same time-scale, relate them, on the basis of their specificity, to the non-discursive practices that surround them and serve as a general element for them. In this, too, they are very different from epistemological or 'architectonic' descriptions, which analyse the internal structure of a theory; archaeological study is always in the plural; it operates in a great number of registers; it crosses interstices and gaps; it has its domain where unities are juxtaposed, separated, fix their crests, confront one another, and accentuate the white spaces between one another. When it is concerned with a particular type of discourse (that of psychiatry in *Madness and Civilization* or that of medicine in *Naissance de la clinique*), it is in order to establish, by comparison, its chronological limits; it is also in order to describe, at the same time as them and in correlation with them, an institutional field, a set of events, practices, and political decisions, a sequence of economic processes that also involve demographic fluctuations, techniques of public assistance, manpower needs, different levels of unemployment, etc. But it may also, by a sort of lateral *rapprochement* (as in *The Order of Things*), put into operation several distinct positivities, whose concomitant states are compared during a particular period, and which are confronted with other types of discourse that have taken place at a given period.

But all these analyses are very different from those usually practised.

1. In archaeological analysis comparison is always limited and regional. Far from wishing to reveal general forms, archaeology tries to outline particular configurations. When one compares General Grammar, the

Analysis of Wealth, and Natural History in the Classical period, it is not in order to regroup three manifestations – particularly charged with expressive value, and hitherto strangely neglected – of a mentality that was general in the seventeenth and eighteenth centuries; it is not in order to reconstitute, on the basis of a reduced model and a particular domain, the forms of rationality that operated in the whole of Classical science; it is not even to illuminate the less well-known profile of what we thought was a familiar cultural face. Our aim was not to show that men in the eighteenth century were generally speaking more interested in order than in history, in classification than development, in signs than the mechanisms of causality. Our aim was to reveal a well-determined set of discursive formations that have a number of describable relations between them. These relations do not spill over into adjacent domains and they cannot be brought gradually closer to the totality of contemporary discourses, even less to what is usually called 'the Classical spirit'; they are closely confined to the triad being studied, and are valid only in the domain specified. This interdiscursive group is itself, in its group form, related to other types of discourse (with the analysis of representation, the general theory of signs, and 'ideology' on the one hand; and with mathematics, algebraic analysis, and the attempt to establish a *mathesis* on the other). They are those internal and external relations that characterize Natural History, the Analysis of Wealth, and General Grammar, as a specific group, and make it possible to recognize in them an *interdiscursive configuration*.

There are those who would say: 'Why did you not speak of cosmology, physiology, or Biblical exegesis? Could not pre-Lavoisier chemistry, or Euler's mathematics, or Vico's history have invalidated all the analyses to be found in *The Order of Things*? Are there not, in the inventive richness of the eighteenth century, many other ideas that do not fit into the rigid framework of archaeology?' To such people, with their quite legitimate impatience, to all the counter-examples which, as I am very well aware, they could supply, I will reply: of course, I not only admit that my analysis is limited, I want it so; I have made it so. What for me would be a counter-example would be precisely the possibility of saying: all these relations that you have described in three particular formations, all these networks in which the theories of attribution, articulation, designation, and derivation are articulated upon one another, all that taxonomy that rests on a discontinuous characterization and a continuity of order are found uniformly, and in the same way, in geometry, rational mechanics, the physiology of humours and germs, Biblical criticism, and emergent crystallography. This would, in fact, prove that I did not describe, as I claimed to have done, a *region of interpositivity;* I would have characterized the spirit or science of a period – the very thing to which my whole enterprise is opposed. The relations that I have described are valid in order to define a particular configuration: they are not signs to describe the face of a culture in its totality. It is the friends of the *Weltanschauung* who will be disappointed; I insist that the description that I have undertaken is quite different from theirs. What, for them, is a lacuna, an omission, an error is, for me, a deliberate, methodical exclusion.

But one might also say: you have compared General Grammar with Natural History and the Analysis of Wealth. But why not with History as it was practised at the time, with Biblical criticism, with rhetoric, with the theory of the fine arts? Wouldn't you then have discovered a quite different field of interpositivity? What privilege, then, has the one that you have described? – Privilege, none; it is only one of the describable groups; if, in fact, one took General Grammar, and tried to define its relations with the historical disciplines and textual criticism, one would certainly see the emergence of a quite different system of relations; and a description would reveal an interdiscursive network that was not identical with the first, but which would overlap at certain points. Similarly, the taxonomy of the naturalists might be compared not with grammar and economics, but with physiology and pathology: there, too, new inter-positivities would emerge (one only has to compare the taxonomy/grammar/economics relations analysed in *The Order of Things* with the taxonomy/pathology relations studied in *Naissance de la clinique*). The number of such networks is not, therefore, defined in advance; only the test of analysis can show whether they exist, and which of them exist (that is, which can be described). Moreover, every discursive formation does not belong (necessarily, at least) to only one of these systems, but enters simultaneously into several fields of relations, in which it does not occupy the same place, or exercise the same function (the taxonomy/pathology relations are not isomorphic with the taxonomy/grammar relations; the grammar/Analysis of Wealth relations are not isomorphic with the grammar/exegesis relations).

The horizon of archaeology, therefore, is not *a* science, *a* rationality, *a* mentality, *a* culture; it is a tangle of interpositivities whose limits and points of intersection cannot be fixed in a single operation. Archaeology is a comparative analysis that is not intended to reduce the diversity of discourses, and to outline the unity that must totalize them, but is intended to divide up their diversity into different figures. Archaeological comparison does not have a unifying, but a diversifying, effect.

2. In confronting General Grammmar, Natural History, and the Analysis of Wealth in the seventeenth and eighteenth centuries, one might wonder what ideas were shared at that time by linguists, naturalists, and economists; one might wonder what implicit postulates they shared despite the diversity of their theories, what general, perhaps unstated principles they obeyed; one might wonder what influence the analysis of language exercised on taxonomy, or what role the idea of an ordered nature played in the theory of wealth; one might also study the respective diffusion of these different types of discourse, the prestige accorded to each, the value attributed to it on account of its age (or, on the contrary, on account of its newness) or of its greater rigour, the channels of communication by which information was exchanged; lastly, one might, as in quite traditional analyses, wonder to what extent Rousseau had transferred to the analysis of languages and their origin his knowledge and experience as a botanist; what common categories Turgot applied to the analysis of coinage and to the theory of language and etymology; how the idea of a universal, artificial, and perfect language had been taken up again and used by such classifiers as Linnaeus and Adanson. Of course, these questions would be legitimate (some of them, at least). But none of them would be relevant to the level of archaeology.

What archaeology wishes to uncover is primarily – in the specificity and distance maintained in various discursive formations – the play of analogies and differences as they appear at the level of rules of formation. This implies five distinct tasks:

(a) To show how quite different discursive elements may be formed on the basis of similar rules (the concepts of General Grammar, like those of verb, subject, complement, root, are formed on the basis of the same arrangements of the enunciative field – theories of attribution, articulation, designation, and derivation – as the very different, radically heterogeneous concepts of Natural History and Economy); to show, between different formations, the *archaeological isomorphisms*.

(b) To show to what extent these rules do or do not apply in the same way, are or are not linked in the same order, are or are not arranged in accordance with the same model in different types of discourse (General Grammar follows, and in that same order, the theory of attribution, the theory of articulation, the theory of designation, and the theory of derivation; Natural History and the Analysis of Wealth regroup the first two and the last two, but they link each of them in the reverse order); to define the *archaeological model* of each formation.

(c) To show how entirely different concepts (like those of value and specific character, or price and generic character) occupy a similar position in the ramification of their system of positivity – that they are therefore endowed with an archaeological isotopia – although their domain of application, their degree of formalization, and above all their historical genesis make them quite alien to one another.

(d) To show, on the other hand, how a single notion (possibly designated by a single word) may cover two archaeologically distinct elements (the notions of origin and evolution have neither the same role, the same place, nor the same formation in the system of positivity of General Grammar and Natural History); to indicate the *archaeological shifts*.

(e) Lastly, to show how, from one positivity to another, relations of subordination or complementarity may be established (thus in relation to the Analysis of Wealth and the analysis of species, the description of language plays a dominant role in the Classical period, in so far as it is the theory of institutional signs that duplicate, mark, and represent the representation itself): to establish the *archaeological correlations*.

None of these descriptions is based on the attribution of influences, exchanges, transmitted information, or communications. Not that I wish to deny their existence, or deny that they could ever be the object of a description. But rather that I have tried to step back from them, to shift the level of attack of the analysis, to reveal what made them possible; to map the points at which the projection of one concept upon another could take place, to fix the isomorphism that made a transference of methods or techniques possible, to show the proximities, symmetries, or analogies that have made generalizations possible; in short, to describe the field of vectors and of differential receptivity (of permeability and impermeability) that has been a condition of historical possibility for the interplay of exchanges. A configuration of interpositivity is not a group of neighbouring disciplines; it is not only an observable phenomenon of resemblance; it is not only the overall relation of several discourses to this or that other discourse; it is the law of their communications. Because Rousseau and others reflected in turn on the ordering of the species and the origin of the languages, this does not mean that relations were made and exchanges occurred between taxonomy and grammar; or because Turgot, after Law and Petty, wished to treat coinage as a sign, that economy and the theory of language were brought close together and that their history still bears the trace of these attempts. It means rather – if, at least, one is attempting to make an archaeological description – that the respective arrangements of these three positivities were such that, at the level of *œuvres*, authors, individual existences, projects, and attempts, one can find such exchanges.

3. Archaeology also reveals relations between discursive formations and non-discursive domains (institutions, political events, economic practices and processes). These *rapprochements* are not intended to uncover great cultural continuities, nor to isolate mechanisms of causality. Before a set of enunciative facts, archaeology does not ask what could have motivated them (the search for contexts of formulation); nor does it seek to rediscover what is expressed in them (the task of hermeneutics); it tries to determine how the rules of formation that govern it – and which characterize the positivity to which it belongs – may be linked to non-discursive systems: it seeks to define specific forms of articulation.

Let us take the example of clinical medicine, whose establishment at the end of the eighteenth century is contemporary with a number of political events, economic phenomena, and institutional changes. Between these facts and the organization of hospital medicine, it is easy enough to suspect the existence of certain links, at least if one operates largely on intuition. But how can such links be analysed? A symbolic analysis would see in the organizing of clinical medicine, and in the historical processes that were concomitant with it, two simultaneous expressions, which reflect and symbolize one another, which serve each other as a mirror, and whose meanings are caught up in an endless play of reflexion: two expressions that express nothing but the form that they share. Thus medical ideas of organic solidarity, functional cohesion, tissular communication – and the abandonment of the classificatory principle of diseases in favour of an analysis of the bodily interactions – might correspond (in order to reflect them, but also to be reflected in them) to a political practice that is discovering, beneath still feudal stratifications, relations of a functional type, economic connexions, a society whose dependences and reciprocities were to provide, in the form of society, the analogon of life. A causal analysis, on the other hand, would try to discover to what extent political changes, or ecomonic processes, could determine the consciousness of scientists – the horizon and direction of their interest, their system of values, their way of perceiving things, the style of their rationality; thus, at a period in which industrial capitalism was beginning to recalculate its manpower requirements, disease took a on social dimension: the maintenance of health, cure, public assistance for the poor and sick, the search for pathological causes and sites, became a collective responsibility that must be assumed by the state. Hence the value placed upon the body as a work tool, the care to rationalize medicine on the basis of the other sciences, the efforts to maintain the level of health of a population, the attention paid to therapy, after-care, and the recording of long-term phenomena.

Archaeology situates its analysis at another level: the phenomena of expression, reflexions, and symbolization are for it merely the effects of an overall reading in search of formal analogies or translations of meaning; as for causal relations, they may be assigned to the level of the context or of the situation and their effect on the speaking subject; both, in any case, can be mapped once one has defined the positivities in which they appear and the rules in accordance with which these positivities have been formed. The field of relations that characterizes a discursive formation is the locus in which symbolizations and effects may be perceived, situated, and determined. If archaeology brings medical discourse closer to a number of practices, it is in order to discover far less 'immediate' relations than expression, but far more direct relations than those of a causality communicated through the consciousness of the speaking subjects. It wishes to show not how political practice has determined the meaning and form of medical discourse, but how and in what form it takes part in its conditions of emergence, insertion, and functioning. This relation may be assigned to several levels. First to that of the division and delimitation of the medical object: not, of course, that it was political practice that from the early nineteenth century imposed on medicine such new objects as tissular lesions or the anatomo-physiological correlations; but it opened up new fields for the mapping of medical objects (these fields are constituted by the mass of the population administratively compartmented and supervised, gauged according to certain norms of life and health, and analysed according to documentary and statistical forms of registration; they are also constituted by the great conscript armies of the revolutionary and Napoleonic period, with their specific form of medical control; they are also constituted by the institutions of hospital assistance that were defined at the end of the eighteenth and the beginning of the nineteenth centuries, in relation to the economic needs of the time, and to the reciprocal position of the social classes). One can also see the appearance of this relation of political practice to medical discourse in the status accorded to the doctor, who becomes not only the privileged, but also virtually the exclusive, enunciator of this discourse, in the form of institutional relation that the doctor may have with the hospitalized patient or with his private practice, in the modalities of teaching and diffusion that are prescribed or authorized for this knowledge. Lastly, one can grasp this relation in the function that is attributed to medical discourse, or in the role that is required of it, when it is a question of judging individuals, making administrative decisions, laying down the norms of a society, translating – in order to 'resolve' or to conceal them – conflicts of another order, giving models of a natural type to analyses of society and to the practices that concern it. It is not a question, then, of showing how the political practice of a given society constituted or modified the medical concepts and theoretical structure of pathology; but how medical discourse as a practice concerned with a particular field of objects, finding itself in the hands of a certain number of statutorily designated individuals, and having certain functions to exercise in society, is articulated on practices that are external to it, and which are not themselves of a discursive order.

If in this analysis archaeology suspends the theme of expression and reflexion, if it refuses to see in discourse the surface of the symbolic projection of events or processes that are situated elsewhere, it is not in order to rediscover a causal sequence that might be described point by point, and which would make it possible to relate a discovery and an event, or a concept and a social structure. But on the other hand if it suspends such a causal analysis, if it wishes to avoid the necessary connexion through the speaking subject, it is not in order to guarantee the sovereign, sole independence of discourse; it is in order to discover the domain of existence and functioning of a discursive practice. In other words, the archaeological description of discourses is deployed in the dimension of a general history; it seeks to discover that whole domain of institutions, economic processes, and social relations on which a discursive formation can be articulated; it tries to show how the autonomy of discourse and its specificity nevertheless do not give it the status of pure ideality and total historical independence; what it wishes to uncover is the particular level in which history can give place to definite types of discourse, which have their own type of historicity, and which are related to a whole set of various historicities.

CHAPTER 5

Change and Transformations

Let us now turn to the archaeological description of change. Whatever theoretical criticisms one can make of the traditional history of ideas, it does at least take as its essential theme the phenomena of temporal succession and sequence, analyses them in accordance with schemata of evolution, and thus describes the historical deployment of discourses. Archaeology, however, seems to treat history only to freeze it. On the one hand, by describing discursive formations, it ignores the temporal relations that may be manifested in them; it seeks general rules that will be uniformly valid, in the same way, and at every point in time: does it not, therefore, impose the constricting figure of a synchrony on a development that may be slow and imperceptible? In this 'world of ideas', which is in itself so untrustworthy, in which apparently the most stable figures disappear so quickly, but in which so many irregularities occur that are later accorded definitive status, in which the future always anticipates itself, whereas the past is constantly shifting, is not archaeology valid as a sort of motionless thought? And, on the other hand, when it does have recourse to chronology, it is only, it seems, in order to fix, at the limits of the positivities, two pinpoints: the moment at which they are born and the moment at which they disappear, as if duration was used only to fix this crude calendar, and was omitted throughout the analysis itself; as if time existed only in the vacant moment of rupture, in that white, paradoxically atemporal crack in which one sudden formulation replaces another. Whether as a synchrony of positivities, or as an instantaneity of substitutions, time is avoided, and with it the possibility of a historical description disappears. Discourse is snatched from the law of development and established in a discontinuous atemporality. It is immobilized in fragments: precarious splinters of eternity. But there is nothing one can do about it: several eternities succeeding one another, a play of fixed images disappearing in turn, do not constitute either movement, time, or history.

But the problem must be examined in greater detail.

I

Let us take first the apparent synchrony of discursive formations. One thing is true: it is no use establishing the rules in every statement, and they cannot therefore be put into operation with every statement, they do not change each time; they can be found at work in statements or groups of statements in widely separated periods. We have seen, for example, that for nearly a century – from Tournefort to Jussieu – the various objects of Natural History obeyed the same rules of formation; we have seen that the theory of attribution is the same and plays the same role in the work of Lancelot, Condillac, and Destutt de Tracy. Moreover, we have seen that the order of statements based on archaeological derivation did not necessarily reproduce the order of successions: one can find in Beauzée statements that are archaeologically anterior to those to be found in the *Grammaire* of Port-Royal. In such an analysis, therefore, there is a suspension of *temporal successions* – or, to be more precise, of the calendar of formulations. But this suspension is intended precisely to reveal the relations that characterize the temporality of discursive formations and articulate them in series whose intersection in no way precludes analysis.

(a) Archaeology defines the rules of formation of a group of statements. In this way it shows how a succession of events may, in the same order in which it is presented, become an object of discourse, be recorded, described, explained, elaborated into concepts, and provide the opportunity for a theoretical choice. Archaeology analyses the degree and form of permeability of a discourse: it provides the principle of its articulation over a chain of successive events; it defines the operators by which the events are transcribed into statements. It does not challenge, for example, the relation between the Analysis of Wealth and the great monetary fluctuations of the seventeenth and early eighteenth centuries; it tries to show what, in these crises, could be given as an object of discourse, how those crises could be conceptualized in such an object, how the interests that were in conflict throughout these processes could deploy their strategy in them. Or again, it does not claim that the cholera epidemic of 1832 was not an event that concerned medicine: it shows how clinical discourse put into operation such a body of rules that a whole domain of medical objects could then be reorganized, that a whole group of methods of recording and notation could be used, that the concept of inflammation could be abandoned and the old theoretical problem of fevers could be resolved definitively. Archaeology does not deny the possibility of new statements in correlation with 'external' events. Its task is to show on what condition a correlation can exist between them, and what precisely it consists of (what are its limits, its form, its code, its law of possibility). It does not try to avoid that mobility of discourses that makes them move to the rhythm of events; it tries to free the level at which it is set in motion – what might be called the level of 'evential' *engagement*. (An engagement that is specific for every discursive formation, and which does not have the same rules, the same operators, or the same sensibility in, for example, the Analysis of Wealth and in Political Economy, in the old medicine of the 'constitutions' and in modern epidemiology.)

(b) Moreover, all the rules of formation assigned by archaeology to a positivity do not have the same generality: some are more specific and derive from others. This subordination may be merely hierarchical but it may also involve a temporal vector. Thus in General Grammar, the theory of the verb-attribution and that of the noun-articulation are linked to one another: and the second derives from the first, but without it being possible to determine an order of succession between them (other than the deductive or rhetorical order that has been chosen for the exposé). On the other hand, the analysis of the complement or the search for roots could appear (or reappear) only when the analysis of the attributive sentence or the notion of the noun as an analytic sign of representation had been developed. Another example: in the Classical period, the principle of the continuity of beings is implied in the classification of species according to structural characters; and in this sense they are simultaneous; on the other hand, it is only when this classification is undertaken that the lacunae and gaps may be interpreted in the categories of a history of nature, of the earth, and of the species. In other words, the archaeological ramification of the rules of formation is not a uniformly simultaneous network: there exist relations, branches, derivations that are temporally neutral; there exist others that imply a particular temporal direction. Archaeology, then, takes as its model neither a purely logical schema of simultaneities; nor a linear succession of events; but it tries to show the intersection between necessarily successive relations and others that are not so. It does not believe, therefore, that a system of positivity is a synchronic figure that one can perceive only by suspending the whole of the diachronic process. Far from being indifferent to succession, archaeology maps the *temporal vectors of derivation.*

Archaeology does not set out to treat as simultaneous what is given as successive; it does not try to freeze time and to substitute for its flux of events correlations that outline a motionless figure.What it suspends is the theme that succession is an absolute: a primary, indissociable sequence to which discourse is subjected by the law of its finitude; it is also the theme that there is in discourse only one form and only one level of succession. For these themes, it substitutes analyses that reveal both the various forms of succession that are superposed in discourse (and by forms I do not simply mean the rhythms or causes, but the series themselves), and the way in which the successions thus specified are articulated. Instead of following the thread of an original calendar, in relation to which one would establish the chronology of successive or simultaneous events, that of short or lasting processes, that of momentary or permanent phenomena, one tries to show how it is possible for there to be succession, and at what different levels distinct successions are to be found. To constitute an archaeological history of discourse, then, one must free oneself of two models that have for so long imposed their image: the linear model of speech (and partly at least of writing), in which all events succeed one another, without any effect of coincidence and superposition; and the model of the stream of consciousness whose presence always eludes itself in its openness to the future and its retention of the past. Paradoxical as it may be, discursive formations do not have the same model of historicity as the flow of consciousness or the linearity of language. Discourse, at least as analysed by archaeology, that is, at the level of its positivity, is not a consciousness that embodies its project in the external form of language (*langage*); it is not a language (*langue*), plus a subject to speak it. It is a practice that has its own forms of sequence and succession.

II

Archaeology is much more willing than the history of ideas to speak of discontinuities, ruptures, gaps, entirely new forms of positivity, and of sudden redistributions. The practice of political economy was, traditionally, to seek everything that led up to Ricardo, everything that could foreshadow his analyses, methods, and principal notions, everything that tended to make his discoveries more probable; the practice of the history of comparative grammar was to rediscover – beyond Bopp and Rask – earlier research into the filiation and kinship of languages; it was to determine how much Anquetil-Duperron contributed towards the constitution of an Indo-European domain; it was to uncover the first comparison (made in 1769) of Sanskrit and Latin conjugations; it may even lead one back to Harris or Ramus. Archaeology proceeds in the opposite direction: it seeks rather to untie all those knots that historians have patiently tied; it increases differences, blurs the lines of communication, and tries to make it more difficult to pass from one thing to another; it does not try to show that the Physiocratic analysis of production foreshadowed that of Ricardo; it does not regard it as relevant to its own analyses to say that Cœurdoux foreshadowed Bopp.

What does this insistence on discontinuities correspond to? In fact, it is paradoxical only in relation to the practice of the historians of ideas. It is rather the history of ideas – with its concern for continuities, transitions, anticipations, and foreshadowings – that plays with paradox. From Daubenton to Cuvier, from Anquetil to Bopp, from Graslin, Turgot, or Forbonnais to Ricardo – even such a chronologically small gap – the differences are innumerable: some are localized, others are more general; some concern methods, others concepts; sometimes they concern the domain of objects, at others the whole linguistic instrument. More striking still is the example of medicine: in a quarter of a century, from 1790 to 1815, medical discourse changed more profoundly than since the seventeenth century, probably than since the Middle Ages, and perhaps even since Greek medicine: a change that revealed new objects (organic lesions, deep sites, tissular alterations, ways and forms of inter-organic diffusion, anatomo-clinical signs and correlations), techniques of observation, of detection of the pathological site, recording; a new perceptual grid, and on almost entirely new descriptive vocabulary; new sets of concepts and nosographical distributions (century-old, sometimes age-old categories such as fever or constitution disappeared, and diseases that are perhaps as old as the world – like tuberculosis – were at last isolated and named). Those who say that archaeology invents differences in an arbitrary way can never have opened *La Nosographie philosophique* and the *Traité des membranes*. Archaeology is simply trying to take such differences seriously: to throw some light on the matter, to determine how they are divided up, how they are entangled with one another, how they govern or are governed by one another, to which distinct categories they belong; in short, to describe these differences, not to establish a system of differences between them. If there is a paradox in archaeology, it is not that it increases differences, but that it refuses to reduce them – thus inverting the usual values. For the history of ideas, the appearance of difference indicates an error, or a trap; instead of examining it, the clever historian must try to reduce it: to find beneath it a smaller difference, and beneath that an even smaller one, and so on until he reaches the ideal limit, the non-difference of perfect continuity. Archaeology, on the other hand, takes as the object of its description what is usually regarded as an obstacle: its aim is not to overcome differences, but to analyse them, to say what exactly they consist of, to *differentiate* them. How does this differentiation operate?

1. Instead of considering that discourse is made up of a series of homogeneous events (individual formulations), archaeology distinguishes several possible levels of events within the very density of discourse: the level of the statements themselves in their unique emergence; the level of the appearance of objects, types of enunciation, concepts, strategic choices (or transformations that affect those that already exist); the level of the derivation of new rules of formation on the basis of rules that are already in operation – but always in the element of a single positivity; lastly, a fourth level, at which the substitution of one discursive formation for another takes place (or the mere appearance and disappearance of a positivity). These events, which are by far the most rare, are, for archaeology, the most important: only archaeology, in any case, can reveal them. But they are not the exclusive object of its description; it would be a mistake to think that they have an absolute control over all the others, and that they lead to similar, simultaneous ruptures at the different levels distinguished above. All the events that occur within the density of discourse are not immediately below one another. Of course, the appearance of a discursive formation is often correlative with a vast renewal of objects, forms of enunciation, concepts, and strategies (a principle that is not universal however: General Grammar was established in the seventeenth century without much apparent alteration in grammatical tradition); but it is not possible to determine the particular concept or object that suddenly manifests its presence. One should not describe such an event, therefore, in accordance with categories that may be suitable for the emergence of a formulation, or the appearance of a new word. It is useless to ask of such an event questions like: 'Who is its author? Who is

speaking? In what circumstances and in what context? With what intentions, what project in mind?' The appearance of a new positivity is not indicated by a new sentence – unexpected, surprising, logically unpredictable, stylistically deviant – that is inserted into a text, and announces either the opening of a new chapter, or the entry of a new speaker. It is an event of a quite different type.

2. In order to analyse such events, it is not enough simply to indicate changes, and to relate them immediately to the theological, aesthetic model of creation (with its transcendence, with all its originalities and inventions), or to the psychological model of the act of consciousness (with its previous obscurity, its anticipations, its favourable circumstances, its powers of restoration), or to the biological model of evolution. We must define precisely what these changes consist of: that is, substitute for an undifferentiated reference to *change* – which is both a general container for all events and the abstract principle of their succession – the analysis of *transformations*. The disappearance of one positivity and the emergence of another implies several types of transformation. By going from the more particular to the more general, one can and must describe: how the different elements of a system of formation were transformed (what, for example, were the variations in the rate of unemployment and labour needs, what were the political decisions concerning the guilds and the universities, what were the new needs and new possibilities of public assistance at the end of the eighteenth century – all these were elements in the system of formation of clinical medicine); how the characteristic relations of a system of formation were transformed (how, in the middle of the seventeenth century, for example, the relation between the perceptual field, the linguistic code, the use of instruments, and information that was put into operation by the discourse on living beings was modified, thus making possible the definition of the objects proper to Natural History); how the relations between different rules of formation were transformed (how, for example, biology modified the order and the dependence that Natural History had established between the theory of characterization and the analysis of temporal derivations); lastly, how the relations between various positivities were transformed (how the relations between philology, biology, and economics transform the relations between General Grammar, Natural History, and the Analysis of Wealth; how the interdiscursive configuration outlined by the privileged relations of these three disciplines is decomposed; how their respective relations with

mathematics and philosophy are modified; how a place emerges for other discursive formations and, in particular, for that interpositivity that was later to assume the name of the human sciences). Rather than refer to the living force of change (as if it were its own principle), rather than seek its causes (as if it were no more than a mere effect), archaeology tries to establish the system of transformations that constitute 'change'; it tries to develop this empty, abstract notion, with a view to according it the analysable status of transformation. It is understandable that some minds are so attached to all those old metaphors by which, for a century and a half, history (movement, flux, evolution) has been imagined, that they see archaeology simply as the negation of history and the crude affirmation of discontinuity; the truth is that they cannot accept that change should be cleansed of all these adventitious models, that it should be deprived of both its primacy as a universal law and its status as a general effect, and that it should be replaced by the analysis of various transformations.

3. To say that one discursive formation is substituted for another is not to say that a whole world of absolutely new objects, enunciations, concepts, and theoretical choices emerges fully armed and fully organized in a text that will place that world once and for all; it is to say that a general transformation of relations has occurred, but that it does not necessarily alter all the elements; it is to say that statements are governed by new rules of formation, it is not to say that all objects or concepts, all enunciations or all theoretical choices disappear. On the contrary, one can, on the basis of these new rules, describe and analyse phenomena of continuity, return, and repetition: we must not forget that a rule of formation is neither the determination of an object, nor the characterization of a type of enunciation, nor the form or content of a concept, but the principle of their multiplicity and dispersion. One of these elements – or several of them – may remain identical (preserve the same division, the same characteristics, the same structures), yet belong to different systems of dispersion, and be governed by distinct laws of formation. One can find in such phenomena therefore: elements that remain throughout several distinct positivities, their form and content remaining the same, but their formations being heterogeneous (such as monetary circulation as an object first in the Analysis of Wealth, and then in political economy; the concept of character first in Natural History, then in biology); elements that are constituted, modified, organized in one discursive formation, and which, stabilized at last, figure in another (such as the concept of reflex, which, as G. Canguilhem

has shown, was formed in Classical science from Willis to Prochaska, then entered modern physiology); elements that appear later, as an ultimate derivation in a discursive formation, and which occupy an important place in a later formation (such as the notion of organism, which appeared at the end of the eighteenth century in Natural History, and as the result of a whole taxonomic enterprise of characterization, and which became the major concept of biology at the time of Cuvier; or the notion of lesional site, which Morgagni discovered, and which became one of the principal concepts of clinical medicine); elements that reappear after a period of desuetude, oblivion, or even invalidation (such as the return to a Linnaean type of fixism in a biologist like Cuvier; or the reactivation in the eighteenth century of the old notion of an original language). The problem for archaeology is not to deny such phenomena, nor to try to diminish their importance; but, on the contrary, to try to describe and measure them: how can such permanences or repetitions, such long sequences or such curves projected through time exist? Archaeology does not hold the content for the primary and ultimate *donnée* that must account for all the rest; on the contrary, it considers that the same, the repetitive, and the uninterrupted are no less problematic than the ruptures; for archaeology, the identical and the continuous are not what must be found at the end of the analysis; they figure in the element of a discursive practice; they too are governed by the rules of formation of positivities; far from manifesting that fundamental, reassuring inertia which we like to use as a criterion of change, they are themselves actively, regularly formed. And to those who might be tempted to criticize archaeology for concerning itself primarily with the analysis of the discontinuous, to all those agoraphobics of history and time, to all those who confuse rupture and irrationality, I will reply: 'It is you who devalue the continuous by the use that you make of it. You treat it as the support-element to which everything else must be related; you treat it as the primary law, the essential weight of any discursive practice; you would like to analyse every modification in the field of this inertia, as one analyses every movement in the gravitational field. But in according this status to continuity, you are merely neutralizing it, driving it out to the outer limit of time, towards an original passivity. Archaeology proposes to invert this arrangement, or rather (for our aim is not to accord to the discontinuous the role formerly accorded to the continuous) to play one off against the other; to show how the continuous is formed in accordance with the same conditions and the same rules as dispersion; and how it enters – neither more nor less than differences, inventions, innovations or deviations – the field of discursive practice.'

4. The appearance and disappearance of positivities, the play of substitutions to which they give rise, do not constitute a homogeneous process that takes place everywhere in the same way. We must not imagine that rupture is a sort of great drift that carries with it all discursive formations at once: rupture is not an undifferentiated interval – even a momentary one – between two manifest phases; it is not a kind of lapsus without duration that separates two periods, and which deploys two heterogeneous stages on either side of a split; it is always a discontinuity specified by a number of distinct transformations, between two particular positivities. The analysis of archaeological breaks sets out, therefore, to establish, between so many different changes, analogies and differences, hierarchies, complementarities, coincidences, and shifts: in short, to describe the dispersion of the discontinuities themselves.

The idea of a single break suddenly, at a given moment, dividing all discursive formations, interrupting them in a single moment and reconstituting them in accordance with the same rules – such an idea cannot be sustained. The contemporaneity of several transformations does not mean their exact chronological coincidence: each transformation may have its own particular index of temporal 'viscosity'. Natural History, General Grammar, and the Analysis of Wealth were constituted in similar ways, and all three in the course of the seventeenth century; but the system of formation of the Analysis of Wealth was linked with a great many conditions and non-discursive practices (the circulation of goods, monetary manipulations and their effects, the system of protecting trade and manufactures, fluctuations in the quantity of metal coined): hence the slowness of a process that lasted for over a century (from Grammont to Cantillon), whereas the transformations that had taken place in General Grammar and Natural History had extended over scarcely more than twenty-five years. Inversely, contemporary, similar, and linked transformations do not belong to a single model that is reproduced several times on the surface of discourses, and imposes on all a strictly identical form of rupture: when one describes the archaeological break that led to philology, biology, and economics, one is showing how these three positivities were linked (by the disappearance of the analysis of the sign, and of the theory of representation), what symmetrical effects it could produce (the idea of a totality and of an organic adaptation among living beings; the idea of morphological coherence, and of a regulated evolution in languages; the idea of a form of production that has its internal laws and its limits of development); but it also shows what were the specific differences of these transformations (how in particular historicity is introduced in a particular way in these three positivities, how their relation to history cannot therefore be the same, even though they all have a particular relation with it).

Lastly, there are important shifts between different archaeological ruptures – and sometimes even between discursive formations that are very close and linked by a great many relations. Let us take the disciplines of languages and historical analysis: the great transformation that gave rise at the beginning of the nineteenth century to a historical, comparative grammar preceded by a good half-century the mutation in historical discourse: as a result, the system of interpositivity in which philology was involved was profoundly affected in the second half of the nineteenth century, without the positivity of philology ever being put into question. Hence phenomena of 'fragmented shift', of which we can cite at least another famous example: concepts like those of surplus value or falling rate of profit, as found in Marx, may be described on the basis of the system of positivity that is already in operation in the work of Ricardo; but these concepts (which are new, but whose rules of formation are not) appear – in Marx himself – as belonging at the same time to a quite different discursive practice: they are formed in that discursive practice in accordance with specific laws, they occupy in it a different position, they do not figure in the same sequences: this new positivity is not a trans-formation of Ricardo's analyses; it is not a new political economy; it is a discourse that occurred around the derivation of certain economic con-cepts, but which, in turn, defines the conditions in which the discourse of economists takes place, and may therefore be valid as a theory and a critique of political economy.

Archaeology disarticulates the synchrony of breaks, just as it destroyed the abstract unity of change and event. The *period* is neither its basic unity, nor its horizon, nor its object: if it speaks of these things it is always in terms of particular discursive practices, and as a result of its analyses. The Classical age, which has often been mentioned in archaeological analyses, is not a temporal figure that imposes its unity and empty form on all discourses; it is the name that is given to a tangle of continuities and discontinuities, modifications within positivities, discursive formations that appear and disappear. Similarly, *rupture* is not for archaeology the prop of its analyses, the limit that it indicates from afar, without being able either to determine it or to give it specificity; rupture is the name given to transformations that bear on the general rules of one or several discursive formations. Thus the French Revolution – since up to now all archaeological analyses have been centred on it – does not play the role of an event exterior to discourse, whose divisive effect one is under some kind of obligation to discover in all discourses; it functions as a complex, articulated, describable group of transformations that left a number of positivities intact, fixed for a number of others rules that are still with us, and also established positivities that have recently disappeared or are still disappearing before our eyes.

CHAPTER 6

Science and Knowledge

A silent delimitation has been imposed on all the preceding analyses, without the principle governing it, or even its outline, being made clear. All the examples referred to belonged without exception to a very small domain. In no way could I be said to have 'covered', let alone analysed, the immense domain of discourse: why did I systematically ignore 'literary', 'philosophical', or 'political' texts? Do not discursive formations and systems of positivities have a place in them too? And if I was re-stricting my attention to the sciences, why did I say nothing of mathematics, physics, or chemistry? Why did I concentrate on so many dubious, still imprecise disciplines that are perhaps doomed for ever to remain below the threshold of scientificity? In short, what is the relation between archaeology and the analysis of the sciences?

(a) Positivities, disciplines, sciences

First question: does not archaeology, under the rather bizarre terms of 'discursive formation' and 'positivity', describe what are quite simply pseudo-sciences (like psychopathology), sciences at the prehistoric stage (like Natural History), or sciences entirely penetrated with ideology (like political economy)? Is it not the privileged analysis of what will always remain quasi-scientific? If one calls 'disciplines' groups of statements that borrow their organization from scientific models, which tend to coherence and demonstrativity, which are accepted, institutionalized, transmitted, and sometimes taught as sciences, could one not say that archaeology describes disciplines that are not really sciences, while epistemology describes sciences that have been formed on the basis of (or in spite of) existing disciplines?

To these questions I can reply in the negative. Archaeology does not describe disciplines. At most, such disciplines may, in their manifest deployment, serve as starting-points for the description of positivities; but they do not fix its limits: they do not impose definitive divisions upon it; at the end of the analysis they do not re-emerge in the same state in which they entered it; one cannot establish a bi-univocal relation between established disciplines and discursive formations.

Let us take an example of this distortion. The linch-pin of *Madness and Civilization* was the appearance at the beginning of the nineteenth century of a psychiatric discipline. This discipline had neither the same content, nor the same internal organization, nor the same place in medicine, nor the same practical function, nor the same methods as the traditional chapter on 'diseases of the head' or 'nervous diseases' to be found in eighteenth-century medical treatises. But on examining this new discipline, we discovered two things: what made it possible at the time it appeared, what brought about this great change in the economy of concepts, analyses, and demonstrations, was a whole set of relations between hospitalization, internment, the conditions and procedures of social exclusion, the rules of jurisprudence, the norms of industrial labour and bourgeois morality, in short a whole group of relations that characterized for this discursive practice the formation of its statements; but this practice is not only manifested in a discipline possessing a scientific status and scientific pretensions; it is also found in operation in legal texts, in literature, in philosophy, in political decisions, and in the statements made and the opinions expressed in daily life. The discursive formation whose existence was mapped by the psychiatric discipline was not coextensive with it, far from it: it went well beyond the boundaries of psychiatry. Moreover, by going back in time and trying to discover what, in the seventeenth and eighteenth centuries, could have preceded the establishment of psychiatry, we realized that there was no such prior discipline: what had been said on the subject of mania, delirium, melancholia, and nervous diseases by the doctors of the Classical period in no way constituted an autonomous discipline, but at most a commentary on the analysis of fevers, of alterations in the humours, or of affections of the brain. However, despite the absence of any established discipline, a discursive practice, with its own regularity and consistency, was in operation. This discursive practice was certainly present in medicine, but it was also to be found in administrative regulations, in literary or philosophical texts, in casuistics, in the theories or projects of obligatory labour or assistance to the poor. In the Classical period, therefore, there were a discursive formation and a positivity perfectly accessible to description, to which corresponded no definite discipline that could be compared with psychiatry.

But although it is true that positivities are not merely the doublets of established disciplines, are they not the prototypes of future sciences? By discursive formation, does one not mean the retrospective projection of sciences on their own past, the shadow that they cast on what preceded them and which thus appears to have foreshadowed them? What we have described, for example, as the Analysis of Wealth or General Grammar, thus according them what was perhaps a highly artificial autonomy, was it not, quite simply, political economy in an inchoate state, or a stage prior to the establishment of a truly rigorous science of language? Is it archaeology trying, by means of a retrograde movement whose legitimacy it would no doubt be difficult to establish, to regroup in an independent discursive practice all the heterogeneous and dispersed elements whose complicity will prove to be necessary to the establishment of a science?

Again, the answer must be in the negative. What was analysed under the name of Natural History does not embrace, in a single figure, everything that in the seventeenth and eighteenth centuries might validly constitute a prototype of the science of life, and figure in its legitimate genealogy. The positivity thus revealed accounts for a number of statements concerning the resemblances and differences between beings, their visible structure, their specific and generic characters, their possible classification, the discontinuities that separate them, and the transitions that connect them; but it ignores a number of other analyses that date nevertheless from the same period, and which also outline the ancestral figures of biology: the analysis of reflex movement (which was to have so much importance in the constitution of an anatomo-physiology of the nervous system), the theory of germs (which seems to anticipate the problems of evolution and genetics), the explanation of animal or vegetal growth (which was to be one of the major questions of the physiology of organisms in general). Moreover: far from anticipating a future biology, Natural History – a taxonomic discourse, linked to the theory of signs and to the project of a science of order – excluded, by its solidity and autonomy, the constitution of a unitary science of life. Similarly, the discursive formation described as General Grammar does not take into account – far from it – everything that could have been said about language in the Classical period, and of which the inheritance or repudiation, development or critique, was to be found later in philology: it ignored the methods of Biblical exegesis, and that philosophy of language as formulated by Vico or Herder. Discursive formations are not, therefore, future sciences at the stage at which, still unconscious of themselves, they are quietly being constituted: they are not, in fact, in a state of teleological subordination in relation to the orthogenesis of the sciences.

Should it be said, therefore, that there can be no science where there is a positivity, and that positivities are always exclusive of the sciences? Should it be supposed that instead of being in a chronological relation to the sciences, they are in fact alternatives? That they are, in a way, the positive figure of a certain epistemological defect. But here, too, one could find a counter-example. Clinical medicine is certainly not a science. Not only because it does not comply with the formal criteria, or attain the level of rigour expected of physics, chemistry, or even of physiology; but also because it involves a scarcely organized mass of empirical observations, uncontrolled experiments and results, therapeutic prescriptions, and institutional regulations. And yet this non-science is not exclusive of science: in the course of the nineteenth century, it established definite relations between such perfectly constituted sciences as physiology, chemistry, or microbiology; moreover, it gave rise to such discourses as that of morbid anatomy, which it would be presumptuous no doubt to call a false science.

Discursive formations can be identified, therefore, neither as sciences, nor as scarcely scientific disciplines, nor as distant prefigurations of the sciences to come, nor as forms that exclude any scientificity from the outset. What, therefore, is the relation between the positivities and the sciences?

(b) Knowledge (savoir)

Positivities do not characterize forms of knowledge – whether they are *a priori*, necessary conditions or forms of rationality that have, in turn, been put into operation by history. But neither do they define the state of knowledge at a given moment in time: they do not draw up a list of what, from that moment, had been demonstrated to be true and had assumed the status of definitively acquired knowledge, and a list of what, on the other hand, had been accepted without either proof or adequate demonstration, or of what had been accepted as a common belief or a belief demanded by the power of the imagination. To analyse positivities is to show in accordance with which rules a discursive practice may form groups of objects, enunciations, concepts, or theoretical choices. The elements thus formed do not constitute a science, with a defined structure of ideality; their system of relations is certainly less strict; but neither are they items of knowledge piled up one on top of another, derived from heterogeneous experiments, traditions, or discoveries, and linked only by the identity of the subject that possesses them. They are that on the basis of which coherent (or incoherent) propositions are built up, more or less exact descriptions developed, verifications carried out, theories deployed. They form the precondition of what is later revealed and which later functions as an item of knowledge or an illusion, an accepted truth or an exposed error, a definitive acquisition or an obstacle surmounted. This precondition may not, of course, be analysed as a *donnée*, a lived experience, still implicated in the imagination or in perception, which mankind in the course of its history took up again in the form of rationality, or which each individual must undergo on his own account if he wishes to redis-cover the ideal meanings that are contained or concealed within it. It is not a pre-knowledge or an archaic stage in the movement that leads from immediate knowledge to apodicticity; it is a group of elements that would have to be formed by a discursive practice if a scientific discourse was to be constituted, specified not only by its form and rigour, but also by the objects with which it deals, the types of enunciation that it uses, the concepts that it manipulates, and the strategies that it employs. Thus science is not linked with that which must have been lived, or must be lived, if the intention of ideality proper to it is to be established; but with that which must have been said – or must be said – if a discourse is to exist that complies, if necessary, with the experimental or formal criteria of scientificity.

This group of elements, formed in a regular manner by a discursive practice, and which are indispensable to the constitution of a science, although they are not necessarily destined to give rise to one, can be called *knowledge*. Knowledge is that of which one can speak in a discursive practice, and which is specified by that fact: the domain constituted by the different objects that will or will not acquire a scientific status (the knowledge of psychiatry in the nineteenth century is not the sum of what was thought to be true, but the whole set of practices, singularities, and deviations of which one could speak in psychiatric discourse); knowledge is also the space in which the subject may take up a position and speak of the objects with which he deals in his discourse (in this sense, the knowledge of clinical medicine is the whole group of functions of observation, interrogation, decipherment, recording, and decision that may be exercised by the subject of medical discourse); knowledge is also the field of coordination and subordination of statements in which concepts appear, and are defined, applied and transformed (at this level, the knowledge of Natural History, in the eighteenth century, is not the sum of what was said, but the whole set of modes and sites in accordance with which one can integrate each new statement with the already said); lastly, knowledge is defined by the possibilities of use and appropriation offered by discourse (thus, the knowledge of political economy, in the Classical period, is not the thesis of the different theses sustained, but the totality of its points of articulation on other discourses or on other practices that are not discursive). There are bodies of knowledge that are independent of the sciences (which are neither their historical prototypes, nor their practical by-products), but there is no knowledge without a particular discursive practice; and any discursive practice may be defined by the knowledge that it forms.

Instead of exploring the consciousness/knowledge (*connaissance*)/science axis (which cannot escape subjectivity), archaeology explores the discursive practice/knowledge (*savoir*)/science axis.[1] And whereas the history of ideas finds the point of balance of its analysis in the element of *connaissance* (and is thus forced, against its will, to encounter the transcendental interrogation), archaeology finds the point of balance of its analysis in *savoir* – that is, in a domain in which the subject is necessarily situated and dependent, and can never figure as titular (either as a transcendental activity, or as empirical consciousness).

It is understandable in these conditions that we should distinguish carefully between *scientific domains* and *archaeological territories*: their articulation and their principles of organization are quite different. Only propositions that obey certain laws of construction belong to a domain of scientificity; affirmations that have the same meaning, that say the same thing, that are as true as they are, but which do not belong to the same systematicity, are excluded from this domain: what Diderot's *Le Rêve de d'Alembert* says about the development of species may well express certain of the concepts or certain of the scientific hypotheses of the period; it may even anticipate a future truth; it does not belong to the domain of scientificity of Natural History, but it does belong to its archaeological territory, if at least one can discover in operation in it the same rules of formation as in Linnaeus, Buffon, Daubenton, or Jussieu. Archaeological territories may extend to 'literary' or 'philosophical' texts, as well as scientific ones. Knowledge is to be found not only in demonstrations, it can also be found in fiction, reflexion, narrative accounts, institutional regulations, and

[1] For the distinction between *connaissance* and *savoir*, cf. note 2, p. 15.

political decisions. The archaeological territory of Natural History includes Bonnet's *Palingénésie philosophique* or Benoît de Maillet's *Telliamed*, although they do not comply to a great extent with the accepted scientific norms of the period, and even less, of course, with those that came to be required later. The archaeological territory of General Grammar embraces the imaginings of Fabre d'Olivet (which were never accorded scientific status, and belong rather to the sphere of mystical thought) no less than the analysis of attributive propositions (which was then accepted as evident truth, and in which generative grammar may now recognize its prefigured truth).

Discursive practice does not coincide with the scientific development that it may give rise to; and the knowledge that it forms is neither an unfinished prototype nor the by-product to be found in daily life of a constituted science. The sciences – ignoring, for the moment, the difference between discourses that have the status of scientificity, or pretensions to it, and those that really present the formal criteria of a science – appear in the element of a discursive formation and against the background of knowledge. This opens up two series of problems: what can be the place or role of a region of scientificity in the archaeological territory in which it appears? In accordance with what order and what processes is the emergence of a region of scientificity in a given discursive formation accomplished? We cannot, at present, provide solutions to these problems: all we can do now is to indicate in what direction they might be analysed.

(c) *Knowledge (savoir) and ideology*

Once constituted, a science does not take up, with all the interconnexions that are proper to it, everything that formed the discursive practice in which it appeared; nor does it dissipate – in order to condemn it to the prehistory of error, prejudice, or imagination – the knowledge that surrounds it. Morbid anatomy did not reduce to the norms of scientificity the positivity of clinical medicine. Knowledge is not an epistemological site that disappears in the science that supersedes it. Science (or what is offered as such) is localized in a field of knowledge and plays a role in it. A role that varies according to different discursive formations, and is modified with their mutations. What, in the Classical period, was offered as the medical knowledge of diseases of the mind occupied a very small place in the knowledge of madness: it constituted scarcely more than one of its many surfaces of contact (the others being jurisprudence, casuistics, police regulations, etc.); on the other hand, the psychopathological analyses of the nineteenth century, which were also offered as scientific knowledge (*connaissance*) of mental diseases, played a very different, much more important role in the knowledge (*savoir*) of madness (the role of model, and decision-making authority). Similarly, scientific discourse (or scientific pretension) does not perform the same function in the economic knowledge of the seventeenth and in that of the nineteenth century. In any discursive formation, one finds a specific relation between science and knowledge; and instead of defining between them a relation of exclusion or subtraction (by trying to discover what in knowledge still eludes and resists science, what in science is still compromised by its proximity to and the influence of knowledge), archaeological analysis must show positively how a science functions in the element of knowledge.

It is probably there, in that space of interplay, that the relations of ideology to the sciences are established. The hold of ideology over scientific discourse and the ideological functioning of the sciences are not articulated at the level of their ideal structure (even if they can be expressed in it in a more or less visible way), nor at the level of their technical use in a society (although that society may obtain results from it), nor at the level of the consciousness of the subjects that built it up; they are articulated where science is articulated upon knowledge. If the question of ideology may be asked of science, it is in so far as science, without being identified with knowledge, but without either effacing or excluding it, is localized in it, structures certain of its objects, systematizes certain of its enunciations, formalizes certain of its concepts and strategies; it is in so far as this development articulates knowledge, modifies it, and redistributes it on the one hand, and confirms it and gives it validity on the other; it is in so far as science finds its place in a discursive regularity, in which, by that very fact, it is or is not deployed, functions or does not function, in a whole field of discursive practices. In short, the question of ideology that is asked of science is not the question of situations or practices that it reflects more or less consciously; nor is it the question of the possible use or misuse to which it could be put; it is the question of its existence as a discursive practice and of its functioning among other practices.

Broadly speaking, and setting aside all mediation and specificity, it can be said that political economy has a role in capitalist society, that it serves the interests of the bourgeois class, that it was made by and for that class, and that it bears the mark of its origins even in its concepts and logical architecture; but any more precise description of the relations between the epistemological structure of political economy and its ideological function must take into account the analysis of the discursive formation that gave rise to it and the group of objects, concepts, and theoretical choices that it had to develop and systematize; and one must then show how the discursive practice that gave rise to such a positivity functioned among other practices that might have been of a discursive, but also of a political or economic, order.

This enables us to advance a number of propositions.

1. Ideology is not exclusive of scientificity. Few discourses have given so much place to ideology as clinical discourse or that of political economy: this is not a sufficiently good reason to treat the totality of their statements as being undermined by error, contradiction, and a lack of objectivity.

2. Theoretical contradictions, lacunae, defects may indicate the ideological functioning of a science (or of a discourse with scientific pretensions); they may enable us to determine at what point in the structure this functioning takes effect. But the analysis of this functioning must be made at the level of the positivity and of the relations between the rules of formation and the structures of scientificity.

3. By correcting itself, by rectifying its errors, by clarifying its formulations, discourse does not necessarily undo its relations with ideology. The role of ideology does not diminish as rigour increases and error is dissipated.

4. To tackle the ideological functioning of a science in order to reveal and to modify it is not to uncover the philosophical presuppositions that may lie within it; nor is it to return to the foundations that made it possible, and that legitimated it: it is to question it as a discursive formation; it is to tackle not the formal contradictions of its propositions, but the system of formation of its objects, its types of enunciation, its concepts, its theoretical choices. It is to treat it as one practice among others.

(d) *Different thresholds and their chronology*

It is possible to describe several distinct emergences of a discursive formation. The moment at which a discursive practice achieves individuality and autonomy, the moment therefore at which a single system for the formation of statements is put into operation, or the moment at which this system is transformed, might be called the *threshold of positivity*. When in the operation of a discursive formation, a group of statements is articulated, claims to validate (even unsuccessfully) norms of verification and coherence, and when it exercises a dominant function (as a model, a critique, or a verification) over knowledge, we will say that the discursive formation crosses a *threshold of epistemologization*. When the epistemological figure thus outlined obeys a number of formal criteria, when its statements comply not only with archaeological rules of formation, but also with certain laws for the construction of propositions, we will say that it has crossed a *threshold of scientificity*. And when this scientific discourse is able, in turn, to define the axioms necessary to it, the elements that it uses, the propositional structures that are legitimate to it, and the transformations that it accepts, when it is thus able, taking itself as a starting-point, to deploy the formal edifice that it constitutes, we will say that it has crossed the *threshold of formalization*.

The distribution in time of these different thresholds, their succession, their possible coincidence (or lack of it), the way in which they may govern one another, or become implicated with one another, the conditions in which, in turn, they are established, constitute for archaeology one of its major domains of exploration. Their chronology, in fact, is neither regular nor homogeneous. The discursive formations do not cross them at regular intervals, or at the same time, thus dividing up the history of human knowledge (*connaissances*) into different ages; at a time when many positivities have crossed the threshold of formalization, many others have not yet attained that of scientificity, or even of epistemologization. Moreover: each discursive formation does not pass through these different thresholds in turn, as through the natural stages of biological maturation, in which the only variable is the latency period or the length of the intervals. They are, in fact, events whose dispersion is not evolutive: their unique order is one of the characteristics of each discursive formation. Here are a few examples of these differences.

In some cases, the threshold of positivity is crossed well before that of epistemologization: thus psychopathology, as a discourse with scientific pretensions, epistemologized at the beginning of the nineteenth century, with Pinel, Heinroth, and Esquirol, a discursive practice that largely antedated it, and that had acquired its autonomy and system of regularity long before. But there are also cases in which these two stages are confused in time, when the establishment of a positivity involves at the same time the emergence of an epistemological figure. Sometimes the thresholds of scientificity are linked with the transition from one positivity to another; sometimes they are different; thus the transition from Natural History (with the scientificity that was proper to it) to biology (as a science not of the classification of beings, but of specific correlations of different

organisms) did not take place at the time of Cuvier without the transformation of one positivity into another: on the other hand, the experimental
medicine of Claude Bernard, then the microbiology of Pasteur, modified
the type of scientificity required by morbid anatomy and physiology,
without the discursive formation of clinical medicine, as then established,
being made inoperable. Similarly, the new scientificity established in the
biological disciplines by evolutionism did not modify the biological
positivity that had been defined at the time of Cuvier. In the case of
economics the disconnexions are particularly numerous. In the seventeenth
century, one can recognize a threshold of positivity: it almost coincides
with the practice and theory of mercantilism; but its epistemologization
did not occur until later, at the very end of the century, or the beginning
of the next century, with Locke and Cantillon. However, the nineteenth
century, with Ricardo, marks both a new type of positivity, a new form of
epistemologization, which were later to be modified in turn by Cournot
and Jevons, at the very time that Marx was to reveal an entirely new
discursive practice on the basis of political economy.

If one recognizes in science only the linear accumulation of truths or
the orthogenesis of reason, and fails to recognize in it a discursive practice
that has its own levels, its own thresholds, its own various ruptures, one
can describe only a single historical division, which one adopts as a model
to be applied at all times and for all forms of knowledge: a division between what is definitively or what is not yet scientific. All the density of
the disconnexions, the dispersion of the ruptures, the shifts in their effects,
the play of the interdependence are reduced to the monotonous act of an
endlessly repeated foundation.

There is perhaps only one science for which one can neither distinguish
these different thresholds, nor describe a similar set of shifts: mathematics,
the only discursive practice to have crossed at one and the same time the
thresholds of positivity, epistemologization, scientificity, and formalization. The very possibility of its existence implied that which, in all other
sciences, remains dispersed throughout history, should be given at the
outset: its original positivity was to constitute an already formalized
discursive practice (even if other formalizations were to be used later).
Hence the fact that their establishment is both so enigmatic (so little
accessible to analysis, so confined within the form of the absolute beginning) and so valid (since it is valid both as an origin and as a foundation);
hence the fact that in the first gesture of the first mathematician one saw
the constitution of an ideality that has been deployed throughout history,

and has been questioned only to be repeated and purified; hence the fact that the beginning of mathematics is questioned not so much as a historical event as for its validity as a principal of history: and hence the fact that, for all the other sciences the description of its historical genesis, its gropings and failures, its late emergence is related to the meta-historical model of a geometry emerging suddenly, once and for all, from the trivial practices of land-measuring. But if one takes the establishment of mathematical discourse as a prototype for the birth and development of all the other sciences, one runs the risk of homogenizing all the unique forms of historicity, of reducing to the authority of a single rupture all the different thresholds that a discursive practice may cross, and reproduce endlessly, at every moment in time, the problem of origin: the rights of the historico-transcendental analysis would thus be reinstated. Mathematics has certainly served as a model for most scientific discourses in their efforts to attain formal rigour and demonstrativity; but for the historian who questions the actual development of the sciences, it is a bad example, an example at least from which one cannot generalize.

(e) *The different types of the history of the sciences*

The multiple thresholds that we have succeeded in mapping make distinct forms of historical analysis possible. First, analysis at the level of formalization: it is this history that mathematics never ceases to recount about itself in the process of its own development. What it possesses at a given moment (its domain, its methods, the objects that it defines, the language that it employs) is never thrown back into the external field of non-scientificity, but is constantly undergoing redefinition (if only as an area that has fallen into disuse or temporary sterility) in the formal structure that mathematics constitutes; this past is revealed as a particular case, a naïve model, a partial and insufficiently generalized sketch, of a more abstract, or more powerful theory, or one existing at a higher level; mathematics retranscribes its real historical trajectory into the vocabulary of vicinities, dependences, subordinations, progressive formalizations, and self-enveloping generalities. For this history of mathematics (the history that is constituted by mathematics itself and which mathematics recounts about itself), the algebra of Diophantus is not an experience that remains in suspense; it is a particular case of Algebra as we have known it since Abel and Galois; the Greek method of exhaustions was not an impasse that had to be escaped from; it is a naïve model of integral calculus. Each historical event has its own formal level and localization. This is a *recurrential analysis,* which can be carried out only within a constituted science, one that has crossed its threshold of formalization.[1]

The second type of historical analysis is situated at the threshold of scientificity, and questions itself as to the way in which it was crossed on the basis of various epistemological figures. Its purpose is to discover, for example, how a concept – still overlaid with metaphors or imaginary contents – was purified, and accorded the status and function of a scientific concept. To discover how a region of experience that has already been mapped, already partially articulated, but is still overlaid with immediate practical uses or values related to those uses, was constituted as a scientific domain. To discover how, in general, a science was established over and against a pre-scientific level, which both paved the way and resisted it in advance, how it succeeded in overcoming the obstacles and limitations that still stood in its way. G. Bachelard and G. Canguilhem have provided models of this kind of history. Unlike recurrential analysis, it has no need to situate itself within the science itself, to redistribute every episode in its construction, to recount its formalization in the formal vocabulary that it still possesses today: indeed, how could it do so, since it shows what the science has freed itself from, everything that it has had to leave behind in its progress towards the threshold of scientificity. Consequently, this description takes as its norm the fully constituted science; the history that it recounts is necessarily concerned with the opposition of truth and error, the rational and the irrational, the obstacle and fecundity, purity and impurity, the scientific and the non-scientific. It is an *epistemological* history of the sciences.

The third type of historical analysis takes as its point of attack the threshold of epistemologization – the point of cleavage between discursive formations defined by their positivity and epistemological figures that are not necessarily all sciences (and which may never, in fact, succeed in becoming sciences). At this level, scientificity does not serve as a norm: in this *archaeological history,* what one is trying to uncover are discursive practices in so far as they give rise to a corpus of knowledge, in so far as they assume the status and role of a science. To undertake a history of the sciences at this level is not to describe discursive formations without regard to epistemological structures; it is to show how the establishment of a science, and perhaps its transition to formalization, have come about in a discursive formation, and in modifications to its positivity. Such an analysis sets out, therefore, to outline the history of the sciences on the

[1] Michel Serres, *Hermès ou la communication,* p. 78.

basis of a description of discursive practices; to define how, in accordance with which regularity, and as a result of which modifications, it was able to give rise to the processes of epistemologization, to attain the norms of scientificity, and, perhaps, to reach the threshold of formalization. In seeking the level of discursive practice in the historical density of the sciences, one is not trying to place the discursive practice at some deep, original level, one is not trying to place it at the level of lived experience (on this earth, which is given, irregular and fragmented, before all geometry; in the heaven that glitters through the grid of all astronomies); one is trying to reveal between positivities, knowledge, epistemological figures, and sciences, a whole set of differences, relations, gaps, shifts, independences, autonomies, and the way in which they articulate their own historicities on one another.

The analysis of discursive formations, of positivities, and knowledge in their relations with epistemological figures and with the sciences is what has been called, to distinguish it from other possible forms of the history of the sciences, the analysis of the *episteme*. This episteme may be suspected of being something like a world-view, a slice of history common to all branches of knowledge, which imposes on each one the same norms and postulates, a general stage of reason, a certain structure of thought that the men of a particular period cannot escape – a great body of legislation written once and for all by some anonymous hand. By *episteme*, we mean, in fact, the total set of relations that unite, at a given period, the discursive practices that give rise to epistemological figures, sciences, and possibly formalized systems; the way in which, in each of these discursive formations, the transitions to epistemologization, scientificity, and formalization are situated and operate; the distribution of these thresholds, which may coincide, be subordinated to one another, or be separated by shifts in time; the lateral relations that may exist between epistemological figures or sciences in so far as they belong to neighbouring, but distinct, discursive practices. The episteme is not a form of knowledge (*connaissance*) or type of rationality which, crossing the boundaries of the most varied sciences, manifests the sovereign unity of a subject, a spirit, or a period; it is the totality of relations that can be discovered, for a given period, between the sciences when one analyses them at the level of discursive regularities.

The description of the episteme presents several essential characteristics therefore: it opens up an inexhaustible field and can never be closed; its aim is not to reconstitute the system of postulates that governs all the branches of knowledge (*connaissances*) of a given period, but to cover an indefinite field of relations. Moreover, the episteme is not a motionless figure that appeared one day with the mission of effacing all that preceded it: it is a constantly moving set of articulations, shifts, and coincidences that are established, only to give rise to others. As a set of relations between sciences, epistemological figures, positivities, and discursive practices, the episteme makes it possible to grasp the set of constraints and limitations which, at a given moment, are imposed on discourse: but this limitation is not the negative limitation that opposes knowledge *connaissance*) to ignorance, reasoning to imagination, armed experience to fidelity to appearances, and fantasy to inferences and deductions; the episteme is not what may be known at a given period, due account taken of inadequate techniques, mental attitudes, or the limitations imposed by tradition; it is what, in the positivity of discursive practices, makes possible the existence of epistemological figures and sciences. Lastly, we see that the analysis of the episteme is not a way of returning to the critical question ('given the existence of something like a science, what is its legitimacy?'); it is a questioning that accepts the fact of science only in order to ask the question what it is for that science to be a science. In the enigma of scientific discourse, what the analysis of the episteme questions is not its right to be a science, but the fact that it exists. And the point at which it separates itself off from all the philosophies of knowledge (*connaissance*) is that it relates this fact not to the authority of an original act of giving, which establishes in a transcendental subject the fact and the right, but to the processes of a historical practice.

(f) *Other archaeologies*

One question remains in suspense: could one conceive of an archaeological analysis that would reveal the regularity of a body of knowledge, but which would not set out to analyse it in terms of epistemological figures and sciences? Is an orientation towards the episteme the only one open to archaeology? Must archaeology be – exclusively – a certain way of questioning the history of the sciences? In other words, by confirming itself up to now to the region of scientific discourses, has archaeology been governed by some insuperable necessity – or has it provided an outline, on the basis of a particular example, of forms of analysis that may have a much wider application?

At the moment I am not sufficiently advanced in my task to answer this question. But I can readily imagine – subject to a great deal of further exploration and examination – archaeologies that might develop in different directions. There is, for example, the archaeological description of 'sexuality'. And I can see very well how it might be orientated towards the episteme: one would show how in the nineteenth century such epistemological figures as the biology and psychology of sexuality were formed; and how a discourse of a scientific type was established through the rupture brought about by Freud. But I can also see another possible direction for analysis: instead of studying the sexual behaviour of men at a given period (by seeking its law in a social structure, in a collective unconscious, or in a certain moral attitude), instead of describing what men thought of sexuality (what religious interpretation they gave it, to what extent they approved or disapproved of it, what conflicts of opinion or morality it gave rise to), one would ask oneself whether, in this behaviour, as in these representations, a whole discursive practice is not at work; whether sexuality, quite apart from any orientation towards a scientific discourse, is not a group of objects that can be talked about (or that it is forbidden to talk about), a field of possible enunciations (whether in lyrical or legal language), a group of concepts (which can no doubt be presented in the elementary form of notions or themes), a set of choices (which may appear in the coherence of behaviour or in systems of pre-scription). Such an archaeology would show, if it succeeded in its task, how the prohibitions, exclusions, limitations, values, freedoms, and transgressions of sexuality, all its manifestations, verbal or otherwise, are linked to a particular discursive practice. It would reveal, not of course as the ultimate truth of sexuality, but as one of the dimensions in accord-ance with which one can describe it, a certain 'way of speaking'; and one would show how this way of speaking is invested not in scientific discourses, but in a system of prohibitions and values. An analysis that would be carried out not in the direction of the episteme, but in that of what we might call the ethical.

But here is an example of another possible orientation. In analysing a painting, one can reconstitute the latent discourse of the painter; one can try to recapture the murmur of his intentions, which are not transcribed into words, but into lines, surfaces, and colours; one can try to uncover the implicit philosophy that is supposed to form his view of the world. It is also possible to question science, or at least the opinions of the period, and to try to recognize to what extent they appear in the painter's work. Arch-aeological analysis would have another aim: it would try to discover whether space, distance, depth, colour, light, proportions, volumes, and contours were not, at the period in question, considered, named, enunciated, and conceptualized in a discursive practice; and whether the knowledge that this discursive practice gives rise to was not embodied perhaps in theories and speculations, in forms of teaching and codes of practice, but also in processes, techniques, and even in the very gesture of the painter. It would not set out to show that the painting is a certain way of 'meaning' or 'saying' that is peculiar in that it dispenses with words. It would try to show that, at least in one of its dimensions, it is discursive practice that is embodied in techniques and effects. In this sense, the painting is not a pure vision that must then be transcribed into the materiality of space; nor is it a naked gesture whose silent and eternally empty meanings must be freed from subsequent interpretations. It is shot through – and independently of scientific knowledge (*connaissance*) and philosophical themes – with the positivity of a knowledge (*savoir*).

It seems to me that one might also carry out an analysis of the same type on political knowledge. One would try to show whether the political behaviour of a society, a group, or a class is not shot through with a particular, describable discursive practice. This positivity would obviously not coincide either with the political theories of the period or with economic determinations: it would define the element in politics that can become an object of enunciation, the forms that this enunciation may take, the concepts that are employed in it, and the strategic choices that are made in it. Instead of analysing this knowledge – which is always possible – in the direction of the episteme that it can give rise to, one would analyse it in the direction of behaviour, struggles, conflicts, decisions, and tactics. One would thus reveal a body of political knowledge that is not some kind of secondary theorizing about practice, nor the application of theory. Since it is regularly formed by a discursive practice that is deployed among other practices and is articulated upon them, it is not an expression that more or less adequately 'reflects' a number of 'objective data' or real practices. It is inscribed, from the outset, in the field of different practices in which it finds its specificity, its functions, and its network of dependences. If such a description were possible, there would be no need of course to pass through the authority of an individual or collective consciousness in order to grasp the place of articulation of a political practice and theory; there would be no need to try to discover to what extent this consciousness may, on the one hand, express silent conditions, and, on the other, show that it is susceptible to theoretical truths; one would not need to pose the psychological problem of an act of consciousness (*prise de conscience*); instead, one would analyse the formation and transformations of a body of knowledge.

The question, for example, would not be to determine from what moment a revolutionary consciousness appears, nor the respective roles of economic conditions and theoretical elucidations in the genesis of this consciousness; it would not attempt to retrace the general, and exemplary, biography of revolutionary man, or to find the origins of his project; but it would try to explain the formation of a discursive practice and a body of revolutionary knowledge that are expressed in behaviour and strategies, which give rise to a theory of society, and which operate the interference and mutual transformation of that behaviour and those strategies.

To the questions posed above – Is archaeology concerned only with sciences? Is it always an analysis of scientific discourse? – we can now give a reply, in each case in the negative. What archaeology tries to describe is not the specific structure of science, but the very different domain of *knowledge*. Moreover, although it is concerned with knowledge in its relation to epistemological figures and the sciences, it may also question knowledge in a different direction and describe it in a different set of relations. The orientation towards the episteme has been the only one to be explored so far. The reason for this is that, because of a gradient that no doubt characterizes our cultures, discursive formations are constantly becoming epistemologized. It is by questioning the sciences, their history, their strange unity, their dispersion, and their ruptures, that the domain of positivities was able to appear; it is in the interstice of scientific discourses that we were able to grasp the play of discursive formations. It is hardly surprising, therefore, that the most fruitful region, the one most open to archaeological description should have been that 'Classical' age, which from the Renaissance to the nineteenth century saw the epistemologization of so many positivities; nor is it surprising that the discursive formations and specific regularities of knowledge are outlined precisely where the levels of scientificity and formalization were most difficult to attain. But that was no more than a preferential point of attack; it is not, for archaeology, an obligatory domain.

PART V

Conclusion

Conclusion

—Throughout this book, you have been at great pains to dissociate yourself from 'structuralism', or at least from what is ordinarily understood by that term. You have tried to show that you used neither the methods nor the concepts of structuralism; that you made no reference to the procedures of linguistic description; that you are not concerned with formalization. But what do these differences amount to, if not that you have failed to avail yourself of what is most positive, most rigorous, and most revealing in structural analysis? That the domain that you have tried to deal with is not susceptible to this kind of enterprise, and that its richness has constantly eluded the schemata in which you wished to enclose it? And with apparent unconcern, you are now trying to disguise the impotence of your method; you are now presenting as an explicitly intended difference the unconquerable distance that separates you, and will always separate you, from a true structural analysis.

For you have not managed to deceive us. It is true that in the void left by the methods that you have chosen not to use, you have precipitated a whole series of notions that seem quite alien to the concepts now accepted by those who describe languages, myths, or works of literature; you have spoken of formations, positivities, knowledge, discursive practices: a whole panoply of terms whose uniqueness and marvellous powers you were proud to point out at every step. But would you have invented so many oddities if you had not tried to apply, in a domain that was irreducible to them, some of the fundamental themes of structuralism – and those very themes that constitute its most debatable and philosophically dubious postulates? It is as if you had used not the empirical, serious work of structural analysis, but two or three themes that are really extrapolations rather than necessary principles.

You have tried to reduce the dimensions proper to discourse, ignore its specific irregularity, hide what initiative and freedom it possesses, and make up for the imbalance that it sets up within the language (*langue*): you have tried to close this openness. Like a certain form of linguistics, you have tried to dispense with the speaking subject; you believed that one could cut off from discourse all its anthropological references, and treat it as if it had never been formulated by anyone, as if it had not come about in particular circumstances, as if it were not imbued with representations, as if it were addressed to no one. Lastly, you have applied to it a principle of simultaneity: you have refused to see that discourse, unlike the language (*langue*) perhaps, is essentially historical, that it was made up not of available elements, but of real, successive events, that it cannot be analysed outside the time in which it occurred.

—You are quite right: I misunderstood the transcendence of discourse; in describing it, I refused to refer it to a subjectivity; I did not give primary consideration, as if it ought to be its general form, to its diachronic character. But this was not intended to extend, beyond the domain of the language (*langue*), concepts and methods that had been tested within it. If I spoke of discourse, it was not to show that the mechanisms or processes of the language (*langue*) were entirely preserved in it; but rather to reveal, in the density of verbal performances, the diversity of the possible levels of analysis; to show that in addition to methods of linguistic structuration (or interpretation), one could draw up a specific description of statements, of their formation, and of the regularities proper to discourse. If I suspended all reference to the speaking subject, it was not to discover laws of construction or forms that could be applied in the same way by all speaking subjects, nor was it to give voice to the great universal discourse that is common to all men at a particular period. On the contrary, my aim was to show what the differences consisted of, how it was possible for men, within the same discursive practice, to speak of different objects, to have contrary opinions, and to make contradictory choices; my aim was also to show in what way discursive practices were distinguished from one another; in short, I wanted not to exclude the problem of the subject, but to define the positions and functions that the subject could occupy in the diversity of discourse. Lastly, as you have observed, I did not deny history, but held in suspense the general, empty category of change in order to reveal transformations at different levels; I reject a uniform model of temporalization, in order to describe, for each discursive practice, its rules of accumulation, exclusion, reactivation, its own forms of derivation, and its specific modes of connexion over various successions.

So I did not wish to carry the structuralist enterprise beyond its legitimate limits. And you must admit that I never once used the word 'structure' in *The Order of Things*. But let us leave off our polemics about 'structuralism'; they hardly survive in areas now deserted by serious workers; this particular controversy, which might have been so fruitful, is now acted out only by mimes and tumblers.

—It's no use trying to avoid these polemics: you won't escape the problem so easily. For the problem does not concern structuralism. I recognize the value of its insights of course: when it is a question of analysing a language (*langue*), mythologies, folk-tales, poems, dreams, works of literature, even films perhaps, structural description reveals relations that could not otherwise be isolated; it makes it possible to define recurrent elements, with their forms of opposition, and their criteria of individualization; it also makes it possible to lay down laws of construction, equivalences, and rules of transformation. And despite a number of reservations that I had at the beginning, I now have no difficulty in accepting that man's languages (*langues*), his unconscious, and his imagination are governed by laws of structure. But what I absolutely cannot accept is what you are doing: I cannot accept that one can analyse scientific discourses in their succession without referring them to something like a constituent activity, without recognizing even in their hesitations the opening of an original project or a fundamental teleology, without discovering the profound continuity that links them, and leads them to the point at which we can grasp them; I cannot accept that one can analyse the development of reason in this way, and free the history of thought from all taint of subjectivity. Let us examine the problem more closely: I agree that one can speak, in terms of elements and rules of construction, of language (*langue*) in general – at least of that language of other times and places which is that of myths, or even of that nevertheless rather strange language which is that of our unconscious or of our literary works; but the language of our knowledge, that language which we are using here and now, the structural discourse itself that enables us to analyse so many other languages (*langages*), that language which, in its historical density, we regard as irreducible. You surely cannot forget that it is on the basis of that language, with its slow genesis, and the obscure development that has brought it to its present state, that we can speak of other discourses in terms of structures; it is that language which has given us the possibility and the right to do so; it forms the blind spot on the basis of which things around us are arranged as we see them today. I don't mind one dealing with elements, relations, and discontinuities when analysing

Indo-European myths or the tragedies of Racine; and I can even accept that one should dispense, as far as one can, with a discussion of the speaking subjects; but I dispute that these successes give one the right to turn the analysis back on to the forms of discourse that made them possible, and to question the very locus in which we are speaking today. The history of those analyses in which subjectivity eludes one retains its own transcendence.

—It seems to me that the difference between us lies there (much more than in the over-discussed question of structuralism). As you know, I have no great liking for interpretation, but allow me, as a kind of game, to say what I understand you to have said earlier. 'Of course,' you say, 'we must now admit, despite all the attacks of the *arrière-garde*, that one formalizes deductive discourses; of course we have to admit that one describes, not so much the history of a soul, not so much a project of existence, as the architecture of a philosophical system; of course, whatever we think about it, we have to tolerate those analyses that link literary *oeuvres*, not to the lived experience of an individual, but to the structures of the language (*langue*). Of course, we have had to abandon all those discourses that once led us to the sovereignty of consciousness. But what we have lost over the last half-century, we are hoping to recover in the second degree, by means of the analysis of those analyses, or at least by the fundamental questioning that we apply to them. We will ask them where they came from, towards what historical destination they are moving without being aware of it, what naïvety blinds them to the conditions that make them possible, and what metaphysical enclosure encloses their rudimentary positivism. And so in the end it will not matter that the unconscious is not, as we believed and affirmed, the implicit edge of consciousness; it will not matter that a mythology is no longer a world-view, and that a novel is something other than the outer slope of a lived experience; for the reason that establishes all these new 'truths' is under strict supervision: neither itself, nor its past, nor that which makes it possible, nor that which makes it ours escapes the attribution of transcendence. For it is to it now – and we are determined never to abandon this – that we will now pose the question of the origin, the first constitution, the teleological horizon, temporal continuity. It is that thought, which is now becoming ours, that we will maintain in historico-transcendental dominance. That is why, if we must tolerate all these structuralisms, whether we like it or not, we will not allow any taint to that history of thought that is our own history; we will not allow the unravelling of those transcendental threads that have bound it since the nineteenth century to the problem of origin and subjectivity. To whomsoever approaches that fortress in which we have taken refuge, and which we are determined to defend and to hold, we repeat, with a gesture that wards off all profanation: *'Noli tangere'*.

But I have obstinately gone on. Not that I am either certain of victory or sure of my weapons. But because it seemed to me that, for the moment, the essential task was to free the history of thought from its subjection to transcendence. For me, the problem was certainly not how to structuralize it, by applying to the development of knowledge or to the genesis of the sciences categories that had proved themselves in the domain of language (*langue*). My aim was to analyse this history, in the discontinuity that no teleology would reduce in advance; to map it in a dispersion that no pre-established horizon would embrace; to allow it to be deployed in an anonymity on which no transcendental constitution would impose the form of the subject; to open it up to a temporality that would not promise the return of any dawn. My aim was to cleanse it of all transcendental narcissism; it had to be freed from that circle of the lost origin, and rediscovered where it was imprisoned; it had to be shown that the history of thought could not have this role of revealing the transcendental moment that rational mechanics has not possessed since Kant, mathematical idealities since Husserl, and the meanings of the perceived world since Merleau-Ponty – despite the efforts that had been made to find it here.

And I think that really, despite the element of doubt introduced by our apparent dispute over structuralism, we understood each other perfectly. I mean, each of us understood perfectly what the other was trying to do. It is quite normal that you should defend the rights of a continuous history, open both to the application of a teleology and to the endless processes of causality; but it was not to protect it from a structural invasion that failed to recognize its movement, spontaneity, and internal dynamism; in fact, you were trying to preserve the powers of a constituent consciousness, since it was really they that were in question. But this defence was to take place elsewhere, and not in the same place as the discussion itself: for if you recognize the right of a piece of empirical research, some fragment of history, to challenge the transcendental dimension, then you have ceded the main point. Hence a series of shifts or displacements. To treat archaeology as a search for the origin, for formal *a prioris*, for founding acts, in short, as a sort of historical phenomenology (when, on the contrary, its aim is to free history from the grip of phenomenology), and then to object that it fails in its task, and that it never discovers more than a series of empirical facts. Then to contrast archaeological description, and its concern to establish thresholds, ruptures, and transformations, with the true work of historians, which is to reveal continuities (when this ceased to be the concern of historians decades ago); and then to reproach it for its lack of concern for empiricities. And then to regard it as an enterprise whose aim is to describe cultural totalities, to homogenize the most obvious differences, and to rediscover the universality of constrictive forms (when its aim is to define the unique specificity of discursive practices), and then to object to differences, changes, and mutations. Lastly, to regard it as an importation of structuralism into the domain of history (when its methods and concepts cannot possibly be confused with structuralism) and then to show that it cannot function as a true structural analysis.

This whole play of displacements and misunderstandings is perfectly coherent and necessary. It brought with it a secondary benefit: being able to approach from an oblique angle all those forms of structuralism that had to be tolerated, and that could no longer be resisted; and to say to them: 'You see what you'll expose yourselves to if you touch those domains that are still ours; your methods may have some validity elsewhere, but they would soon be brought to recognize their limitations; all the concrete content that you would like to analyse would elude them; you would be forced to give up your prudent empiricism; and, against your will, you would fall into a strange ontology of structure. So be prudent enough to keep to those domains which you have no doubt conquered, but which we will pretend to have conceded to you, since we have fixed their boundaries.' But the major benefit, of course, is that it conceals the crisis in which we have been involved for so long, and which is constantly growing more serious: a crisis that concerns that transcendental reflexion with which philosophy since Kant has identified itself; which concerns that theme of the origin, that promise of the return, by which we avoid the difference of our present; which concerns an anthropological thought that orders all these questions around the question of man's being, and allows us to avoid an analysis of practice; which concerns all humanist ideologies; which, above all, concerns the status of the subject. It is this discussion that you would like to suppress, and from which you hope, I think, to divert attention, by pursuing the pleasant games of genesis and system, synchrony and development, relation and cause, structure and history. Are you sure you are not practising a theoretical metathesis?

*   *   *

—Let us suppose that our dispute is where you say it is; let us suppose that our aims are to attack or to defend the last bastion of transcendental thought, and let us admit that this discussion is in fact situated in the crisis you describe: what then is the title of your discourse? Where does it come from and from where does it derive its right to speak? How could it be legitimated? If you have done nothing more than carry out an empirical inquiry devoted to the appearance and transformation of discourses, if you have described groups of statements, epistemological figures, the historical forms of a body of knowledge, how can you escape the naïvety of all positivisms? And how could your enterprise prevail against the question of origin, and the necessary recourse to a constituent subject? But if you claim that you are opening up a radical interrogation, if you wish to place your discourse at the level at which we place ourselves, you know very well that it will enter our game, and, in turn, extend the very dimension that it is trying to free itself from. Either it does not reach us, or we claim it. In any case, you have promised to tell us what these discourses are that you have been pursuing so obstinately for the past ten years, without ever bothering to define their status. In short, what are they: history or philosophy?

—I admit that this question embarrasses me more than your earlier objections. I am not entirely surprised by it; but I would have preferred to leave it in suspense a little longer. This is because, for the moment, and as far ahead as I can see, my discourse, far from determining the locus in which it speaks, is avoiding the ground on which it could find support. It is a discourse about discourses: but it is not trying to find in them a hidden law, a concealed origin that it only remains to free; nor is it trying to establish by itself, taking itself as a starting-point, the general theory of which they would be the concrete models. It is trying to deploy a dispersion that can never be reduced to a single system of differences, a scattering that is not related to absolute axes of reference; it is trying to operate a decentring that leaves no privilege to any centre. The role of such a discourse is not to dissipate oblivion, to rediscover, in the depths of things said, at the very place in which they are silent, the moment of their birth (whether this is seen as their empirical creation, or the transcendental act that gives them origin); it does not set out to be a recollection of the original or a memory of the truth. On the contrary, its task is to *make* differences: to constitute them as objects, to analyse them, and to define their concept. Instead of travelling over the field of discourses in order to recreate the suspended totalizations for its own use, instead of seeking in what has been said that *other* hidden discourse, which nevertheless remains the *same* (and instead of playing endlessly with *allegory* and *tautology*), it is continually making *differentiations*, it is a *diagnosis*. If philosophy is memory or a return of the origin, what I am doing cannot, in any way, be regarded as philosophy; and if the history of thought consists in giving life to half-effaced figures, what I am doing is not history either.

—From what you have just said, one must at least deduce that your archaeology is not a science. You allow it to fluctuate, with the uncertain status of a description. Yet another of those discourses that would like to be taken as a discipline still in its early stages, no doubt; which gives their authors the double advantage of not having to establish their explicit, rigorous scientificity, and of opening up for it a future generality that frees it from the hazards of its birth; yet another of those projects that justify themselves on the basis of what they are not, always leaving their essential task, the moment of their verification, and the definitive establishment of their coherence until later; yet another of those foundations, so many of which have been announced since the nineteenth century: for we know very well that, in the modern theoretical field, what one is pleased to invent are not demonstrable systems, but disciplines for which one opens up possibilities, outlines a programme, and leaves its future development to others. But no sooner have they been outlined than they disappear together with their authors. And the field that they were supposed to tend remains sterile for ever.

—It is true that I have never presented archaeology as a science, or even as the beginnings of a future science. And I have tried to draw up a survey – and in the process to make a good many corrections – of the work that I had done in certain fields of concrete research, rather than produce plans for some future building. The word archaeology is not supposed to carry any suggestion of anticipation; it simply indicates a possible line of attack for the analysis of verbal performances: the specification of a level – that of the statement and the archive; the determination and illumination of a domain – the enunciative regularities, the positivities; the application of such concepts as rules of formation, archaeological derivation, and historical *a priori*. But in almost all its dimensions and over almost all its crests, the enterprise is related to the sciences, and to analyses of a scientific type, or to theories subject to rigorous criteria. First of all, it is related to

the sciences that are constituted and establish their norms in the knowledge archaeologically described: for the archaeological enterprise, these
sciences are so many *science-objects*, as morbid anatomy, philology,
political economy, and biology have already been. It is also related to
scientific forms of analysis, but is distinguished from them either in level,
domain, or methods, and juxtaposed to them by characteristic lines of
division; by seizing, out of the mass of things said, upon the statement
defined as a function of realization of the verbal *performance*, it distinguishes itself from a search whose privileged field is linguistic *competence:*
while such a description constitutes a generative model, in order to define
the acceptability of statements, archaeology tries to establish rules of
formation, in order to define the conditions of their realization;
between these two modes of analysis, there are, therefore, a number of
analogies, but there are also a number of differences (in particular, concerning the possible level of formalization); in any case, for archaeology,
a generative grammar plays the role of a *related analysis*. Moreover, in their
deployment and in the fields that they cover, archaeological descriptions
are articulated upon other disciplines; in seeking to define, outside all
reference to a psychological or constituent subjectivity, the different
positions of the subject that may be involved in statements, archaeology
touches on a question that is being posed today by psychoanalysis; in
trying to reveal the rules of formation of concepts, the modes of succession,
connexion, and coexistence of statements, it touches on the problem of
epistemological structures; in studying the formation of objects, the fields
in which they emerge and are specified, in studying too the conditions of
appropriation of discourses, it touches on the analysis of social formations.
For archaeology, these are so many *correlative spaces*. Lastly, in so far as it
is possible to constitute a general theory of productions, archaeology, as the
analysis of the rules proper to the different discursive practices, will find
what might be called its *enveloping theory*.

If I situate archaeology among so many other, already constituted,
discourses, it is not in order to give it some kind of status by association
that it would be incapable of acquiring in isolation; it is not in order to
give it a definitive place in an unmoving constellation; but in order to
reveal, with the archive, the discursive formations, the positivities, the
statements, and their conditions of formation, a specific domain. A domain
that has not so far been made the object of any analysis (at least, of what is
most specific and most irreducible to interpretations and formalizations
about it); but a domain that has no means of guaranteeing – at the still

rudimentary stage of mapping at which I am at present – that it will remain stable and autonomous. After all, it may be that archaeology is doing nothing more than playing the role of an instrument that makes it possible to articulate, in a less imprecise way than in the past, the analysis of social formations and epistemological descriptions; or which makes it possible to relate an analysis of the positions of the subject to a theory of the history of the sciences; or which makes it possible to situate the place of intersection between a general theory of production and a generative analysis of statements. Lastly, it may turn out that archaeology is the name given to a part of our contemporary theoretical conjuncture. Whether this conjuncture is giving rise to an individualizable discipline, whose initial characteristics and overall limits are being outlined here, or whether it is giving rise to a set of problems whose present coherence does not mean that it will not be taken up later elsewhere, in a different way, at a higher level, or using different methods, I am in no position at the moment to decide. And, to tell you the truth, it is probably not up to me to decide. I accept that my discourse may disappear with the figure that has borne it so far.

—You make curious use of the freedom that you question in others. For you give yourself the whole field of a free space that you even refuse to qualify. But are you forgetting the care with which you enclosed the discourse of others within systems of rules? Are you forgetting all those constraints that you described so meticulously? Have you not deprived individuals of the right to intervene personally in the positivities in which their discourses are situated? You have linked their slightest words to obligations that condemn their slightest innovations to conformity. You make revolution very easy for yourself, but very difficult for others. It might be better if you had a clearer awareness of the conditions in which you speak, and a greater confidence in the real action of men and in their possibilities.

—I'm afraid you are making a double mistake: about the discursive practices that I have tried to define and about the role that you yourself accord to human freedom. The positivities that I have tried to establish must not be understood as a set of determinations imposed from the out-side on the thought of individuals, or inhabiting it from the inside, in advance as it were; they constitute rather the set of conditions in accord-ance with which a practice is exercised, in accordance with which that practice gives rise to partially or totally new statements, and in accordance with which it can be modified. These positivities are not so much limitations imposed on the initiative of subjects as the field in which that initiative is articulated (without, however, constituting its centre), rules that it puts into operation (without it having invented or formulated them), relations that provide it with a support (without it being either their final result or their point of convergence). It is an attempt to reveal discursive practices in their complexity and density; to show that to speak is to do something – something other than to express what one thinks; to translate what one knows, and something other than to play with the structures of a language (*langue*); to show that to add a statement to a pre-existing series of statements is to perform a complicated and costly gesture, which involves conditions (and not only a situation, a context, and motives), and rules (not the logical and linguistic rules of construction); to show that a change in the order of discourse does not presuppose 'new ideas', a little invention and creativity, a different mentality, but transformations in a practice, perhaps also in neighbouring practices, and in their common articulation. I have not denied – far from it – the possibility of changing discourse: I have deprived the sovereignty of the subject of the exclusive and instantaneous right to it.

And now I should like to ask you a question: how do you see change, or, let us say, revolution, at least in the scientific order and in the field of discourses, if you link it with the themes of meaning, project, origin and return, constituent subject, in short with the entire thematic that ensures for history the universal presence of the Logos? What possibility do you accord it if you analyse it in accordance with dynamic, biological, evolutionist metaphors in which the difficult, specific problem of historical mutation is usually dissolved? More precisely still: what political status can you give to discourse if you see in it merely a thin transparency that shines for an instant at the limit of things and thoughts? Has not the practice of revolutionary discourse and scientific discourse in Europe over the past two hundred years freed you from this idea that words are wind, an external whisper, a beating of wings that one has difficulty in hearing in the serious matter of history? Or must we conclude that in order to refuse this lesson, you are determined to misunderstand discursive practices, in their own existence, and that you wished to maintain, in spite of that lesson, a history of the mind, of rational knowledge, ideas, and opinions? What is that fear which makes you reply in terms of consciousness when someone talks to you about a practice, its conditions, its rules, and its historical transformations? What is that fear which makes you seek, beyond all boundaries, ruptures, shifts, and divisions, the great historico-transcendental destiny of the Occident?

It seems to me that the only reply to this question is a political one. But let us leave that to one side for today. Perhaps we will take it up again soon in another way.

This book was written simply in order to overcome certain preliminary difficulties. I know as well as anyone how 'thankless' is the task that I undertook some ten years ago. I know how irritating it can be to treat discourses in terms not of the gentle, silent, intimate consciousness that is expressed in them, but of an obscure set of anonymous rules. How unpleasant it is to reveal the limitations and necessities of a practice where one is used to seeing, in all its pure transparency, the expression of genius and freedom. How provocative it is to treat as a set of transformations this history of discourses which, until now, has been animated by the reassuring metaphors of life or the intentional continuity of the lived. How unbearable it is, in view of how much of himself everyone wishes to put, thinks he is putting of 'himself' into his own discourse, when he speaks, how unbearable it is to cut up, analyse, combine, rearrange all these texts that have now returned from silence, without ever the transfigured face of the author appearing: 'What! All those words, piled up one after another, all those marks made on all that paper and presented to innumerable pairs of eyes, all that concern to make them survive beyond the gesture that articulated them, so much piety expended in preserving them and inscribing them in men's memories – all that and nothing remaining of the poor hand that traced them, of the anxiety that sought appeasement in them, of that completed life that has nothing but them to survive in? Is not discourse, in its most profound determination, a "trace"? And is its murmur not the place of insubstantial immortalities? Must we admit that the time of discourse is not the time of consciousness extrapolated to the dimensions of history, or the time of history present in the form of consciousness? Must I suppose that in my discourse I can have no survival? And that in speaking I am not banishing my death, but actually establishing it; or rather that I am abolishing all interiority in that exterior that is so indifferent to my life, and so *neutral*, that it makes no distinction between my life and my death?'

I understand the unease of all such people. They have probably found it difficult enough to recognize that their history, their economics, their social practices, the language (*langue*) that they speak, the mythology of their ancestors, even the stories that they were told in their childhood, are governed by rules that are not all given to their consciousness; they can hardly agree to being dispossessed in addition of that discourse in which they wish to be able to say immediately and directly what they think, believe, or imagine; they prefer to deny that discourse is a complex, differentiated practice, governed by analysable rules and transformations, rather than be deprived of that tender, consoling certainty of being able to change, if not the world, if not life, at least their 'meaning', simply with a fresh word that can come only from themselves, and remain for ever close to the source. So many things have already eluded them in their language (*langage*): they have no wish to see *what they say* go the same way; at all costs, they must preserve that tiny fragment of discourse – whether written or spoken – whose fragile, uncertain existence must perpetuate their lives. They cannot bear (and one cannot but sympathize) to hear someone saying: 'Discourse is not life: its time is not your time; in it, you will not be reconciled to death; you may have killed God beneath the weight of all that you have said; but don't imagine that, with all that you are saying, you will make a man that will live longer than he.'

APPENDIX

and

INDEX

APPENDIX

The Discourse on Language*

I would really like to have slipped imperceptibly into this lecture, as into all the others I shall be delivering, perhaps over the years ahead. I would have preferred to be enveloped in words, borne way beyond all possible beginnings. At the moment of speaking, I would like to have perceived a nameless voice, long preceding me, leaving me merely to enmesh myself in it, taking up its cadence, and to lodge myself, when no one was looking, in its interstices as if it had paused an instant, in suspense, to beckon to me. There would have been no beginnings: instead, speech would proceed from me, while I stood in its path – a slender gap – the point of its possible disappearance.

Behind me, I should like to have heard (having been at it long enough already, repeating in advance what I am about to tell you) the voice of Molloy, beginning to speak thus: 'I must go on; I can't go on; I must go on; I must say words as long as there are words, I must say them until they find me, until they say me – heavy burden, heavy sin; I must go on; maybe it's been done already; maybe they've already said me; maybe they've already borne me to the threshold of my story, right to the door opening onto my story; I'd be surprised if it opened'.

A good many people, I imagine, harbour a similar desire to be freed from the obligation to begin, a similar desire to find themselves, right from the outside, on the other side of discourse, without having to stand outside it, pondering its particular, fearsome, and even devilish features. To this all too common feeling, institutions have an ironic reply, for they solemnise beginnings, surrounding them with a circle of silent attention; in order that they can be distinguished from far off, they impose ritual forms upon them.

Inclination speaks out: 'I don't want to have to enter this risky world of discourse; I want nothing to do with it insofar as it is decisive and final; I would like to feel it all around me, calm and transparent, profound, infinitely open, with others responding to my expectations, and truth emerging, one

* This lecture was delivered in French at the Collège de France on December 2, 1970. The original French text has been published with the title *L'ordre du discours* (Paris, Gallimard, 1971). The English translation by Rupert Swyer was first published in *Social Science Information*, April 1971, pp. 7-30.

by one. All I want is to allow myself to be borne along, within it, and by it, a happy wreck'. Institutions reply: 'But you have nothing to fear from launching out; we're here to show you discourse is within the established order of things, that we've waited a long time for its arrival, that a place has been set aside for it – a place which both honours and disarms it; and if it should happen to have a certain power, then it is we, and we alone, who give it that power'.

Yet, maybe this institution and this inclination are but two converse responses to the same anxiety: anxiety as to just what discourse is, when it is manifested materially, as a written or spoken object; but also, uncertainty faced with a transitory existence, destined for oblivion – at any rate, not belonging to us; uncertainty at the suggestion of barely imaginable powers and dangers behind this activity, however humdrum and grey it may seem; uncertainty when we suspect the conflicts, triumphs, injuries, dominations and enslavements that lie behind these words, even when long use has chipped away their rough edges.

What is so perilous, then, in the fact that people speak, and that their speech proliferates? Where is the danger in that?

Here then is the hypothesis I want to advance, tonight, in order to fix the terrain – or perhaps the very provisional theatre – within which I shall be working. I am supposing that in every society the production of discourse is at once controlled, selected, organised and redistributed according to a certain number of procedures, whose role is to avert its powers and its dangers, to cope with chance events, to evade its ponderous, awesome materiality.

In a society such as our own we all know the rules of *exclusion*. The most obvious and familiar of these concerns what is *prohibited*. We know perfectly well that we are not free to say just anything, that we cannot simply speak of anything, when we like or where we like; not just anyone, finally, may speak of just anything. We have three types of prohibition, covering objects, ritual with its surrounding circumstances, the privileged or exclusive right to speak of a particular subject; these prohibitions interrelate, reinforce and complement each other, forming a complex web, continually subject to modification. I will note simply that the areas where this web is most tightly woven today, where the danger spots are most numerous, are those dealing with politics and sexuality. It is as though discussion, far from being a transparent, neutral element, allowing us to disarm sexuality and to pacify politics, were one of those privileged areas in which they exercised some of their more awesome powers. In appearance, speech may well be of little account, but the prohibitions surrounding it soon reveal its links with desire and power. This should not be very surprising, for psychoanalysis has already shown us that speech is not merely the medium which manifests – or dissembles – desire; it is also the object of desire. Similarly, historians have constantly impressed upon us that speech is no mere verbalisation of conflicts and systems of domination, but that it is the very object of man's conflicts.

But our society possesses yet another principle of exclusion; not another prohibition, but a division and a rejection. I have in mind the opposition:

reason and folly. From the depths of the Middle Ages, a man was mad if his speech could not be said to form part of the common discourse of men. His words were considered nul and void, without truth or significance, worthless as evidence, inadmissible in the authentification of acts or contracts, incapable even of bringing about transubstantiation – the transformation of bread into flesh – at Mass. And yet, in contrast to all others, his words were credited with strange powers, of revealing some hidden truth, of predicting the future, of revealing, in all their naivete, what the wise were unable to perceive. It is curious to note that for centuries, in Europe, the words of a madman were either totally ignored or else were taken as words of truth. They either fell into a void – rejected the moment they were proffered – or else men deciphered in them a naive or cunning reason, rationality more rational than that of a rational man. At all events, whether excluded or secretly invested with reason, the madman's speech did not strictly exist. It was through his words that one recognised the madness of the madman; but they were certainly the medium within which this division became active; they were neither heard nor remembered. No doctor before the end of the eighteenth century had ever thought of listening to the content – how it was said and why – of these words; and yet it was these which signalled the difference between reason and madness. Whatever a madman said, it was taken for mere noise; he was credited with words only in a symbolic sense, in the theatre, in which he stepped forward, unarmed and reconciled, playing his role: that of masked truth.

Of course people are going to say all that is over and done with, or that it is in the process of being finished with, today; that the madman's words are no longer on the other side of this division; that they are no longer nul and void, that, on the contrary, they alert us to the need to look for a sense behind them, for the attempt at, or the ruins of some '*œuvre*'; we have even come to notice these words of madmen in our own speech, in those tiny pauses when we forget what we are talking about. But all this is no proof that the old division is not just as active as before; we have only to think of the systems by which we decipher this speech; we have only to think of the network of institutions established to permit doctors and psychoanalysts to listen to the mad and, at the same time, enabling the mad to come and speak, or, in desperation, to withhold their meagre words; we have only to bear all this in mind to suspect that the old division is just as active as ever, even if it is proceeding along different lines and, via new institutions, producing rather different effects. Even when the role of the doctor consists of lending an ear to this finally liberated speech, this procedure still takes place in the context of a hiatus between listener and speaker. For he is listening to speech invested with desire, crediting itself – for its greater exultation or for its greater anguish – with terrible powers. If we truly require silence to cure monsters, then it must be an attentive silence, and it is in this that the division lingers.

It is perhaps a little risky to speak of the opposition between true and false as a third system of exclusion, along with those I have mentioned already. How could one reasonably compare the constraints of truth with those other divisions, arbitrary in origin if not developing out of historical contingency – not merely modifiable but in a state of continual flux, supported by a system of institutions imposing and manipulating them, acting not without constraint, nor without an element, at least, of violence?

Certainly, as a proposition, the division between true and false is neither arbitrary, nor modifiable, nor institutional, nor violent. Putting the question in different terms, however – asking what has been, what still is, throughout our discourse, this will to truth which has survived throughout so many centuries of our history; or if we ask what is, in its very general form, the kind of division governing our will to knowledge – then we may well discern something like a system of exclusion (historical, modifiable, institutionally constraining) in the process of development.

It is, undoubtedly, a historically constituted division. For, even with the sixth century Greek poets, true discourse – in the meaningful sense – inspiring respect and terror, to which all were obliged to submit, because it held sway over all and was pronounced by men who spoke as of right, according to ritual, meted out justice and attributed to each his rightful share; it prophesied the future, not merely announcing what was going to occur, but contributing to its actual event, carrying men along with it and thus weaving itself into the fabric of fate. And yet, a century later, the highest truth no longer resided in what discourse *was*, nor in what it *did*: it lay in what was *said*. The day dawned when truth moved over from the ritualised act – potent and just – of enunciation to settle on what was enunciated itself: its meaning, its form, its object and its relation to what it referred to. A division emerged between Hesiod and Plato, separating true discourse from false; it was a new division for, henceforth, true discourse was no longer considered precious and desirable, since it had ceased to be discourse linked to the exercise of power. And so the Sophists were routed.

This historical division has doubtless lent its general form to our will to knowledge. Yet it has never ceased shifting: the great mutations of science may well sometimes be seen to flow from some discovery, but they may equally be viewed as the appearance of new forms of the will to truth. In the nineteenth century there was undoubtedly a will to truth having nothing to do, in terms of the forms examined, of the fields to which it addressed itself, nor the techniques upon which it was based, with the will to knowledge which characterised classical culture. Going back a little in time, to the turn of the sixteenth and seventeenth centuries – and particularly in England – a will to knowledge emerged which, anticipating its present content, sketched out a schema of possible, observable, measurable and classifiable objects; a will to knowledge which imposed upon the knowing subject – in some ways taking precedence over all experience – a certain position, a certain viewpoint, and a certain function (look rather than read, verify rather than comment), a will to knowledge which prescribed (and, more generally speaking, all instruments determined) the technological level at which knowledge could be employed in order to be verifiable and useful (navigation, mining, pharmacopoeia). Everything seems to have occurred as though, from the time of the great

Platonic division onwards, the will to truth had its own history, which is not at all that of the constraining truths: the history of a range of subjects to be learned, the history of the functions of the knowing subject, the history of material, technical and instrumental investment in knowledge.

But this will to truth, like the other systems of exclusion, relies on institutional support: it is both reinforced and accompanied by whole strata of practices such as pedagogy – naturally – the book-system, publishing, libraries, such as the learned societies in the past, and laboratories today. But it is probably even more profoundly accompanied by the manner in which knowledge is employed in a society, the way in which it is exploited, divided and, in some ways, attributed. It is worth recalling at this point, if only symbolically, the old Greek adage, that arithmetic should be taught in democracies, for it teaches relations of equality, but that geometry alone should be reserved for oligarchies, as it demonstrates the proportions within inequality.

Finally, I believe that this will to knowledge, thus reliant upon institutional support and distribution, tends to exercise a sort of pressure, a power of constraint upon other forms of discourse – I am speaking of our own society. I am thinking of the way Western literature has, for centuries, sought to base itself in nature, in the plausible, upon sincerity and science – in short, upon true discourse. I am thinking, too, of the way economic practices, codified into precepts and recipes – as morality, too – have sought, since the eighteenth century, to found themselves, to rationalise and justify their currency, in a theory of wealth and production; I am thinking, again, of the manner in which such prescriptive ensembles as the Penal Code have sought their bases or justifications. For example, the Penal Code started out as a theory of Right; then, from the time of the nineteenth century, people looked for its validation in sociological, psychological, medical and psychiatric knowledge. It is as though the very words of the law had no authority in our society, except insofar as they are derived from true discourse. Of the three great systems of exclusion governing discourse – prohibited words, the division of madness and the will to truth – I have spoken at greatest length concerning the third. With good reason: for centuries, the former have continually tended toward the latter; because this last has, gradually, been attempting to assimilate the others in order both to modify them and to provide them with a firm foundation. Because, if the two former are continually growing more fragile and less certain to the extent that they are now invaded by the will to truth, the latter, in contrast, daily grows in strength, in depth and implacability.

And yet we speak of it least. As though the will to truth and its vicissitudes were masked by truth itself and its necessary unfolding. The reason is perhaps this: if, since the time of the Greeks, true discourse no longer responds to desire or to that which exercises power in the will to truth, in the will to speak out in true discourse, what, then, is at work, if not desire and power? True discourse, liberated by the nature of its form from desire and power, is incapable of recognising the will to truth which pervades it; and the will to truth, having imposed itself upon us for so long, is such that the truth it seeks to reveal cannot fail to mask it.

Thus, only one truth appears before our eyes: wealth, fertility and sweet strength in all its insidious universality. In contrast, we are unaware of the prodigious machinery of the will to truth, with its vocation of exclusion. All those who, at one moment or another in our history, have attempted to re-mould this will to truth and to turn it against truth at that very point where truth undertakes to justify the taboo, and to define madness; all those, from Nietzsche to Artaud and Bataille, must now stand as (probably haughty) sign-posts for all our future work.

There are, of course, many other systems for the control and delimitation of discourse. Those I have spoken of up to now are, to some extent, active on the exterior; they function as systems of exclusion; they concern that part of discourse which deals with power and desire.

I believe we can isolate another group: internal rules, where discourse exercises its own control; rules concerned with the principles of classification, ordering and distribution. It is as though we were now involved in the mastery of another dimension of discourse: that of events and chance.

In the first place, commentary. I suppose, though I am not altogether sure, there is barely a society without its major narratives, told, retold and varied; formulae, texts, ritualised texts to be spoken in well-defined circum-stances; things said once, and conserved because people suspect some hidden secret or wealth lies buried within. In short, I suspect one could find a kind of gradation between different types of discourse within most societies: discourse 'uttered' in the course of the day and in casual meetings, and which disappears with the very act which gave rise to it; and those forms of discourse that lie at the origins of a certain number of new verbal acts, which are reiterated, transformed or discussed; in short, discourse which *is spoken* and remains spoken, indefinitely, beyond its formulation, and which remains to be spoken. We know them in our own cultural system: religious or juridical texts, as well as some curious texts, from the point of view of their status, which we term 'literary'; to a certain extent, scientific texts also.

What is clear is that this gap is neither stable, nor constant, nor absolute. There is no question of there being one category, fixed for all time, reserved for fundamental or creative discourse, and another for those which reiterate, expound and comment. Not a few major texts become blurred and disap-pear, and commentaries sometimes come to occupy the former position. But while the details of application may well change, the function remains the same, and the principle of hierarchy remains at work. The radical denial of this gradation can never be anything but play, utopia or anguish. Play, as Borges uses the term, in the form of commentary that is nothing more than the reappearance, word for word (though this time it is solemn and anticipated) of the text commented on; or again, the play of a work of criticism talking endlessly about a work that does not exist. It is a lyrical dream of talk reborn, utterly afresh and innocent, at each point; continually reborn in all its vigour, stimulated by things, feelings or thoughts. Anguish, such as that of Janet when sick, for whom the least utterance sounded as the 'word of the Evangelist', concealing an inexhaustible wealth of meaning, worthy to be broadcast, rebegun, commented upon indefinitely: 'When I think', he said on reading or listening; 'When I think of this phrase, continuing its journey through eternity, while I, perhaps, have only incompletely understood it . . .'

But who can fail to see that this would be to annul one of the terms of the relationship each time, and not to suppress the relationship itself? A relationship in continual process of modification; a relationship taking multiple and diverse forms in a given epoch: juridical exegesis is very different – and has been for a long time – from religious commentary; a single work of literature can give rise, simultaneously, to several distinct types of discourse. The *Odyssey*, as a primary text, is repeated in the same epoch, in Berand's translation, in infinite textual explanations and in Joyce's *Ulysses*.

For the time being, I would like to limit myself to pointing out that, in what we generally refer to as commentary, the difference between primary text and secondary text plays two interdependent roles. On the one hand, it permits us to create new discourses ad infinitum: the top-heaviness of the original text, its permanence, its status as discourse ever capable of being brought up to date, the multiple or hidden meanings with which it is credited, the reticence and wealth it is believed to contain, all this creates an open possibility for discussion. On the other hand, whatever the techniques employed, commentary's only role is to say *finally*, what has silently been articulated *deep down*. It must – and the paradox is ever-changing yet inescapable – say, for the first time, what has already been said, and repeat tirelessly what was, nevertheless, never said. The infinite rippling of commentary is agitated from within by the dream of masked repetition: in the distance there is, perhaps, nothing other than what was there at the point of departure: simple recitation. Commentary averts the chance element of discourse by giving it its due: it gives us the opportunity to say something other than the text itself, but on condition that it is the text itself which is uttered and, in some ways, finalised. The open multiplicity, the fortuitousness, is transferred, by the principle of commentary, from what is liable to be said to the number, the form, the masks and the circumstances of repetition. The novelty lies no longer in what is said, but in its reappearance.

I believe there is another principle of rarefaction, complementary to the first: the author. Not, of course, the author in the sense of the individual who delivered the speech or wrote the text in question, but the author as the unifying principle in a particular group of writings or statements, lying at the origins of their significance, as the seat of their coherence. This principle is not constant at all times. All around us, there are sayings and texts whose meaning or effectiveness has nothing to do with any author to whom they might be attributed: mundane remarks, quickly forgotten; orders and contacts that are signed, but have no recognisable author; technical prescriptions anonymously transmitted. But even in those fields where it is normal to attribute a work to an author – literature, philosophy, science – the principle does not always play the same role; in the order of scientific discourse, it was, during the Middle Ages, indispensable that a scientific text be attributed to an author, for the author was the index of the work's truthfulness. A proposition was held to derive its scientific value from its author. But since the seventeenth century this function has been steadily declining; it barely survives now, save to give a name to a theorem, an effect, an example or a syndrome. In literature, however, and from about the same period, the author's function has become steadily more important. Now, we demand of all those narratives, poems, dramas and comedies which circulated relatively anonymously throughout the Middle Ages, whence they come, and we virtually insist they tell us who wrote them. We ask authors to answer for the unity of the works published in their names; we ask that they reveal, or at least display the hidden sense pervading their work; we ask them to reveal their personal lives, to account for their experiences and the real story that gave birth to their writings. The author is he who implants, into the troublesome language of fiction, its unities, its coherence, its links with reality.

I know what people are going to say: 'But there you are speaking of the author in the same way as the critic reinvents him after he is dead and buried, when we are left with no more than a tangled mass of scrawlings. Of course, then you have to put a little order into what is left, you have to imagine a structure, a cohesion, the sort of theme you might expect to arise out of an author's consciousness or his life, even if it is a little fictitious. But all that cannot get away from the fact the author existed, irrupting into the midst of all the words employed, infusing them with his genius, or his chaos'.

Of course, it would be ridiculous to deny the existence of individuals who write, and invent. But I think that, for some time, at least, the individual who sits down to write a text, at the edge of which lurks a possible *œuvre*, resumes the functions of the author. What he writes and does not write, what he sketches out, even preliminary sketches for the work, and what he drops as simple mundane remarks, all this interplay of differences is prescribed by the author-function. It is from his new position, as an author, that he will fashion – from all he might have said, from all he says daily, at any time – the still shaky profile of his *œuvre*.

Commentary limited the hazards of discourse through the action of an *identity* taking the form of *repetition* and *sameness*. The author principle limits this same chance element through the action of an *identity* whose form is that of *individuality* and the *I*.

But we have to recognise another principle of limitation in what we call, not sciences, but 'disciplines'. Here is yet another relative, mobile principle, one which enables us to construct, but within a narrow framework.

The organisation of disciplines is just as much opposed to the commentary-principle as it is to that of the author. Opposed to that of the author, because disciplines are defined by groups of objects, methods, their corpus of propositions considered to be true, the interplay of rules and definitions, of techniques and tools: all these constitute a sort of anonymous system, freely available to whoever wishes, or whoever is able to make use of them, without there being any question of their meaning or their validity being derived from whoever happened to invent them. But the principles involved in the formation of disciplines are equally opposed to that of commentary. In a discipline, unlike in commentary, what is supposed at the point of departure is not some meaning which must be rediscovered, nor an identity to be reiterated; it is that which is required for the construction of new statements. For a discipline to exist, there must be the possibility of formulating – and of doing so ad infinitum – fresh propositions.

But there is more, and there is more, probably, in order that there may be less. A discipline is not the sum total of all the truths that may be uttered concerning something; it is not even the total of all that may be accepted, by virtue of some principle of coherence and systematisation, concerning some given fact or proposition. Medicine does not consist of all that may be truly said about disease; botany cannot be defined by the sum total of the truths one could say about plants. There are two reasons for this, the first being that botany and medicine, like other disciplines, consist of errors as well as truths, errors that are in no way residuals, or foreign bodies, but having their own positive functions and their own valid history, such that their roles are often indissociable from that of the truths. The other reason is that, for a proposition to belong to botany or pathology, it must fulfil certain conditions, in a stricter and more complex sense than that of pure and simple truth: at any rate, other conditions. The proposition must refer to a specific range of objects; from the end of the seventeenth century, for example, a proposition, to be 'botanical', had to be concerned with the visible structure of plants, with its system of close and not so close resemblances, or with the behavior of its fluids; (but it could no longer retain, as had still been the case in the sixteenth century, references to its symbolic value or to the virtues and properties accorded it in antiquity). But without belonging to any discipline, a proposition is obliged to utilize conceptual instruments and techniques of a well-defined type; from the nineteenth century onwards, a proposition was no longer medical – it became 'non-medical', becoming more of an individual fantasy or item of popular imagery – if it employed metaphorical or qualitative terms or notions of essence (congestion, fermented liquids, dessicated solids); in return, it could – it had to – appeal to equally metaphorical notions, though constructed according to a different functional and physiological model (concerning irritation, inflammation or the decay of tissue). But there is more still, for in order to belong to a discipline, a proposition must fit into a certain type of theoretical field. Suffice it to recall that the quest for primitive language, a perfectly acceptable theme up to the eighteenth century, was enough, in the second half of the nineteenth century, to throw any discourse into, I hesitate to say error, but into a world of chimera and reverie – into pure and simple linguistic monstrosity.

Within its own limits, every discipline recognises true and false propositions, but it repulses a whole teratology of learning. The exterior of a science is both more, and less, populated than one might think: certainly, there is immediate experience, imaginary themes bearing on and continually accompanying immemorial beliefs; but perhaps there are no errors in the strict sense of the term, for error can only emerge and be identified within a well-defined process;

there are monsters on the prowl, however, whose forms alter with the history of knowledge. In short, a proposition must fulfil some onerous and complex conditions before it can be admitted within a discipline; before it can be pronounced true or false it must be, as Monsieur Canguilhem might say, 'within the true'.

People have often wondered how on earth nineteenth-century botanists and biologists managed not to see the truth of Mendel's statements. But it was precisely because Mendel spoke of objects, employed methods and placed himself within a theoretical perspective totally alien to the biology of his time. But then, Naudin had suggested that hereditary traits constituted a separate element before him; and yet, however novel or unfamiliar the principle may have been, it was nevertheless reconcilable, if only as an enigma, with biological discourse. Mendel, on the other hand, announced that hereditary traits constituted an absolutely new biological object, thanks to a hitherto untried system of filtrage: he detached them from species, from the sex transmitting them, the field in which he observed being that infinitely open series of generations in which hereditary traits appear and disappear with statistical regularity. Here was a new object, calling for new conceptual tools, and for fresh theoretical foundations. Mendel spoke the truth, but he was not *dans le vrai* (within the true) of contemporary biological discourse: it simply was not along such lines that objects and biological concepts were formed. A whole change in scale, the deployment of a totally new range of objects in biology was required before Mendel could enter into the true and his propositions appear, for the most part, exact. Mendel was a true monster, so much so that science could not even properly speak of him. And yet Schleiden, for example, thirty years earlier, denying, at the height of the nineteenth century, vegetable sexuality, was committing no more than a disciplined error.

It is always possible one could speak the truth in a void; one would only be in the true, however, if one obeyed the rules of some discursive 'policy' which would have to be reactivated every time one spoke.

Disciplines constitute a system of control in the production of discourse, fixing its limits through the action of an identity taking the form of a permanent reactivation of the rules.

We tend to see, in an author's fertility, in the multiplicity of commentaries and in the development of a discipline so many infinite resources available for the creation of discourse. Perhaps so, but they are nonetheless principles of constraint, and it is probably impossible to appreciate their positive, multiplicatory role without first taking into consideration their restrictive, constraining role.

There is, I believe, a third group of rules serving to control discourse. Here, we are no longer dealing with the mastery of the powers contained within discourse, nor with averting the hazards of its appearance; it is more a question of determining the conditions under which it may be employed, of imposing a certain number of rules upon those individuals who employ it, thus denying access to everyone else. This amounts to a rarefaction among speaking subjects: none may enter into discourse on a specific subject unless he has satisfied certain conditions or if he is not, from the outset, qualified to do so. More exactly, not all areas of discourse are equally open and penetrable; some are forbidden territory (differentiated and differentiating) while others are virtually open to the winds and stand, without any prior restrictions, open to all.

Here, I would like to recount a little story so beautiful I fear it may well be true. It encompasses all the constraints of discourse: those limiting its powers, those controlling its chance appearances and those which select from among speaking subjects. At the beginning of the seventeenth century, the Shogun heard tell of European superiority in navigation, commerce, politics and the military arts, and that this was due to their knowledge of mathematics. He wanted to obtain this precious knowledge. When someone told him of an English sailor possessed of this marvelous discourse, he summoned him to his palace and kept him there. The Shogun took lessons from the mariner in private and familiarised himself with mathematics, after which he retained power and lived to a very old age. It was not until the nineteenth century that there were *Japanese* mathematicians. But that is not the end of the anecdote, for it has its European aspect as well. The story has it that the English sailor, Will Adams, was a carpenter and an autodidact. Having worked in a shipyard he had learnt geometry. Can we see in this narrative the expression of one of the great myths of European culture? To the monopolistic, secret knowledge of oriental tyranny, Europe opposed the universal communication of knowledge and the infinitely free exchange of discourse.

This notion does not, in fact, stand up to close examination. Exchange and communication are positive forces at play within complex but restrictive systems; it is probable that they cannot operate independently of these. The most superficial and obvious of these restrictive systems is constituted by what we collectively refer to as ritual; ritual defines the qualifications required of the speaker (of who in dialogue, interrogation or recitation, should occupy which position and formulate which type of utterance); it lays down gestures to be made, behaviour, circumstances and the whole range of signs that must accompany discourse; finally, it lays down the supposed, or imposed significance of the words used, their effect upon those to whom they are addressed, the limitations of their constraining validity. Religious discourse, juridical and therapeutic as well as, in some ways, political discourse are all barely dissociable from the functioning of a ritual that determines the individual properties and agreed roles of the speakers.

A rather different function is filled by 'fellowships of discourse', whose function is to preserve or to reproduce discourse, but in order that it should circulate within a closed community, according to strict regulations, without those in possession being dispossessed by this very distribution. An archaic model of this would be those groups of Rhapsodists, possessing knowledge of poems to recite or, even, upon which to work variations and transformations. But though the ultimate object of this knowledge was ritual recitation, it was protected and preserved within a determinate group, by the, often extremely complex, exercises of memory implied by such a process. Apprenticeship gained access both to a group and to a secret which recitation made manifest, but did not divulge. The roles of speaking and listening were not interchangeable.

Few such 'fellowships of discourse' remain, with their ambiguous interplay of secrecy and disclosure. But do not be deceived; even in true discourse, even in the order of published discourse, free from all ritual, we still find secret-appropriation and non-interchangeability at work. It could even be that the act of writing, as it is institutionalised today, with its books, its publishing system and the personality of the writer, occurs within a diffuse, yet constraining, 'fellowship of discourse'. The separateness of the writer, continually opposed to the activity of all other writing and speaking subjects, the intransitive character he lends to his discourse, the fundamental singularity he has long accorded to 'writing', the affirmed dissymmetry between 'creation' and any use of linguistic systems – all this manifests in its formulation (and tends moreover to accompany the interplay of these factors in practice) the existence of a certain 'fellowship of discourse'. But there are many others, functioning according to entirely different schemas of exclusivity and disclosure: one has only to think of technical and scientific secrets, of the forms of diffusion and circulation in medical discourse, of those who have appropriated economic or political discourse.

At first sight, 'doctrine' (religious, political, philosophical) would seem to constitute the very reverse of a 'fellowship of discourse'; for among the latter, the number of speakers were, if not fixed, at least limited, and it was among this number that discourse was allowed to circulate and be transmitted. Doctrine, on the other hand, tends to diffusion: in the holding in common of a single ensemble of discourse that individuals, as many as you wish, could define their reciprocal allegiance. In appearance, the sole requisite is the recognition of the same truths and the acceptance of a certain rule – more or less flexible – of conformity with validated discourse. If it were a question of just that, doctrines would barely be any different from scientific disciplines, and discursive control would bear merely on the form or content of what was uttered, and not on the speaker. Doctrinal adherence, however, involves both speaker and the spoken, the one through the other. The speaking subject is involved through, and as a result of, the spoken, as is demonstrated by the rules of exclusion and the rejection mechanism brought into play when a speaker formulates one, or many, inassimilable utterances; questions of heresy and unorthodoxy in no way arise out of fanatical exaggeration of doctrinal mechanisms; they are a fundamental part of them. But conversely, doctrine involves the utterances of speakers in the sense that doctrine is, permanently, the sign, the manifestation and the instrument of a prior adherence – adherence to a class, to a social or racial status, to a nationality or an interest, to a struggle, a revolt, resistance or acceptance. Doctrine links individuals to certain types of utterance while consequently barring them from all others. Doctrine effects a dual subjection, that of speaking subjects to discourse, and that of discourse to the group, at least virtually, of speakers.

Finally, on a much broader scale, we have to recognise the great cleavages in what one might call the social appropriation of discourse. Education may well be, as of right, the instrument whereby every individual, in a society like our own, can gain access to any kind of discourse. But we well know that in its distribution, in what it permits and in what it prevents, it follows the well-trodden battle-lines of social conflict. Every educational system is a political means of maintaining or of modifying the appropriation of discourse, with the knowledge and the powers it carries with it.

I am well aware of the abstraction I am performing when I separate, as I have just done, verbal rituals, 'fellowships of discourse', doctrinal groups and social appropriation. Most of the time they are linked together, constituting great edifices that distribute speakers among the different types of discourse, and which appropriate those types of discourse to certain categories of subject. In a word, let us say that these are the main rules for the subjection of discourse. What is an educational system, after all, if not a ritualisation of the word; if not a qualification of some fixing of roles for speakers; if not the constitution of a (diffuse) doctrinal group; if not a distribution and an appropriation of discourse, with all its learning and its powers? What is 'writing' (that of 'writers') if not a similar form of subjection, perhaps taking rather different forms, but whose main stresses are nonetheless analogous? May we not also say that the judicial system, as well as institutionalised medicine, constitute similar systems for the subjection of discourse?

I wonder whether a certain number of philosophical themes have not come to conform to this activity of limitation and exclusion and perhaps even to reinforce it.

They conform, first of all, by proposing an ideal truth as a law of discourse, and an immanent rationality as the principle of their behaviour. They accompany, too, an ethic of knowledge, promising truth only to the desire for truth itself and the power to think it.

They then go on to reinforce this activity by denying the specific reality of discourse in general.

Ever since the exclusion of the activity and commerce of the sophists, ever since their paradoxes were muzzled, more or less securely, it would seem that Western thought has seen to it that discourse be permitted as little room as possible between thought and words. It would appear to have ensured that *to discourse* should appear merely as a certain interjection between speaking and thinking; that it should constitute thought, clad in its signs and rendered visible by words or, conversely, that the structures of language themselves should be brought into play, producing a certain effect of meaning.

This very ancient elision of the reality of discourse in philosophical thought has taken many forms in the course of history. We have seen it quite recently in the guise of many themes now familiar to us.

It seems to me that the theme of the founding subject permits us to elide the reality of discourse. The task of the founding subject is to animate the empty forms of language with his objectives; through the thickness and inertia of empty things, he grasps intuitively the meanings lying within them. Beyond time, he indicates the field of meanings – leaving history to make them explicit –

in which propositions, sciences, and deductive ensembles ultimately find their foundation. In this relationship with meaning, the founding subject has signs, marks, tracks, letters at his disposal. But he does not need to demonstrate these passing through the singular instance of discourse.

The opposing theme, that of originating experience, plays an analogous role. This asserts, in the case of experience, that even before it could be grasped in the form of a *cogito*, prior significations, in some ways already spoken, were circulating in the world, scattering it all about us, and from the outset made possible a sort of primitive recognition. Thus, a primary complicity with the world founds, for us, a possibility of speaking of experience, in it, to designate and name it, to judge it and, finally, to know it in the form of truth. If there is discourse, what could it legitimately be if not a discrete reading? Things murmur meanings our language has merely to extract; from its most primitive beginnings, this language was already whispering to us of a being of which it forms the skeleton.

The theme of universal mediation is, I believe, yet another manner of eliding the reality of discourse. And this despite appearances. At first sight it would seem that, to discover the movement of a logos everywhere elevating singularities into concepts, finally enabling immediate consciousness to deploy all the rationality in the world, is certainly to place discourse at the centre of speculation. But, in truth, this logos is really only another discourse already in operation, or rather, it is things and events themselves which *insensibly* become discourse in the unfolding of the essential secrets. Discourse is no longer much more than the shimmering of a truth about to be born in its own eyes; and when all things come eventually to take the form of discourse, when everything may be said and when anything becomes an excuse for pronouncing a discourse, it will be because all things having manifested and exchanged meanings, they will then all be able to return to the silent interiority of self-consciousness.

Whether it is the philosophy of a founding subject, a philosophy of originating experience or a philosophy of universal mediation, discourse is really only an activity, of writing in the first case, of reading in the second and exchange in the third. This exchange, this writing, this reading never involve anything but signs. Discourse thus nullifies itself, in reality, in placing itself at the disposal of the signifier.

What civilization, in appearance, has shown more respect towards discourse than our own? Where has it been more and better honoured? Where have men depended more radically, apparently, upon its constraints and its universal character? But, it seems to me, a certain fear hides behind this apparent supremacy accorded, this apparent logophilia. It is as though these taboos, these barriers, thresholds and limits were deliberately disposed in order, at least partly, to master and control the great proliferation of discourse, in such a way as to relieve its richness of its most dangerous elements; to organise its disorder so as to skate round its most uncontrollable aspects. It is as though people had wanted to efface all trace of its irruption into the activity of our thought and language. There is undoubtedly in our society, and I would not be surprised to see it in others, though taking different forms and modes, a profound logophobia, a sort of dumb fear of these events, of this mass of spoken things, of everything that could possibly be violent, discontinuous, querulous, disordered even and perilous in it, of the incessant, disorderly buzzing of discourse.

If we wish – I will not say to efface this fear – but to analyse it in its conditions, its activity and its effects, I believe we must resolve ourselves to accept three decisions which our current thinking rather tends to resist, and which belong to the three groups of function I have just mentioned: to question our will to truth; to restore to discourse its character as an event; to abolish the sovereignty of the signifier.

These are the tasks, or rather, some of the themes which will govern my work in the years ahead. One can straight away distinguish some of the methodological demands they imply.

A principle of *reversal*, first of all. Where, according to tradition, we think we recognise the source of discourse, the principles behind its flourishing and continuity, in those factors which seem to play a positive role, such as the author discipline, will to truth, we must rather recognise the negative activity of the cutting-out and rarefaction of discourse.

But, once we have distinguished these principles of rarefaction, once we have ceased considering them as a fundamental and creative action, what do we discover behind them? Should we affirm that a world of uninterrupted discourse would be virtually complete? This is where we have to bring other methodological principles into play.

Next, then, the principle of *discontinuity*. The existence of systems of rarefaction does not imply that, over and beyond them lie great vistas of limitless discourse, continuous and silent, repressed and driven back by them, making it our task to abolish them and at last to restore it to speech. Whether talking in terms of speaking or thinking, we must not imagine some unsaid thing, or an unthought, floating about the world, interlacing with all its forms and events. Discourse must be treated as a discontinuous activity, its different manifestations sometimes coming together, but just as easily unaware of, or excluding each other.

The principle of *specificity* declares that a particular discourse cannot be resolved by a prior system of significations; that we should not imagine that the world presents us with a legible face, leaving us merely to decipher it; it does not work hand in glove with what we already know; there is no pre-discursive fate disposing the word in our favour. We must conceive discourse as a violence that we do to things, or, at all events, as a practice we impose upon them; it is in this practice that the events of discourse find the principle of their regularity.

The fourth principle, that of *exteriority*, holds that we are not to burrow to the hidden core of discourse, to the heart of the thought or meaning manifested in it; instead, taking the discourse itself, its appearance and its regularity, that we should look for its external conditions of existence, for that which gives rise to the chance series of these events and fixes its limits.

As the regulatory principles of analysis, then, we have four notions: event series, regularity and the possible conditions of existence. Term for term we find the notion of event opposed to that of creation, the possible conditions of existence opposing signification. These four notions (signification, originality, unity, creation) have, in a fairly general way, dominated the traditional history of ideas; by general agreement one sought the point of creation, the unity of a work, of a period or a theme, one looked also for the mark of individual originality and the infinite wealth of hidden meanings.

I would like to add just two remarks, the first of which concerns history. We frequently credit contemporary history with having removed the individual event from its privileged position and with having revealed the more enduring structures of history. That is so. I am not sure, however, that historians have been working in this direction alone. Or, rather, I do not think one can oppose the identification of the individual event to the analysis of long term trends quite so neatly. On the contrary, it seems to me that it is in squeezing the individual event, in directing the resolving power of historical analysis onto official price-lists (*mercuriales*), title deeds, parish registers, to harbour archives analysed year by year and week by week, that we gradually perceive – beyond battles, decisions, dynasties and assemblies – the emergence of those massive phenomena of secular or multi-secular importance. History, as it is practised today, does not turn its back on events; on the contrary, it is continually enlarging the field of events, constantly discovering new layers – more superficial as well as more profound – incessantly isolating new ensembles – events, numerous, dense and interchangeable or rare and decisive: from daily price fluctuations to secular inflations. What is significant is that history does not consider an event without defining the series to which it belongs, without specifying the method of analysis used, without seeking out the regularity of phenomena and the probable limits of their occurrence, without enquiring about variations, inflexions and the slope of the curve, without desiring to know the conditions on which these depend. History has long since abandoned its attempts to understand events in terms of cause and effect in the formless unity of some great evolutionary process, whether vaguely homogeneous or rigidly hierarchised. It did not do this in order to seek out structures anterior to, alien or hostile to the event. It was rather in order to establish those diverse converging, and sometimes divergent, but never autonomous series that enable us to circumscribe the 'locus' of an event, the limits to its fluidity and the conditions of its emergence.

The fundamental notions now imposed upon us are no longer those of consciousness and continuity (with their correlative problems of liberty and causality), nor are they those of sign and structure. They are notions, rather, of events and of series, with the group of notions linked to these; it is around such an ensemble that this analysis of discourse I am thinking of is articulated, certainly not upon those traditional themes which the philosophers of the past took for 'living' history, but on the effective work of historians.

But it is also here that this analysis poses some, probably awesome philosophical or theoretical problems. If discourses are to be treated first as ensembles of discursive events, what status are we to accord this notion of event, so rarely taken into consideration by philosophers? Of course, an event is neither substance, nor accident, nor quality nor process; events are not corporeal. And yet, an event is certainly not immaterial; it takes effect, becomes effect, always on the level of materiality. Events have their place; they consist in relation to, coexistence with, dispersion of, the cross-checking accumulation and the selection of material elements; it occurs as an effect of, and in, material dispersion. Let us say that the philosophy of event should advance in the direction, at first sight paradoxical, of an incorporeal materialism. If, on the other hand, discursive events are to be dealt with as homogeneous, but discontinuous series, what status are we to accord this discontinuity? Here we are not dealing with a succession of instants in time, nor with the plurality of thinking subjects; what is concerned are those caesurae breaking the instant and dispersing the subject in a multiplicity of possible positions and functions. Such a discontinuity strikes and invalidates the smallest units, traditionally recognised and the least readily contested: the instant and the subject. Beyond them, independent of them, we must conceive – between these discontinuous series of relations which are not in any order of succession (or simultaneity) within any (or several) consciousnesses – and we must elaborate – outside of philosophies of time and subject – a theory of discontinuous systematisation. Finally, if it is true that these discursive, discontinuous series have their regularity, within certain limits, it is clearly no longer possible to establish mechanically causal links or an ideal necessity among their constitutive elements. We must accept the introduction of chance as a category in the production of events. There again, we feel the absence of a theory enabling us to conceive the links between chance and thought.

In the sense that this slender wedge I intend to slip into the history of ideas consists not in dealing with meanings possibly lying behind this or that discourse, but with discourse as regular series and distinct events, I fear I recognise in this wedge a tiny (odious, too, perhaps) device permitting the introduction, into the very roots of thought, of notions of *chance, discontinuity* and *materiality*. This represents a triple peril which one particular form of history attempts to avert by recounting the continuous unfolding of some ideal necessity. But they are three notions which ought to permit us to link the history of systems of thought to the practical work of historians; three directions to be followed in the work of theoretical elaboration.

Following these principles, and referring to this overall view, the analyses I intend to undertake fall into two groups. On the one hand, the 'critical' group which sets the reversal-principle to work. I shall attempt to distinguish the forms of exclusion, limitation and appropriation of which I was speaking earlier; I shall try to show how they are formed, in answer to which needs, how they are modified and displaced, which constraints they have effectively exercised, to what extent they have been worked on. On the other hand, the 'genealogical' group, which brings the three other principles into play:

how series of discourse are formed, through, in spite of, or with the aid of these systems of constraint: what were the specific norms for each, and what were their conditions of appearance, growth and variation.

Taking the critical group first, a preliminary group of investigations could bear on what I have designated functions of exclusion. I have already examined one of these for a determinate period: the disjunction of reason and madness in the classical age. Later, we could attempt an investigation of a taboo system in language, that concerning sexuality from the sixteenth to the nineteenth century. In this, we would not be concerned with the manner in which this has progressively – and happily – disappeared, but with the way it has been altered and rearticulated, from the practice of confession, with its forbidden conduct, named, classified, hierarchised down to the smallest detail, to the belated, timid appearance of the treatment of sexuality in nineteenth-century psychiatry and medicine. Of course, these only amount to somewhat symbolic guidelines, but one can already be pretty sure that the stresses will not fall where we expect, and that taboos are not always to be found where we imagine them to be.

For the time being, I would like to address myself to the third system of exclusion. I will envisage it in two ways. Firstly, I would like to try to visualise the manner in which this truth within which we are caught, but which we constantly rene·./, was selected, but at the same time, was repeated, extended and displaced. I will take first of all the age of the Sophists and its beginning with Socrates, or at least with Platonic philosophy, and I shall try to see how effective, ritual discourse, charged with power and peril, gradually arranged itself into a disjunction between true and false discourse. I shall next take the turn of the sixteenth and seventeenth centuries and the age which, above all in England, saw the emergence of an observational, affirmative science, a certain natural philosophy inseparable, too, from religious ideology – for this certainly constituted a new form of the will to knowledge. In the third place, I shall turn to the beginning of the nineteenth century and the great founding acts of modern science, as well as the formation of industrial society and the accompanying positivist ideology. Three slices out of the morphology of our will to knowledge; three staging posts in our philistinism.

I would also like to consider the same question from quite another angle. I would like to measure the effect of a discourse claiming to be scientific – medical, psychiatric or sociological – on the ensemble of practices and prescriptive discourse of which the penal code consists. The study of psychiatric skills and their role in the penal system will serve as a point of departure and as basic material for this analysis.

It is within this critical perspective, but on a different level, that the analysis of the rules for the limitation of discourse should take place, of those among which I earlier designated the author principle, that of commentary and that of discipline. One can envisage a certain number of studies in this field. I am thinking, for example, of the history of medicine in the sixteenth to nineteenth centuries; not so much an account of discoveries made and concepts developed, but of grasping – from the construction of medical discourse, from all its supporting institutions, from its transmission and its reinforcement, – how the principles of author, commentary and discipline worked in practice; of seeking to know how the great author principle, whether Hippocrates, Galen, Paracelsus and Sydenham, or Boerhaave, became a principle of limitation in medical discourse; how, even late into the nineteenth century, the practice of aphorism and commentary retained its currency and how it was gradually replaced by the emphasis on case-histories and clinical training on actual cases; according to which model medicine sought to constitute itself as a discipline, basing itself at first on natural history and, later, on anatomy and biology.

One could also envisage the way in which eighteenth and nineteenth-century literary criticism and history have constituted the character of the author and the form of the work, utilising, modifying and altering the procedures of religious exegesis, biblical criticism, hagiography, the 'lives' of historical or legendary figures, of autobiography and memoirs. One day, too, we must take a look at Freud's role in psycho-analytical knowledge, so different from that of Newton in physics, or from that an author might play in the field of philosophy (Kant, for example, who originated a totally new way of philosophizing).

These, then, are some of the projects falling within the critical aspect of the task, for the analysis of instances of discursive control. The genealogical aspect concerns the effective formation of discourse, whether within the limits of control, or outside of them, or as is most frequent, on both sides of the delimitation. Criticism analyses the processes of rarefaction, consolidation and unification in discourse; genealogy studies their formation, at once scattered, discontinuous and regular. To tell the truth, these two tasks are not always exactly complementary. We do not find, on the one hand, forms of rejection, exclusion, consolidation or attribution, and, on a more profound level, the spontaneous pouring forth of discourse, which immediately before or after its manifestation, finds itself submitted to selection and control. The regular formation of discourse may, in certain conditions and up to a certain point, integrate control procedures (this is what happens, for example, when a discipline takes on the form and status of scientific discourse). Conversely, modes of control may take on life within a discursive formation (such as literary criticism as the author's constitutive discourse) even though any critical task calling instances of control into play must, at the same time, analyse the discursive regularities through which these instances are formed. Any genealogical description must take into account the limits at play within real formations. The difference between the critical and the genealogical enterprise is not one of object or field, but of point of attack, perspective and delimitation.

Earlier on I mentioned one possible study, that of the taboos in discourse on sexuality. It would be difficult, and in any case abstract, to try to carry out this study, without at the same time analysing literary, religious and ethical, biological and medical, as well as juridical discursive ensembles: wherever sexuality is discussed, wherever it is named or described, metaphorised, explained or judged. We are a very long way from having constituted a unitary, regular discourse concerning sexuality; it may be that we never will, and that we are not even travelling in that direction. No matter. Taboos are homogeneous neither in their forms nor their behaviour whether in literary or medical discourse, in that of psychiatry or of the direction of consciousness. Conversely, these different discursive regularities do not divert or alter taboos in the same manner. It will only be possible to undertake this study, therefore, if we take into account the plurality of series within which the taboos, each one to some extent different from all the others, are at work.

We could also consider those series of discourse which, in the sixteenth and seventeenth centuries, dealt with wealth and poverty, money, production and trade. Here, we would be dealing with some pretty heterogeneous ensembles of enunciations, formulated by rich and poor, the wise and the ignorant, protestants and catholics, royal officials, merchants or moralists. Each one has its forms of regularity and, equally, its systems of constraint. None of them precisely prefigures that other form of regularity that was to acquire the momentum of a discipline and which was later to be known, first as 'the study of wealth' and, subsequently, 'political economy'. And yet, it was from the foregoing that a new regularity was formed, retrieving or excluding, justifying or rejecting, this or that utterance from these old forms.

One could also conceive a study of discourse concerning heredity, such as it can be gleaned, dispersed as it was until the beginning of the twentieth century, among a variety of disciplines, observations, techniques and formulae; we would be concerned to show the process whereby these series eventually became subsumed under the single system, now recognised as epistemologically coherent, known as genetics. This is the work François Jacob has just completed, with unequalled brilliance and scholarship.

It is thus that critical and genealogical descriptions are to alternate, support and complete each other. The critical side of the analysis deals with the systems enveloping discourse; attempting to mark out and distinguish the principles of ordering, exclusion and rarity in discourse. We might, to play with our words, say it practises a kind of studied casualness. The genealogical side of discourse, by way of contrast, deals with series of effective formation of discourse: it attempts to grasp it in its power of affirmation, by which I do not mean a power opposed to that of negation, but the power of constituting domains of objects, in relation to which one can affirm or deny true or false propositions. Let us call these domains of objects positivist and, to play on words yet again, let us say that, if the critical style is one of studied casualness, then the genealogical mood is one of felicitous positivism.

At all events, one thing at least must be emphasised here: that the analysis of discourse thus understood, does not reveal the universality of a meaning, but brings to light the action of imposed rarity, with a fundamental power of affirmation. Rarity and affirmation; rarity, in the last resort of affirmation – certainly not any continuous outpouring of meaning, and certainly not any monarchy of the signifier.

And now, let those who are weak on vocabulary, let those with little comprehension of theory call all this – if its appeal is stronger than its meaning for them – structuralism.

I am well aware that I could never have begun to undertake these researches I have just outlined to you, were I not able to benefit from the aid of certain models and props. I believe I owe much to Monsieur Dumézil, for it was he who encouraged me to work at an age when I still thought writing a pleasure. But I owe a lot, too, to his work; may he forgive me if I have wandered from the meaning and rigour of his texts, which dominate us today. It is he who taught me to analyse the internal economy of discourse quite differently from the traditional methods of exegesis or those of linguistic formalism. It is he who taught me to refer the system of functional correlations from one discourse to another by means of comparison. It was he, again, who taught me to describe the transformations of a discourse, and its relations to the institution. If I have wished to apply a similar method to discourse quite other than legendary or mythical narratives, it is because before me lay the works of the historians of science, above all, that of Monsieur Canguilhem. I owe it to him that I understood that the history of science did not necessarily involve, either an account of discoveries, or descriptions of the ideas and opinions bordering science either from the side of its doubtful beginnings, or from the side of its fall-out; but that one could – that one should – treat the history of science as an ensemble, at once coherent, and transformable into theoretical models and conceptual instruments.

A large part of my indebtedness, however, is to Jean Hyppolite. I know that, for many, his work is associated with that of Hegel, and that our age, whether through logic or epistemology, whether through Marx or through Nietzsche, is attempting to flee Hegel: and what I was attempting to say earlier concerning discourse was pretty disloyal to Hegel.

But truly to escape Hegel involves an exact appreciation of the price we have to pay to detach ourselves from him. It assumes that we are aware of the extent to which Hegel, insidiously perhaps, is close to us; it implies a knowledge, in that which permits us to think against Hegel, of that which remains Hegelian. We have to determine the extent to which our anti-Hegelianism is possibly one of his tricks directed against us, at the end of which he stands, motionless, waiting for us.

If, then, more than one of us is indebted to Jean Hyppolite, it is because he has tirelessly explored, for us, and ahead of us, the path along which we may escape Hegel, keep our distance, and along which we shall find ourselves brought back to him, only from a different angle, and then, finally, be forced to leave him behind, once more.

First, Hyppolite took the trouble to give some presence to this great, slightly phantomlike shadow that was Hegel, prowling through the nineteenth century, with whom men struggled in the dark. He gave Hegel this presence with his translation of the *Phenomonology of the mind*; proof of the extent to which Hegel came to life in this text was the number of Germans who came to consult this text in order to understand what, for a moment at least, had become the German version.

From this text, Hyppolite sought out and explored all the issues, as though his chief concern had become: can one still philosophize where Hegel is no longer possible? Can any philosophy continue to exist that is no longer Hegelian? Are the non-Hegelian elements in our thought necessarily non-philosophical? Is that which is antiphilosophical necessarily non-Hegelian? As well as giving us this Hegelian presence, he sought not merely a meticulous historical description: he wanted to turn Hegel into a schema for the experience of modernity (is it possible to think of the sciences, politics and daily suffering as a Hegelian?) and he wanted, conversely, to make modernity the test of Hegelianism and, beyond that, of philosophy. For Hyppolite, the relationship with Hegel was the scene of an experiment, of a confrontation in which it was never certain that philosophy would come out on top. He never saw the Hegelian system as a reassuring universe; he saw in it the field in which philosophy took the ultimate risk.

From this stem, I believe, the alterations he worked, not within Hegelian philosophy, but upon it, and upon philosophy as Hegel conceived it; from this also, a complete inversion of themes. Instead of conceiving philosophy as a totality ultimately capable of dispersing and regrouping itself in the movement of the concept, Jean Hyppolite transformed it into an endless task, against the background of an infinite horizon. Because it was a task without end, it was also a task in process of continuous recommencement, given over to the forms and paradoxes of repetition. For Hyppolite, philosophy, as the thought of the inaccessible totality, was that which could be rejected in the extreme irregularity of experience; it was that which presents and reveals itself as the continually recurring question in life, death and in memory. Thus he transformed the Hegelian theme of the end of self-consciousness into one of repeated interrogation. But because it consisted in repetition, this philosophy did not lie beyond concepts; its task was not that of abstraction, it was, rather, to maintain a certain reticence, to break with acquired generalisations and continually to reestablish contact with the non-philosophical; it was to draw as close as possible, not to its final fulfilment, but to that which precedes it, that which has not yet stirred its uncertainty. In order not to reduce them, but to think them, this philosophy was to examine the singularity of history, the regional rationalities of science, the depths of memory in consciousness; thus arose the notion of a philosophy that was present, uncertain, mobile all along its line of contact with non-philosophy, existing on its own, however, and revealing the meaning this non-philosophy has for us. But, if it is in repeated contact with non-philosophy, where then lies the beginning of philosophy? Is it already there, secretly present in that which is not philosophy, beginning to formulate itself half under its breath, amid the murmuring of things? But, perhaps, from that point on, philosophy has no *raison d'être*, or, maybe, philosophy should start out on a priori foundations? We see, thus, the theme of the foundations of discourse and its formal structure substituting itself for the Hegelian one of present movement.

The final alteration Jean Hyppolite worked upon Hegelian philosophy was this: if philosophy really must begin as absolute discourse, then what of history, and what is this beginning which starts out with a singular individual, within a society and a social class, and in the midst of struggle?

These five alterations, leading to the very extremities of Hegelian philosophy, doubtless forcing it to spill over its own limits, evoke by turns the great figures of modern philosophy Jean Hyppolite ceaselessly opposed to Hegel: Marx, with his questions of history; Fichte, and the problem of the absolute beginnings of philosophy; Bergson's theme of contact with non-philosophy; Kierkegaard, with the problem of repetition and truth; Husserl, and the theme of philosophy as an infinite task, linked to the history of our rationality. Beyond these philosophical figures we can perceive all those fields of knowledge Hyppolite invoked around his own questions: psychoanalysis, with its strange logic of desire; mathematics and the formalisation of discourse; information theory and its application to the analysis of life – in short, all those fields giving rise to questions of logic and existence, continually intertwining and unravelling their links.

I think this work, articulated in a small number of major books, but, even more, invested in research, teaching, in a perpetual attentiveness, in an everyday alertness and generosity, in its apparently administrative and pedagogic responsibilities (*i.e.*, doubly political), has traversed and formulated the most fundamental problems of our age. Many of us are infinitely indebted to him.

It is because I have borrowed both the meaning and the possibility of what I am doing from him; because, often, he enlightened me when I struck out blindly; because I would like to dedicate my work to him, that I end this presentation of my projected work by invoking the name of Jean Hyppolite. It is towards him, towards that hiatus – where I feel at once his absence and my failings – that the questions I now ask myself are pointing.

Because I owe him so much, I well understand that your choice, in inviting me to teach here is, in good part, a homage to Jean Hyppolite. I am profoundly grateful to you for the honour you have done me, but I am no less equal to the challenge of succeeding him, I know nonetheless that, if that happiness should have been granted us, I should have been encouraged by his indulgence this evening.

I now understand better why I experienced so much difficulty when I began speaking, earlier on. I now know which voice it was I would have wished for, preceding me, supporting me, inviting me to speak and lodging within my own speech. I know now just what was so awesome about beginning; for it was here, where I speak now, that I listened to that voice, and where its possessor is no longer, to hear me speak.

Index

Abel, N., 189
accumulation, 122–25, 130, 141, 200
Adanson, M., 59, 160
analysis, linguistic (philosophy), 48, 80–84, 107–8
Analysis of Wealth (and economics, political economy), 6, 10, 13, 16, 31, 35–38, 46, 56, 63–70, 72–73, 108, 110, 126, 135, 158, 159, 160–61, 167–69, 172–73, 175–76, 178, 180, 183, 185, 188, 207, 210
  coinage, 36, 66
  emergent capitalism, 68–69
  formation of value, 36, 66, 69
  ground rents, 35–36, 66
  mercantilism, 188
  Utilitarists, 36, 65–66, 69, 73
Anquetil-Duperron, A., 142, 170
anthropology (-ical), 12, 16, 131
archaeology and history
  archive, 126, 131, 135, 206–7
  causality (causal), 4, 6, 7, 42, 92, 139, 163, 203
  connexion, 4–5, 11, 33, 75, 207
  continuity, 3–5, 6, 12–13, 21, 25, 31, 58, 64, 127, 131, 137–38, 141, 146, 148, 150–51, 158, 162, 171, 173, 201–2, 204
  contradictions (oppositions), 151–55, 201
  development, 11–14, 16, 21, 32, 76, 127–28, 137, 149, 154, 166, 176, 189, 204
  difference(s), differentiation(s), 6, 12–14, 21, 37, 41, 43–46, 63, 73, 92, 115, 121, 131, 142, 144–46, 148–49, 160, 170–71, 175, 180, 191, 204–7

discontinuity (break, displacement, gap, interruption, mutation, rupture, shift, threshold), 3–10, 12–15, 21, 31, 33–35, 37, 40–41, 44, 54, 58, 60, 66, 70, 72, 74, 79, 89, 103, 108, 110–14, 117, 119, 121, 127–28, 131, 136, 141, 142, 151–52, 157, 161, 166, 169, 170–71, 173–77, 180, 186–88, 189–93, 195, 201, 203–4, 210
division, 5, 10, 13, 22, 33–34, 37–38, 117, 119, 139, 142, 152, 163, 173, 179, 188, 207, 210
event(s), 3–4, 7–8, 10, 22, 25, 31, 46, 62, 74, 76, 80, 83, 101–2, 104, 109, 121, 124, 127–30, 142–43, 146, 157, 162, 164, 167–69, 171–72, 176, 189, 200
history, general and universal, 3–17, 164
level, 3–6, 8–10, 13, 24, 37–38, 43, 60, 62, 65–67, 69, 72–76, 85–86, 90–91, 93, 95–96, 98–99, 101, 108–9, 112, 115–16, 122, 125–26, 130–31, 145–46, 149–51, 155, 162, 165, 171, 185, 188–89, 191, 200, 206–7
limit(s), 9–10, 13–15, 17, 21, 23, 31, 46, 71, 86, 103, 106, 108, 110, 113, 117–119, 168, 176, 179, 208
origin, 4–6, 8, 11–14, 21, 25, 38, 59, 74, 95, 107, 113, 123, 125–26, 131, 140–48, 150, 161, 188–89, 202–5, 209
period (-ization), 4, 8–9, 148, 176

archaeology and history—*contd.*

relations, 4, 7, 9, 11, 13–14, 22–23, 31,
33, 43–46, 48, 57–62, 67–68, 71–74,
76, 80, 89–93, 98–99, 122, 124–25,
129, 142, 146, 148, 158–59, 163–64,
169, 181, 191–92, 201, 204, 209

repetition, 5, 21, 42, 57, 101–3, 115,
141, 143, 173

resemblance, 21, 44, 180

resumption, 5

return, 137, 173, 204, 209

the same, 21, 139, 174, 206

series (sequences, successions), 3, 7, 8, 10,
12–14, 21–22, 31, 41–43, 56–57, 60,
62, 65, 66, 70, 74–75, 81–86, 88–89,
92, 94–96, 99, 101, 107, 110–11, 115,
122, 126–27, 142–44, 148, 166–69,
174, 187, 201, 204

totality (-ies) (-izations), 3, 7–8, 10, 12,
14–16, 39, 108, 119–20, 122, 125, 138,
204, 206

transformation(s), 4–5, 10, 12–15, 21,
33–34, 37–38, 44, 58, 62, 69, 71, 74,
81, 99, 109, 117, 120–22, 124, 136,
140–41, 147, 154, 166–77, 188, 194,
200, 201, 204–5, 209–11

transmissions, 5, 21

unity(-ies), 4–7, 12, 21–35, 37, 46, 54,
58, 68–72, 76, 79–81, 87, 108, 111,
114, 116–17, 126, 135, 139, 149–52,
155, 157, 160, 176, 191, 195

archive, *see* archaeology and history

Aristotle, 143

Arnauld, A., 142

art (painting), 136, 193

Artaud, Antonin, 24

author, 92–95, 102–3, 115–16, 122, 126,
135, 137, 139, 141, 150, 162, 171, 206

Bachelard, Gaston, 4, 190

Balzac, Honoré de, 23

Beauzée, N., 167

Benoît de Maillet, 36, 143, 151, 184

Bernard, Claude, 188

Bichat, M. F., 33–34, 126, 144

biology, *see* Natural History

Bleuler, E., 32, 40

Blumenbach, J., 143

Bonnet, C., 184

books, *see under* literature

Bopp, F., 142, 170

Bordeu, T. de, 36, 151

break, *see* discontinuity *under* discourse

Broussais, F.-J.V., 126

Buffon, G., 35, 58, 59, 65, 126, 143, 144,
151–52, 183

Butor, Michel, 23

Canguilhem, Georges, 4, 144, 173, 190

Cantillon, 66, 68, 175, 188

clinic (-al), *see* medicine

Coeurdoux, R.-P., 142, 170

cogito, *see under* subject

coinage, *see under* Analysis of Wealth

Colbert, J. B., 68

Comédie humaine, La, see Balzac

competence, linguistic, *see under* language

concepts, 4–5, 9, 12, 15, 21, 33–38, 45, 65,
67, 70, 72–75, 79, 108, 116, 127–28,
137, 145, 147–50, 153–55, 161, 167,
170–71, 173, 181–82, 185–86, 190,
193–94, 205–7

rules of formation of concepts, 37–38,
56–63, 65, 67, 72–73

Condillac, E., 167

connexion, *see under* archaeology and history

conscious (-ness), *see under* subject

continuity(-ies), *see under* archaeology and
history

contradiction, *see under* archaeology and
history

Copernicus, 103

Coup de dés, Un, see Mallarmé

Cournot, A. A., 188

culture, 128, 130, 150

customs, 7

Cuvier, G., 143–44, 170, 174, 188

Darwin, Charles, 35–36, 103–4, 126, 143,
145, 153

Daubenton, L.-J.-M., 143, 170, 183

Désargues, 23
desire, *see under* subject
Destutt de Tracy, 167
development, *see under* archaeology and
    history
diachrony, 169, 200,
    see also synchrony
Diderot, D., 36, 126, 143, 151, 183
Diophantus, 189
discontinuity, *see under* archaeology and
    history
discourse (discursive), 7, 9, 12–13, 17,
    22–23, 25, 31–36, 40–50, 52–55, 57–58,
    60–66, 70–76, 79–81, 93, 95, 99,
    107–8, 113–14, 117–20, 122, 125–29,
    131, 135, 137–39, 141–44, 146, 148–51,
    153, 155–56, 158, 160–71, 175–76,
    178, 180, 182, 184–87, 192–93, 199–
    202, 205–11
  discursive formation, 31–41, 44–45, 55,
    58–59, 62, 64–65, 67–68, 71, 73–76,
    79–81, 106–7, 113–20, 124–26, 128,
    131, 135, 139, 145, 147–48, 153, 155,
    157–60, 162–64, 166–69, 171–81,
    184–88, 190–91, 195, 199–200, 206–7
  discursive objects, 40–49, 63, 65, 67, 70,
    72–75, 78, 85, 91, 95, 97, 99, 102,
    105–8, 111, 115–16, 118, 120, 124,
    136, 140, 145, 147, 151–55, 167–68,
    171, 173, 176, 181–82, 185–86, 193–94,
    205, 207
  discursive practice, 46, 48–49, 57, 62, 72,
    74–76, 80, 87, 117, 127–28, 131, 135,
    139, 144–46, 154–55, 164, 174–76,
    179–95, 199–200, 208–9, 211
  discursive regularities, 62–63, 74–76, 80,
    114, 122, 128–29, 141–48, 179, 185,
    187, 191–92, 195
  discursive strategies (theoretical choices
    and options), 36–37, 64–74, 79–80,
    105, 116, 147, 153, 167, 171, 173, 181–
    82, 186, 193–95
  discursive unities, 21–30, 35
displacement, *see* discontinuity *under*
    archaeology and history
division, *see under* archaeology and history

documents, 6–7, 10, 129–30, 138
Dostoevsky, F. M., 23
Duclos, C., 35
Du Laurens, H.-J., 40

Ecce Homo, see Nietzsche
economy (-ics), *see* Analysis of Wealth
emergent capitalism, *see under* Analysis of
    Wealth
enunciation, 59, 64–65, 74, 94–95, 100–5,
    110–13, 115, 112–23, 145–46, 148,
    154, 160, 162, 171, 173, 181, 185–86,
    193–94
  enunciative analysis, 118, 121, 124–25
  enunciative events, 98–99, 119, 131, 135
  formation of enunciations, 50–55
  enunciative field, 98–99, 119, 131, 135
  enunciative function, 86–106, 112, 115–
    117, 127, 131, 144, 153–54
  enunciative level, 91–92, 111–12, 116
  enunciative modes and modalities, 75, 79
  enunciative rules, 65, 115, 153
  enunciative series, 67, 72–73, 147, 154–56
  enunciative system, 116
  enunciative types, 63
  thresholds of enunciation, 89
epistemology (-ical), (-ization), 5, 38,
    187–88, 190–92, 207
Esquirol, J. E. D., 32, 40, 43, 187
ethnology, 11–13
etymology, 160
Euclidean geometry, 124
Euler, L., 158
events, *see under* archaeology and history
evolution, 143, 161, 173
    see also Darwin *and* Natural History
exteriority and interiority, 120–22, 125, 140

fantasies, *see under* subject
Fortbonnais, Véron de, 170
formation, *see* discursive formation *under*
    discourse
formation of value, *see under* Analysis of
    Wealth
formulation, 107–8, 110, 115, 141, 146–47,
    167, 171

French Revolution, 177
Freud, Sigmund, 103, 193
  see also psychoanalysis

Galois, 189
gap, *see* discontinuity *under* archaeology
  and history
General Grammar (*and* philology, grammar), 31, 34, 37–38, 46, 56, 60–61,
  63–68, 71, 84, 108–9, 115, 119, 127,
  142, 145, 150, 157–62, 168, 171–72,
  175–76, 180, 184, 207
  generative grammar, 184, 207
Genera Plantarum, see Linnaeus
Grammaire of Port-Royal, 31, 34–35, 56,
  67, 144, 146, 167
  see also General Grammar
Grammont, S. de, 175
Graslin, 170
Gresham, Sir Thomas, 145
Grimm, J., 142
ground rent(s), *see under* Analysis of
  Wealth
Guéroult, M., 5

Harris, J., 170
Heinroth, J. C. A., 40, 187
Herder, J. G., 180
hermeneutics, 162
Hermès et la communication, see Serres
Histoire de France, see Michelet
Histoire de la folie, see Madness and Civilization
history, *see separate headings under* archaeology and history
humanism, 12–13, 16
human sciences, 173
Husserl, E. 203

ideology (-ical), 5, 158, 184–86
ideas (and history of), 4, 6, 7–8, 14, 21, 38,
  63–64, 70, 72, 117, 128, 135–42, 149,
  151, 166, 169, 171, 209
identity(-ies), (-ical), 17, 35, 63, 81, 100–6,
  127, 129, 131, 139, 141, 143, 145–46,
  148, 174, 182

influence(s), 5, 21, 38, 56, 64, 126, 149–
  150, 161
institutions, 6–7, 10, 41–42, 45, 68, 72, 74,
  103, 118, 120, 123, 129, 137, 157, 162,
  164
interruptions, *see* discontinuities *under*
  archaeology and history

Jevons, W. S., 126, 188
Jonston, 148
Joyce, James, 23
Jussieu, B. de, 59, 143, 167, 183

Kant, I., 203–4
Keynes, J. M., 145
knowledge (*savoir, connaissance*), 4–6, 12,
  14–15, 21, 33, 35, 42–43, 54, 57, 79,
  128, 136–37, 152, 178–95, 199, 201,
  205, 207, 209
Kraepelin, E., 40

Laennec, R. T. H., 34, 126
Lamarck, J. B., 143
Lancelot, C., 35, 142, 145–46, 167
language (*langage, langue*), linguistic, 13,
  16, 24, 34, 42, 46, 48–49, 59, 61–62,
  64, 68–69, 76, 82, 84–86, 88, 90, 94–97,
  99, 101, 104, 107–9, 111–13, 118–19,
  127, 130–31, 135, 137, 139, 142,
  145–46, 148, 150, 160, 162, 169, 176,
  180, 189, 199, 200–3, 209–11
  linguistic competence, 96, 117, 207
  linguistic performances, verbal perform-
    ances, speech acts, 80, 83–84, 86, 107–
    110, 115–16, 125, 129, 144–45, 200,
    206–7
  linguistics, 11–13, 98, 112–13, 199
  metalanguage, metalinguistics, 95, 99
  rules of grammar, of construction of a
    language, 96–97, 99, 107, 112
  speech, 108, 125, 130, 169
Lavoisier, A., 158
Law, J., 66, 69, 162
level, *see under* archaeology and history
life, living beings, *see* Natural History
linguistics, *see under* language

Linnaeus, C., 56, 58–59, 65, 67, 69, 126, 143–44, 148, 151–53, 160, 174, 183

literature, 4–6, 10, 22, 42, 93, 98–99, 136–137, 179, 183, 199, 201
  books, 5, 7, 15, 17, 23, 25, 37, 60, 71–72, 79, 95, 101–3, 116, 123, 126, 128, 135
  novel, the (and fiction), 90, 93, 98, 100, 202
  œuvres, 5, 21, 23–24, 37–38, 60, 71–72, 79, 95, 116, 126, 135–39, 142, 149, 162, 202
  texts, 5, 7, 17, 23–24, 37, 57–60, 73, 75–76, 92–93, 95, 98, 101–4, 106, 111, 116, 118–19, 123–24, 126–28, 143–45, 149–50, 155, 172–73, 179, 183, 210
  writings, 118, 136

limit, see archaeology and history

Locke, J., 145, 188

logic (-al), 84, 100–1, 107–8, 112–13, 115–16, 145

logos, 121, 209

madness, 16, 32, 40–43, 47–48, 68, 184–85

Madness and Civilization, 14–16, 47, 65, 157, 179

Mallarmé, S., 23–24

Marx, Karl, 12–14, 176–88

mathematics, 5, 158, 173, 188–89

meaning(s), 7, 10, 14, 48, 90–93, 97, 100–1, 106–7, 109–13, 118–20, 123–25, 127, 143, 149, 150, 163, 209–10

mechanical sciences, 127

medicine (medical, clinic, clinical), 16, 31–34, 37–38, 41–42, 44, 46, 51, 53–54, 64–65, 67, 72, 75, 108, 126–27, 157, 159, 162–64, 167–68, 170, 172, 174, 179, 181–82, 184, 186, 188, 207

mercantilism, see under Analysis of Wealth

Merleau-Ponty, M., 203

metalanguage, metalinguistic, see under language

Michelet, J., 23

monuments, 7, 137, 139

Morgagni, G. B., 174

Mots et les choses, Les, see Order of Things, The

mutations, see discontinuities under archaeology and history

myth(s), (-ology, -ologies), 199, 201–2

Naissance de la clinique, 14–16, 54, 157

Natural History (and biology, and life and living beings), 12, 16, 31, 35–36, 57–58, 61, 63–65, 67–73, 76, 108, 126, 135, 147, 152–55, 158–61, 167, 172–75, 178, 180, 183–84, 187–88, 193, 207, 210

Neumann, 31

neurology, 46

Nietzsche, F. W., 13–14, 24

Nosographie philosophique, La, 170

novel, the, see under literature

objects, formation of, see discursive objects under discourse

Odyssey, the, 23

œuvres, see under literature

Order of Things, The, 15–16, 60–65, 157–59, 201

origin, see under archaeology and history

Other, the, 12

painting, see art

Palingénésie philosophique, see Bonnet

Paris-Duverney, J., 69

Pasteur, L., 188

Peirce, C. S., 142

performances, linguistic, see under language

period (-ization), see under archaeology and history

Petty, Sir William, 31, 66, 144–45, 162

phenomenology, 203

philology, see General Grammar

philosophy (and history of), 4, 6, 12, 37, 58, 136–38, 173, 179, 205–6

Physiocrats, the (Physiocratic, Physiocracy), 35–36, 64–66, 69, 73, 126, 170

Pinel, P., 32, 40, 144, 187

Plato, 103

Poe, Edgar Allen, 24

political economy, *see* Analysis of Wealth
polysemia, 110
Port-Royal, *see Grammaire* of
positivism(s), 202, 205
positivities (of discourse), (interpositivity), 125–28, 153, 155, 157, 161–63, 166, 168–69, 171–81, 184, 186–88, 190–91, 194–95, 199, 206–8
practices (non-discursive), 42, 46, 54, 68–69, 74, 118, 123, 130, 137, 157, 162, 164, 209–10
practices, discursive, *see under* discourse
Prochaska, J., 144, 174
production, theory of, 207–8
propositions, 81, 91, 92, 94–97, 99–101, 103, 106–8, 111–12, 114–16, 126, 149, 153, 155, 184
psychiatry, 48, 65, 67, 75, 108, 135, 157, 179, 182
psychoanalysis, 13, 207
see also Freud
psychopathology, 31–32, 40–42, 44–45, 47, 187
psychology, 16, 46

Quesnay, F., 36, 126

Racine, J., 202
Rais, Gilles de, 23
Ramus, P., 170
rarity (of statements), 118–21, 125, 130, 141
Rask, 170
rationality, rationalization, *see* reason
reason, rationality, rationalization, 4, 8, 13, 41, 45, 121, 125, 131, 158, 181, 188, 191, 201–2
referent, the, 89, 97
regularity(-ies), *see* discursive regularities *under* discourse
relations, *see under* archaeology and history
repetition, *see under* archaeology and history
resemblance, *see under* archaeology and history
resumption, *see under* archaeology and history

return, *see under* archaeology and history
Rêve d'Alembert, Le, see Diderot
Ricardo, D., 36, 56, 144, 169–70, 176, 188
Rousseau, Jean Jacques, 160, 162
rules of discursive formation, *see* discursive formation *under* discourse
rules of grammar, of construction of a language, *see under* language
rupture, *see* discontinuity *under* archaeology and history

Saint-Hilaire, Geoffroy, 143
same, the, *see under* archaeology and history
San Marco, see Butor
Saussure, F. de, 142, 145
sciences (and history of), 4–5, 8, 10, 21–22, 37–39, 126, 136–37, 206–7
classical science, 158, 175
sentences, 80–82, 84, 86, 91–98, 100–1, 104, 107–12, 114, 116–17, 130, 149, 168
sequences, *see* series *under* archaeology and history
series, *see under* archaeology and history
Serres, M., 5, 190
sexuality, 13, 40–41, 44, 48, 193
shift, *see* discontinuity *under* archaeology and history
sign(s), 9, 23, 33–34, 44, 47, 49, 50, 57, 61, 66–67, 69, 73, 84–86, 88–89, 92, 95–96, 98, 100, 106–9, 111, 138, 142, 158, 161, 168, 175
signified(s), 11, 89, 111, 118
signifier(s) (and signifying elements), 11, 89, 100, 109, 111, 118, 143
Simpson, 104
speech, *see under* language
speech acts, *see* linguistic performances *under* language
statements, 31–35, 37–38, 56–62, 65–68, 70, 72–74, 79–96, 98–100, 102–25, 127–30, 135, 141, 144–45, 147, 167, 173, 178–80, 186–87, 200, 206–9
Stendhal, 23
Stoics, 142

strategy(-ies), *see* discursive strategies *under* discourse

structure(s), (-ural), (-uralism), 5–6, 10–11, 13–16, 21, 37, 46, 48, 57, 59–60, 62–63, 70, 73, 75, 82, 84, 86–87, 89, 97, 102, 104, 110–12, 127–28, 142, 145, 147, 150, 152, 155, 157, 168, 173, 181, 185–86, 190–91, 195, 199–204, 207, 209

subject, the (and subjectivity), 12–14, 16, 21, 37, 40, 54, 70, 88, 91, 94–95, 106–7, 111–12, 115, 121, 125, 131, 139, 181, 185, 191, 200–5, 207

cogito, knowing subject, 63, 122

conscious (-ness), 8, 12–14, 39, 63, 94, 121–22, 150, 183, 185, 202–3, 210

desire, 13, 47, 67–69, 105, 115, 117, 123, 149

enunciating subject, 122

fantasies, 123

positions of the subject, of subjectivity, 55, 73, 108, 115–16, 153, 207–8

speaking subject, 55, 65, 72–73, 79, 92–99, 117, 150, 163–64, 169, 200, 202, 209

transcendental subject, 55, 113, 122, 125, 192

unconscious, the, 13–14, 24, 121, 150, 201

successions, *see* series *under* archaeology and history

synchrony, 13, 148, 166–67, 169, 176, 204 *see also* diachrony

systems, 13–14, 22, 33–35, 37–38, 41, 42, 47, 56–57, 61–62, 70, 72–76, 79, 96, 99, 116–17, 120, 123, 127–31, 136, 139, 143, 148–50, 154–55, 162, 171, 173, 178, 205, 208

taxonomy (taxonomic tables), 64, 67, 70, 158, 160, 162, 180

Telliamed, see Benoît de Maillet

telos, teleology, 5, 8, 11–13, 16, 39, 70, 121, 125, 131, 201–3

text, *see under* literature

Théâtre et son Double, Le, see under Artaud

theology, 127

theoretical choices and options, *see* discursive strategies *under* discourse

thought(s), 39, 76, 123, 125, 128–29, 137, 139, 142, 150, 152, 155, 204–5

history of thought, 4, 6, 8, 12–14, 21, 39, 76, 201–3, 206

threshold(s), *see* discontinuities *under* archaeology and history

totality(-ies), (-izations), *see under* archaeology and history

Tournefort, 58–59, 145, 148, 167

Tractatus, see Wittgenstein

tradition(s), 5, 12, 21, 33, 38, 46–47, 56–57, 63, 130

Traité des Coniques, see Désargues

Traité des membranes, 170

transformation(s), *see under* archaeology and history

transmissions, *see under* archaeology and history

Turgot, A. R., 126, 160, 162, 170

Ulysses, see Joyce

unconscious (-ness), *see under* subject

unity(-ies), *see under* archaeology and history

see also discursive unities *under* discourse

Utilitarists, 36, 65–66, 69, 73

Van Swieten, 40, 126

verbal performances, *see* linguistic performances *under* language

Vico, G. 158, 180

Wealth, *see* Analysis of

Willis, T., 31, 144, 174

Wittgenstein, Ludwig, 24

writing, *see under* literature

Zarathustra, see Nietzsche

ABOUT THE AUTHOR

Michel Foucault was born in Poitiers, France, in 1926. He has lectured in many universities throughout the world and served as director of the Institut Français in Hamburg and the Institut de Philosophie at the Faculté des Lettres in the University of Clermont-Ferrand. He writes frequently for French newspapers and reviews, and is the holder of a chair at France's most prestigious institution, the Collège de France.

M. Foucault is the author of *Madness and Civilization, The Order of Things, The Archaeology of Knowledge, The Birth of the Clinic, Discipline and Punish: The Birth of the Prison, The History of Sexuality,* vol. 1, and *Power/Knowledge.* In addition, he has edited two documentary studies, *I, Pierre Rivière* and *Herculine Barbin.*